Gangs of America

The Rise of Corporate Power and the
Disabling of Democracy

Ted Nace

BK

BERRETT-KOEHLER PUBLISHERS, INC.
San Francisco

Berrett-Koehler Publishers, Inc.
235 Montgomery Street, Suite 650
San Francisco, CA 94104-2916
Tel: (415) 288-0260   Fax: (415) 362-2512   www.bkconnection.com

Ordering Information
Quantity sales. Special discounts are available on quantity purchases by corporations,
associations, and others. For details, contact the "Special Sales Department" at the
Berrett-Koehler address above.
Individual sales. Berrett-Koehler publications are available through most bookstores. They
can also be ordered direct from Berrett-Koehler: Tel: (800) 929-2929; Fax: (802) 864-7626;
www.bkconnection.com
Orders for college textbook/course adoption use. Please contact Berrett-Koehler:
Tel: (800) 929-2929; Fax: (802) 864-7626.
Orders by U.S. trade bookstores and wholesalers. Please contact Publishers Group West,
1700 Fourth Street, Berkeley, CA 94710. Tel: (510) 528-1444; Fax (510) 528-3444.

Berrett-Koehler and the BK logo are registered trademarks of Berrett-Koehler Publishers, Inc.

Printed in the United States of America

Berrett-Koehler books are printed on long-lasting acid-free paper. When it is available,
we choose paper that has been manufactured by environmentally responsible processes.
These may include using trees grown in sustainable forests, incorporating recycled paper,
minimizing chlorine in bleaching, or recycling the energy produced at the paper mill.

Library of Congress Cataloging-in-Publication Data
Nace, Ted
    Gangs of America : the rise of corporate power and the disabling of democracy / Ted
Nace.—Updated ed.
        p. cm.
    "Updated with new chapter 'So what's the alternative?'".
    Includes bibliographical references and index.
    ISBN-10 1-57675-319-0; ISBN-13 978-1-57675-319-4 (pbk.)
        1. Corporations—United States—History. 2. Business and politics—United States—
History. I. Title.
HD2785.N32 2005
338.7'4'0973—dc22   2005048159

First Edition
10 09 08 07 06 05   10 9 8 7 6 5 4 3 2 1

Copyeditor: Sandra Beris   Proofreader: Donna Bettencourt
Interior Designer: Gopa & Ted2, Books & Design   Indexer: Medea Bogdanovich
Production: Linda Jupiter, Jupiter Productions

Praise for *Gangs of America*

"An important and highly accessible book about the legal and
political environments that shaped the modern corporation.
Highly recommended."

—*Choice*

"A joy to read . . . clear, straight-forward, and very accessible . . .
one of those books that can awaken people's consciousness."

—*Corporate Reform Weekly*

"Entertaining and sometimes arresting . . . the book is a lively read,
and Nace is an interesting companion."

—*New Leader*

"*Gangs of America* is a brilliant page-turner revealing how
powerful, greedy corporations wage institutional terrorism.
Reading it is the first step to saving our communities, our
democracy, and our planet's environment."

—John Stauber, coauthor of *Toxic Sludge Is Good for You!*

"A beautifully documented and readable history."

—Ben H. Bagdikian, author of *The Media Monopoly*

"The essential guide to the history of the American corporation.
Nace explodes the myth of inevitability surrounding the corporate
takeover of our lives."

—Maria Elena Martinez, executive director, CorpWatch

Gangs of America

"The modern corporation as an institution is entitled to much more respect than it has frequently received. The dangers inherent in its use are also great enough to require serious attention. The possibilities of its continued development are, so far as one can see, unlimited. It is, in fact, an institution at a cross road in history, capable of becoming one of the master tools of society—capable also of surprising abuse; worthy of the attention of the community as well as of scholars."
—Adolph Berle, Jr., *The Twentieth Century Capitalist Revolution*

"Corporations just naturally grab all the power they can."
—Juliette Beck

Contents

Acknowledgments

This book owes its existence to a computer made by Toshiba Corporation, software from Microsoft Corporation and Google, Inc., electricity supplied by Pacific Gas & Electric Company, and coffee roasted by Peet's Coffee & Tea, Inc. Some actual human beings helped as well.

First, thanks to the many friends and family members—Jennifer Beach, Wendell Brooks, Marcus Chamberlain, Robin Chinn, Gregor Clark, Sally Douglass, Lee Goldberg, John Grimes, Helen Hampton, Noelle Hanrahan, Keasley Jones, Martha Johnson, Steve Johnson, Gaen Murphree, Emma Nace, Julia Nace, Lovina Nace, Ted K. Nace, Jasper Patch, Lisa Roth, and Nancy Ruenzel—who commented on the manuscript, helped think up a title, critiqued the design, sent clippings, asked how things were going, and in various ways sustained the comforting illusion that I was actually getting anything done. Many thanks as well to colleagues and editorial reviewers for insightful critiques: John Cavanagh, Robert Clark, Eugene Coyle, Charles Derber, Mark Dowie, Jonathan Frieman, Richard Grossman, Earl Killian, David Korten, Arthur Naiman, and Steve Roth. Special thanks to Sarah Rabkin for crucial editorial advice.

To those who think that book publishing has become a cold and bruising business, I have two words: Berrett-Koehler. I am most grateful to Steve Piersanti and his associates for the collegial and supportive atmosphere they have created and sustained. Special thanks to Jeevan Sivasubramaniam for taking an early interest in the book and to Rick Wilson for welcoming me into the inner sanctum of the design process. Thanks to Mark Ouimet and the rest of the folks at Publishers Group West for their creativity and book smarts. Thanks also to the freelancers who contributed their skills: production coordinator Linda Jupiter, interior designers Gopa and Veetam, copyeditor Sandra Beris, proofreader Donna Bettencourt, indexer Medea Bogdanovich, cover designer Frances Baca, Web site designer Daniel Will-Harris (www.GangsofAmerica.com), and publicist Celia Alario. And thanks to Roslyn Bullas for timely talent scouting.

I want to acknowledge three people in particular. Jennifer Beach, my partner, aimed her heavy artillery at some of my illusions about American history, for which I am most grateful. Her enthusiasm for this project encouraged me more than I can say. I want to also express my deep gratitude to my parents, Lovina Nace and Ted K. Nace, not just for helping me with this book but also for their sheer joy, passion, and curiosity in this world.

Introduction

O N THE MORNING OF August 2, 2002, millions of Americans turned on their TVs to see an unusual spectacle: a high-level corporate executive in handcuffs, being paraded by law enforcement officials in front of the news media. The executive was Scott Sullivan, chief financial officer of the telecommunications firm WorldCom. Along with fellow executive David Myers, Sullivan was charged with hiding $3.85 billion in company expenses, conspiring to commit securities fraud, and filing false information with the Securities and Exchange Commission. The combined maximum penalties from the charges were sixty-five years. In response to the arrests, Attorney General John Ashcroft told reporters, "Corporate executives who cheat investors, steal savings, and squander pensions will meet the judgment they fear and the punishment they deserve."

Now consider a different crime, committed by the leadership of General Motors together with Standard Oil of California, Firestone Tire and Rubber Company, B. F. Phillips Petroleum, and Mac Manufacturing. In 1936, the five companies formed National City Lines, a holding company that proceeded to buy electric trolley lines and tear up the tracks in cities across the nation. Each time it destroyed a local trolley system, National City would license the rights to operate a new system to a local franchisee, under the stipulation that the system convert to diesel-powered General Motors buses.

By 1949, more than one hundred electric transit systems in forty-five cities had been torn up and converted. In April of that year, a federal jury convicted GM and the other firms of conspiracy to commit antitrust violations. But the penalty turned out to be negligible. The judge set the fine at $5,000 for each company. H. C. Grossman, treasurer of General Motors and a key player in the scheme, was fined one dollar. After the conviction, the companies went back to purchasing transit systems, removing electric trolley lines, and replacing them with buses. By 1955, 88 percent of the country's electric streetcar network was gone.

Both the Scott Sullivan case and the National City Lines case fit the traditional definition of crime: laws were broken, the legal system intervened. But the second case suggests that the larger the crime, the more the boundaries between "crime" and "business as usual" begin to blur. As Atlanta mayor and former United Nations ambassador Andrew Young once said, "Nothing is illegal if one hundred businessmen decide to do it."

Young may have overstated things a bit, but the observation encapsulates a basic truth about American society. Business does tend to get its way, acting by means of a nebulous force known as "corporate power" that drives much of what happens in both the public and private spheres. But there are a few details to work out. What is the nature of this power? Exactly how does it work? Does the law *instantly* conform to the needs and wants of those one hundred businessmen? What happens when corporate America finds its wishes thwarted by constitutional barriers? Who decides what is "public" and what is "private?" Who defines the nature of "crime" versus "business as usual?"

In order to answer such questions, one challenge is merely to begin seeing a phenomenon that surrounds us so completely and continuously. I've spent most of my working life in the corporate world, founding and running a company that publishes how-to books about computers. In that world the corporation is the air you breathe. There is no questioning whether it is a good thing or a bad thing. It just is. Nor is there any thought about where the corporation—this particular institutional form—comes from. You assume that corporations have always been a natural part of the American system of "democracy and free enterprise." But even as I pursued my business, questions lurked in the back of my mind, some of which had been triggered as early as my high school years.

I grew up in southwestern North Dakota, and my first summer job was building trails in the Badlands for the U.S. Forest Service. One day, I learned that a large energy corporation had applied to strip-mine a spot called the Burning Coal Vein, a rugged area where at night deep fissures emitted a glow caused by smoldering veins of coal, ignited long ago by lightning strikes or prairie fires. Along the hillsides, columnar junipers reminiscent of the trees in Van Gogh's "Starry Night" stood like silent watchers draped in tunics. Piles of scoria—brilliant red, orange, and purple ceramic shards—covered the ground, the metamorphosed products of shale baked by the intense underground heat. It was like being in an immortal potter's workshop, where every footstep made a tinkling sound as the scoria broke under your feet. That someone could dare propose destroying a place of such beauty in exchange for a few thousand tons of low-grade coal stunned me. But, of course, the entity planning the mine wasn't a *someone* but a *something*—a corporation. Although people in the company may well have cared, the corporation itself didn't.

After college, I started working as a community organizer for a group of farmers and ranchers in North Dakota who were opposed to a vast expansion of strip-mining being proposed by a number of large companies. The shadow cast by these corporations across farms and ranches was not just a metaphorical one. The machines used in strip mines are quite literally of an awesome physical scale. When I saw *Jurassic Park* I experienced a feeling of *déja vu*—it reminded me of being in a strip mine. To extract the coal underneath millions of acres of productive farmland and ranchland, the mining companies have to peel away the overlying layers of plant-nurturing soil, water-bearing aquifers, and rock. The peeling is done by immense, crane-like earth-eaters called draglines, which soar into the air the length of a football field. Like long-necked dinosaurs, the draglines make their way slowly amid ridges of rubble. Using tooth-edged buckets large enough to hold three Greyhound buses, they perform a drop-drag-lift-swivel maneuver, dropping the giant bucket, dragging it until it overflows, then suddenly jerking tons of dirt and rock high into the air, swiveling with surprising grace, and finally dumping the load onto the spoil piles. Especially at night, when intense lights illuminate the machinery and the rubble, the impression is hair-raising—a specter of monsters feeding upon the earth. And then you remember that the rubble being moved and dumped had been someone's pasture, favorite hillside, or alfalfa field. Reclamation? The companies promised that they would restore the land, but given the semiarid conditions, the fragility of the soil, and the complexities of such critical factors as hydrology and salinity, such assurances rang hollow.

You couldn't help but be affected by the courage of the families who carried on a daily existence next to the mines. I recall sitting in the kitchen of a wheat farmer named Werner Benfit and his elderly mother Anna, looking out at the advancing edge of North American Coal Company's Indian Head Mine near Zap, an ordinary town except for its Dr. Seussian name. Even though the towering spoil piles of the mine had come literally to the edge of the Benfits' property, chain-smoking Werner never lost his sense of humor. Anna brought out a plate of cookies and Werner told about the "suit" from North American Coal who had recently paid a visit. The executive had told Anna that she could name any price in the world for her land. "I don't know about that," replied Anna, "but do you think you could move your spoil pile back a little ways so the rocks stop rolling onto my lawn?"

My boss was a genial Norwegian-American rancher named Randolph Nodland. Randolph had spent years fighting a company called Nokota, which had surreptitiously acquired the mining rights to thousands of acres of land and now threatened a number of farms and ranches with the possibility of an immense strip mine and an accompanying synthetic fuels plant.

One summer evening, as Randolph and I passed the time over pitchers of beer in the Shamrock Bar downstairs from our small office, he told me about a funeral he had attended the previous week at his local country church, Vang Lutheran. Flowers had been brought by the family of the deceased, but as Randolph took his place in the pews, a particularly large bouquet caught his eye. On a card the inscription read: "With deepest sympathies, Nokota, Inc."

The memory of the funeral raised a mixture of emotions, which passed like prairie clouds across Randolph's weathered face—disgust, anger, amusement. The funeral bouquet was just one of a variety of "personal" gestures by the company, including congratulatory cards sent to graduating high school seniors, booths at local fairs, and sponsorship of sports teams, all designed to ingratiate Nokota Inc. with the local community.

This particular gesture, though, crossed the line, and I knew Randolph would make sure the story of the grotesque social miscue made the rounds. In relating the encounter with the bouquet, the mere raising of an eyebrow would be enough to define and convey the insult—and having delivered that cue himself, Randolph could be assured that the message would pass from person to person. Such is the nature of a rural community.

But it occurred to me that Nokota's weird social gesture also stood for something else. In a curious way, the ineptness of the funeral bouquet dramatized the mindless persistence that only a corporation can sustain. Randolph's own energies, along with the combined energies of all his neighbors, were ultimately limited. In contrast, the energies of the corporation had no clear bottom. Maybe all the public relations activities of the company weren't really about making Nokota popular.

Maybe they were simply a way of saying, "We're here, we won't go away, get used to it." You can laugh at or hate a corporation, you can turn it into an object of contempt. You may experience it as a tenacious foe, you can get mad at it one day and ignore it the next. Nothing you may feel or do really matters, because in the end there is no getting around the fact that you are not fighting a normal opponent—your opponent is simply *nobody*. As Baron Thurlow said some three centuries ago, "Did you ever expect a corporation to have a conscience, when it has no soul to be damned, and no body to be kicked?"

From the inside, the view is different. I've repeatedly been struck by the paradox that even the most destructive corporations are populated by friendly, caring people. Sure, there are exceptions to that—corrupt companies, companies with poisonous internal cultures, even companies that ought to be classified as instances of organized crime. But in general, far more harm is caused by corporations acting in ways that are utterly legal and that seem, from the perspective of those inside the corporation, to be perfectly appropriate. Quite obviously, if corporations do harm, it is not because the people inside them lack souls. Rather, it's because the company as a whole, like any organization, is a complex entity that acts according to its own autonomous set of motives and dynamics.

I was to learn that basic fact firsthand after I moved from North Dakota to California and started my computer book publishing business on the outskirts of Silicon Valley. The company started on my kitchen table with a single book that I had painstakingly written and printed on a first-generation laser printer. At that point the farthest thought from my mind was that I might be giving birth to an impersonal, monstrous entity, another Nokota. Indeed, nothing could have been more personal than this funky little company, Peachpit Press. For the first five years the business was in our house, with marketing meetings in the kitchen and kids' toys under the desks. In the early days there were just a handful of us. I would write my how-to books in an office next to the bedroom. I would also answer the phones, and my wife would do the accounting. A friend would come in every few days and help ship books to people who had ordered them.

Over time, the company grew, and as it grew it subtly changed. Gradually our revenues advanced into the millions of dollars. In airports I picked up magazines like *Inc.* and *Business Week*. I opened my laptop computer on the plane and made cash-flow projections. I thoroughly bought into the "win-win" notion of the self-made entrepreneur, pro-viding useful things to help people solve their problems—and of course making money in the process.

Occasionally my company enclosed software with our books. I dealt with my production manager, who worked through an independent con-tractor with an assembly company that inserts floppy disks into vinyl en-velopes that are stuck into the backs of books. After a while, I rarely thought much about the physical aspects of these various stages, or about the people who performed the tedious manual labor involved in assem-bling our book-and-software packages.

One particular day stands out in my memory, a day when things had gone slightly awry and I needed to step into an aspect of the business that I rarely got involved with. My production manager was on vacation, there had been a miscommunication of instructions, the warehouse staff called to say that the assembly company was applying our floppy disk la-bels in the wrong way, and someone needed to straighten things out.

I drove over to the assembly company in South San Francisco and met an account manager, who walked me through a warehouse with tow-ering metal shelves. I saw clerks behind glass walls, line managers, work-ers lined up along the steel rollers of assembly lines.

Suddenly it dawned on me. All the clerks in the offices and all the foremen on the floor had white faces. All the workers on the assembly had brown faces. I speculated that they were Filipino immigrants. I had no idea how much they were paid, whether they were unionized, what sort of benefits they received, or what their hours were. So many aspects of the world economy became illuminated at once: the division of labor be-tween haves and have-nots; the distancing of those who benefit from that division by means of "independent contractors"; my own personal in-volvement, which I had so conveniently compartmentalized and not thought about as long as it remained abstract.

"So this is how it works," I thought, realizing that somewhere along the line, my little company's operations had changed quite profoundly. But I had no time to let my thoughts go deeper. The pace was simply too fast to dwell on it. The thought passed quickly, vanishing into a crazy day embedded in a crazy month.

I had promised several key people that they would receive ownership shares of the company, and so one day my accountant called, saying, "Time to incorporate." Until this point we had been operating as a sole proprietorship, meaning simply that in the eyes of the state of California my wife and I were operating the business merely as individuals.

"What's involved?" I asked. "What does it give us?"

"You go to a lawyer. He'll give you some paperwork, register you with the state, and charge you a couple thousand. In theory it gives you a bit of protection from lawsuits, and it means that if the company goes bankrupt you won't lose your personal assets. The company now will be owned by its shareholders, and your family will have more security because the company is now immortal—if you get run over by a bus, it will go on without you."

"That's it?"

"Yeah, that's it—pretty much."

Fair enough, I thought, adding "call lawyer re: incorp" to my to-do list. A week later, I made the call.

As I jumped through the hoops of the incorporation process, meeting with the lawyer and signing forms, I saw little significance in the whole exercise. I knew that our company could now put "Inc." after its name and that the several people to whom I had promised shares could receive certificates documenting their ownership. But it struck me as little more than a necessary formality—like putting on a necktie when you go to ask for a loan. When the certificate of incorporation arrived one day, I stuck it in a file and got back to work. Still, an idea had begun to form in my mind, something like this: "Here I am, building a company. I enjoyed it when it was seven people, and I enjoyed it when it was twenty. But in struggling to survive, we inevitably keep growing. The larger the company gets, the more I feel that it is becoming something strange and separate—something that is taking on a life of its own."

FOUNDING A COMPANY is a deeply personal act. After all, you invest years of your life and all of your creative energies in bringing that company into existence. Ironically, if you do your work well, you build something that gains momentum and eventually becomes capable of functioning without you—or any other single individual. Seemingly by magic, the company develops an existence of its own.

As the father of children both grown-up and on-the-way-to-being-grown-up, the sensation was familiar for me. As your children become capable of functioning on their own two feet, there's always a slight feeling of sadness: childhood is fading away. But that sadness is more than compensated for by a feeling of exhilaration, a sense of discovery and possibility.

With a corporation growing into maturity, you definitely feel a sense of creative pride, but alongside that pride you also feel a chill. Something complex and even alive has come into existence, but it is no longer governed by intuitively familiar human motives and values. Instead, it is a sophisticated, complex, adaptive, continually evolving system—a sort of mindless yet intelligent being—governed by an array of internal and external programming.

Is this really a problem? It all depends on your assumptions about the behavior of the complex systems we call institutions. Economists, for example, tend to see the profit-maximizing orientation of the corporation as a healthy thing. The interaction of numerous such actors, left to their own devices, produces an efficient allocation of resources. But economists, in their myopic fascination with the workings of markets, have little to say about the tendency of corporations, like all institutions, to seek goals beyond simple profit maximization, including that of gaining political power.

Much of what determines the behavior of such a system is internal, starting of course with the ethics, personality, and style of the leadership, in addition to innumerable other elements that make up the ineffable thing we called "corporate culture." But a significant portion of a corporation's programming is actually external to the corporation, embedded in the framework of laws that define the corporation's powers and proscribe certain behaviors. For example, a city ordinance that excludes giant chain retailers or a statute that allows farmers to sue a nearby polluting facility for reducing their crop yields are both ways in which society attempts to program corporate behavior. So what happens when a corporation is able to interject itself into the political process and successfully undermine such controls? This question has been a persistent one in America for a long time—beginning even in the colonial era. But I'm getting ahead of myself. . . .

Eleven years after starting my company, I knew the time had come for a change. Business was booming, and one month I counted seven of our books on the computer-book best-seller lists. Yet I had the feeling I was living on borrowed time. I knew that unpredictability is the only constant in the tech industry, and that a small company like ours might well be capsized by whatever round of unforeseeable craziness would present itself next. So I did what countless other nervous entrepreneurs have done—I sought out a business broker, who began quietly approaching potential buyers. Eventually a deal was done on terms that seemed as good as could reasonably be expected: a guarantee of two years of employment as well as a sizable bonus for each person on our staff, and a promise of autonomy for our company within the larger organization.

But my inner gyroscope forced me to call it what it was: a sellout. There was no getting around the fact that Peachpit Press was no longer an independent company. Instead it was now the colony of an immense empire—Pearson, Ltd., a multinational corporation with over ten thousand employees. On my last day I put a rose on each person's desk, thanked them all for our time together, and walked away.

ONE OF THE DISABILITIES of being an American is that when we try to talk—or even think—about the workings of power, we often find ourselves strangely hobbled, swinging wildly between naiveté and cynicism. We live in a world of complex and finely tuned institutions and legal structures, yet our outlook is often formed through incoherent images, shallow concepts, and simplistic ideologies. We easily lapse into false dichotomies: if you're not gung ho for capitalism, you must be against it. I understand fully why most Americans, although well aware of the reality of corporate power, tend to accept it as a given. There seems to be an attitude that inquiring into the substantive aspects of corporate capitalism is vaguely unpatriotic—a holdover, perhaps, from the fears and witch hunts of the Cold War.

The story of American government is familiar to all of us: the backdrop of colonial settlement under a monarchical system of rule, the rebellion against that rule, the crafting of a constitutional system, the national crisis over slavery, the extension of suffrage to women, and so on. In contrast, the story of how the central institution of our economic system—the corporation—developed is not part of our culture. In my own life, I had experienced the corporation from two drastically different angles: first, from the outside perspective of watching giant energy corporations assault a rural community; second, from the inside perspective of creating a business from scratch. Still, I knew next to nothing about the origins and evolution of the corporation as an institution. It certainly wasn't something I had learned in school, even though I had studied American history in high school and majored in economics in college.

After the sale of Peachpit Press I took a vacation, and then I went back to work—this time alone, probing the questions that had slowly been forming in my mind: *What is a corporation? How did corporations get so much power? Where did corporations come from? How did this particular institution develop?* I began haunting the libraries at the nearby college campus. I fired up Google to see what people out in the world were saying about corporations. Not surprisingly, the story seemed scattered. Sociologists, political scientists, historians, legal scholars, economists, political activists, and even philosophers have taken up the question of corporate power, each within the confines of a particular discipline. But little has been done to reconcile these varying accounts and weld them into a coherent story. This book represents my effort to fill the gap.

CHAPTER ONE

How Did Corporations Get So Much Power?

In which the author reads a poll, feels provoked and befuddled, and organizes his investigation

As corporations gain in autonomous institutional power and become more detached from people and place, the human interest and the corporate interest increasingly diverge. It is almost as though we were being invaded by alien beings intent on colonizing our planet, reducing us to serfs, and then excluding as many of us as possible. —David Korten, *When Corporations Rule the World*

I T'S NOT OFTEN that Americans get asked by pollsters what they think about corporate power. Usually the questions are on issues like abortion and gun control. But in September 2000, *Business Week* published the results of a series of polls about how people felt about the power wielded by large corporations in American society. These polls were conducted more than a year before the corporate scandals involving Enron, Tyco, WorldCom, and other large companies emerged.

The polls suggested a massive cultural stomachache: too much corporate power, too much corporate *everything*. When the Harris pollsters commissioned by *Business Week* asked people what they thought of the statement "Business has too much power over too many aspects of our lives," 52 percent said they agreed "strongly" and an additional 30 percent said they agreed "somewhat."

Two months after doing its first poll, Harris asked a more specific question: "How would you rate the power of different business groups in influencing government policy, politicians, and policymakers in Washington?" Only 5 percent said that big companies had "too little" power; 74 percent said "too much."

Why do large corporations have so much power? The *Business Week* polls didn't include that question. But one can perhaps imagine what people would have said if they had been asked. They would certainly have mentioned the power that large corporations derive from their political action committees, their lobbyists, their lawyers, their control over millions of jobs. They might have also mentioned the "revolving door" that moves corporate people in and out of government agencies, the corporate ownership of media conglomerates, and so forth.

All those factors are well known. Others are less so. As I began my research on the rise of the large corporation, I saw repeated references to aspects of corporate power whose roots lie buried in history, especially in obscure Supreme Court decisions that "discovered" corporate rights hidden in the language of the Constitution.

How do these corporate constitutional rights translate into political power? The answer is that they complement the other political resources available to corporations (especially large ones), providing a trump card to be played when more direct political tactics fail. When threatened by an unwanted regulation or a pesky piece of legislation, corporations have plenty of tools to draw on: lobbyists, publicity campaigns, threats to transfer factories overseas, and so forth. Even so, laws opposed by corporate interests do get enacted, regardless of conventional corporate clout, especially in times of heightened public mobilization. And this is when having a few constitutional rights comes in handy. The CEO or the vice president for legal affairs directs the corporation's lawyers to challenge the nefarious legislation in court. The court then finds the law "unconstitutional" and invalidates it.

I had heard and read repeatedly that the case in which the Supreme Court declared corporations to be persons for constitutional purposes was the 1886 ruling in *Santa Clara County v. Southern Pacific Railroad*. I figured that if *Santa Clara* was the key case in this century-long process of corporate rights decisions, then the text of the decision must be worth reading. I was curious how the Supreme Court had been able to justify declaring corporations to be persons. Typing "Santa Clara County v. Southern Pacific Railroad" into Google, I quickly found the decision online at www.tourolaw.edu/patch/ SupremeCourtcases.html.

The very first sentence of the online version reads as follows: "The defendant Corporations are persons within the intent of the clause of section I of the Fourteenth Amendment to the Constitution of the United States, which forbids a State to deny to any person within its jurisdiction the equal protection of the laws."

"All right," I thought. "Let's see how they justify this." The idea that corporations should be considered "persons" seemed to be quite a radical metaphysical assertion, and I wanted to find out how the Court had backed it up. But rather than an explanation, I soon came upon a rather curious paragraph. Chief Justice Waite, it seems, was in an exceedingly crabby mood on January 26, the first day of oral arguments by the lawyers:

> One of the points made and discussed at length in the brief of counsel for defendants in error was that "Corporations are persons within the meaning of the Fourteenth Amendment to the Constitution of the United States." Before argument, Mr. Chief Justice Waite said: The Court does not wish to hear argument on the question whether the provision in the Fourteenth Amendment to the Constitution, which forbids a State to deny to any person within its jurisdiction the equal protection of the laws, applies to these corporations. We are all of opinion that it does.

Wow! I thought. "The Court does not wish to hear argument." How injudicious. Was the chief justice experiencing a bout of dyspepsia? Gout perhaps? (I'd read somewhere that King George III suffered greatly from this.) Or was this simply a glimpse into that whisky-soaked, hard-living era of railroad barons, alcoholic ex-generals, and their cronies? Maybe he had a hangover.

I read on, until I got to another sentence: "Mr. Justice Harlan delivered the opinion of the Court."

Hmmm. Perhaps this would be the explanation I had been waiting for. So I read and read and read until my eyes glazed over—thirty-six exceedingly dry paragraphs about roadbeds, rails, rolling stock, fences, and rights of way. I went back and checked. Nope, nothing about corporate personhood. And finally I got to a passage where Justice Harlan declares the railroad to be the winner of the case, but not on "personhood" grounds. Instead, he awards the Southern Pacific a thumbs-up on highly technical grounds having to do with how the assessors categorized the fences attached to the railroad's property. Indeed, Justice Harlan declares that the Court doesn't need to invoke any weighty principles to solve the case; the technical issues are sufficient.

Now I felt doubly provoked, first, by the idea that corporations should be treated on the same legal and moral plane as human beings, and second, by the absence of any discussion of *why,* and in fact, a disavowal that any constitutional issue had been decided by the case at all!

All this left me more than a bit befuddled. If those involved in the case itself did not believe they had decided a constitutional issue, then why had this case been heralded in the years since as doing exactly that? Furthermore, the whole notion of corporate personhood struck me as preposterously, intuitively wrong. I reflected on the common observation that there is something impersonal, alien, soulless, even Franken-stein-like about corporations, especially when they become extremely large. "If anything," I ruminated, "it is the people inside the corporation who need to have rights, not the corporation."

As I continued researching the *Santa Clara* decision, I found out that I wasn't the only person to find it confusing. The case is surrounded with complexities and even intrigue. As chapters 9 to 11 of this volume explain, researchers into this case over the decades have discovered schemers with hidden agendas, handwritten notes of untold consequence, false clues, deliberate obfuscation, even a "secret journal." Studying it is like peeling an onion. Beneath one layer of myth is another, and then another. The whole thicket of complications makes the *Santa Clara* decision interesting—perhaps a bit *too* interesting. Because of all the intrigue and complexity, this case tends to distract attention from other things, especially aspects of corporate empowerment that are hidden even further back in history. *Santa Clara* has become its own myth—leading to the mistaken idea that the entire octopus of corporate power stems from that one Supreme Court decision.

One tip-off that there is more to the story of corporate power than *Santa Clara* is the date of the decision: 1886. Yet something was surely going on earlier, because beginning in the mid-1860s a number of prominent Americans began issuing a stream of near-hysterical alarms about corporate power. For example, in 1864 Abraham Lincoln wrote the following in a letter to his friend William Elkins:

We may congratulate ourselves that this cruel war is nearing its end. It has cost a vast amount of treasure and blood. . . . It has indeed been a trying hour for the Republic; but I see in the near future a crisis approaching that unnerves me and causes me to tremble for the safety of my country. As a result of the war, corporations have been enthroned and an era of corruption in high places will follow, and the money power of the country will endeavor to prolong its reign by working upon the prejudices of the people until all wealth is aggregated in a few hands and the Republic is destroyed. I feel at this moment more anxiety for the safety of my country than ever before, even in the midst of war. God grant that my suspicions may prove groundless.

Similarly, in 1870, Henry Adams, grandson and great-grandson of presidents, wrote:

The belief is common in America that the day is at hand when corporations . . . after having created a system of quiet but irresistible corruption—will ultimately succeed in directing government itself. Under the American form of society, there is no authority capable of effective resistance. . . . Nor is this danger confined to America alone. The corporation is in its nature a threat against the popular institutions which are spreading so rapidly over the whole world, . . . and unless some satisfactory solution of the problem can be reached, popular institutions may yet find their very existence endangered.

Clearly, the process by which corporations accumulated the political and legal power they enjoy today neither started nor ended with *Santa Clara* in 1886. Although that case is important, it represents a single gene on the entire chromosome of corporate empowerment. To map this chromosome, we need to consider three overlapping phases of empowerment, summarized in Table 1.1 on the following two pages.

❖ *Legislative creation of corporate quasi-rights:* After the United States gained its independence, the various states constructed a highly restrictive system for regulating corporations. Over time, that system was undermined and dismantled through a series of legislative and judicial actions that can be fairly characterized as creating a growing body of *quasi-rights.* These new corporate

Table 1.1

Three Phases in the Development of Corporate Rights

PHASE I: 1820–1900
LEGISLATIVE CREATION OF CORPORATE QUASI-RIGHTS

QUASI-RIGHT	AVAILABLE TO PEOPLE?	AVAILABLE TO CORPORATIONS?
Limited liability for shareholders	No	Gradual statutory revision by states (1820–1900)
Perpetual existence	No	Switch by states from custom charters to general incorporation (late 1800s)
Virtual location	No	New Jersey general incorporation law (1889)
Indefinite entity or "shape shifting"	No	New Jersey general incorporation law (1889)

PHASE II: 1886–1986
JUDICIAL CREATION OF CORPORATE CONSTITUTIONAL RIGHTS

RIGHT	AVAILABLE TO PEOPLE?	AVAILABLE TO CORPORATIONS?
Equal protection (state legislation)	Fourteenth Amendment	*Santa Clara v. Southern Pacific* (1886)
Due process (state legislation)	Fourteenth Amendment	*Chicago, Milwaukee and St. Paul Railway v. Minnesota* (1890)
Due process (federal legislation)	Fifth Amendment	*Noble v. Union River Logging Railroad Company* (1893)
Freedom from unreasonable searches	Fourth Amendment	*Hale v. Henkel* (1906)
Jury trial in a criminal case	Sixth Amendment	*Armour Packing Company v. U.S.* (1908)
Compensation for government takings	Fifth Amendment	*Pennsylvania Coal Company v. Mahon* (1922)

Right	Available to People?	Available to Corporations?
Freedom from double jeopardy	Fifth Amendment	*Fong Foo v. U.S.* (1962)
Jury trial in a civil case	Seventh Amendment	*Ross v. Bernhard* (1970)
Commercial speech	First Amendment	*Virginia Board of Pharmacy v. Virginia Citizens Consumer Council* (1976)
Political speech	First Amendment	*First National Bank of Boston v. Bellotti* (1978)
Negative speech (the right to abstain from association with the speech of others)	First Amendment	*Pacific Gas & Electric Co. v. Public Utilities Commission* (1986)

PHASE III: 1987–PRESENT
TRADE AGREEMENT CREATION OF CORPORATE GLOBAL RIGHTS

Right	Available to People?	Available to Corporations?
Minimum standard of treatment	No	U.S.–Canada Free Trade Agreement (1987)
National treatment	No	U.S.–Canada Free Trade Agreement (1987)
Compensation for regulatory takings	No	North American Free Trade Agreement (1993)

Source: Phase I, see chapters 6 and 7. Phase II "Corporate Bill of Rights" follows a list compiled by Carl J. Mayer, "Personalizing the Impersonal: Corporations and the Bill of Rights," *Hastings Law Journal,* 1990, 41, 664–667. Phase III, see chapter 16.

privileges included features such as limited liability and perpetual existence. This process continues today with new legislation
such as tort reform laws that exempt particular industries from
lawsuits. (The story is told in chapters 6 and 7.)

❖ *Judicial creation of corporate constitutional rights:* As shown in
the table, corporations have gained at least eleven distinct constitutional rights as a result of a string of Supreme Court decisions over the course of a century. The first decisions granted
corporations Fourteenth Amendment protections, which mainly
became shields against attempts by states to enact taxes and
workplace regulations. The most recent decisions have created
a body of First Amendment protections, whose most significant
effect is to impede campaign finance reform. (The creation of
corporate constitutional rights is described in chapters 8
through 14.)

❖ *Trade agreement creation of corporate global rights:* The most
recent phase of corporate empowerment began with the enactment of the U.S.–Canada Free Trade Agreement in 1987. International agreements have the effect of producing new rights that
corporations can use to overturn the environmental, labor, consumer, and other laws enacted by sovereign states. (This process
is described in chapter 16.)

Together, these three phases of corporate empowerment account for
much of the embedded institutional power of the corporation today. But
to fully understand the roots of corporate power, we need to look even
further back—to the evolutionary antecedents of the modern corporation, which, as we will see in the next chapter, lie in the craft guilds of late
medieval London.

CHAPTER TWO

From Street Fights to Empire

The British roots of the American corporation
(1267–1773)

T HE YEAR WAS 1267, and blood flowed in the muddy streets of London. A dispute between two guilds—the Goldsmiths and the Tailors— had escalated until it turned into armed conflict. The issues that led to the fighting are not recorded, but history does tell us that over five hundred men were involved, including members of the Clothworkers' Guild and the Cordwainers' Guild, and that many were injured or killed.

Such rumbles broke out from time to time among the scores of craft guilds that had arisen during the thirteenth and fourteenth centuries. In 1340 it was the Skinners fighting the Fishmongers in the Cheapside district of the city. In 1378, the Goldsmiths attacked the Grocers. Though bloody, those conflicts were both mere skirmishes compared with the all-out war of the 1390s, when a grand alliance consisting of the Drapers, the Mercers, the Tailors, the Goldsmiths, the Saddlers, the Haberdashers, and the Cordwainers went to battle against the Fishmongers and the Victuallers. The issues were a complex blend of the lofty and the mundane, including fish prices and the religious teachings of John Wyclif.

What, if anything, do these quaint-sounding medieval guilds and their conflicts over obscure and long-forgotten issues have to do with today's goliaths—General Electric, Microsoft, Merck, Wal-Mart, and so on? The Skinners, Fishmongers, and Haberdashers of the late Middle Ages did not yet display the particular features that would allow us to call them corporations. They were not unified businesses, but rather umbrella groups for the members of particular crafts. Yet already, some seeds of the corporation can be seen in them.

One such seed was a tendency toward exclusion and hierarchy as organizing principles. Even by the fourteenth century, the craft guild had moved a considerable distance from its communal roots in a Saxon tribal institution known as the *frith gild,* an association that included both men and women and served a variety of protective, religious, and mutual-aid functions. Medieval craft guilds had originally been "commonalities," in which all members were equal. But over time a stratification occurred, with the elite members of each guild assuming uniforms known as *liveries*. In time, nonliveried members were shut out entirely, and eligibility for membership was determined not by competency at a craft but by ability to pay a fee of capital. Among the London guilds, a strict ranking developed. Twelve became known as the "great livery guilds," with the Mercers occupying the top slot, followed in order of prestige by the Grocers, the Drapers, the Fishmongers, the Goldsmiths, the Skinners, the Merchant Tailors, the Haberdashers, the Salters, the Ironmongers, the Vintonners, and the Clothworkers. Scores of other guilds were known as the "lesser livery guilds."

Guilds didn't just fight—they also feasted. At one feast in 1516, the Drapers entertained the mayor and the sheriffs with "brawn and mustard, capon boiled, swan roasted, pike, venison baked and roast; jellies, pastry, quails, sturgeon, salmon, wafers and hippocras . . . six sheep, a calf, forty gallons of curds . . . swan's puddings, a neck of mutton in pike broth, two shoulders of mutton roast, four conies, eight chickens, six pigeons, and cold meat plenty."

Indeed, centuries after guilds such as the Skinners, Salters, and Long-Bow Stringmakers had outlived their economic functionality, many of them lived on as vehicles for networking and socializing. (Lately, the guilds have been rediscovered by London's young professionals, who have been forming new ones at a record pace, with names such as the Worshipful Company of Information Technologists, the Worshipful Company of Management Consultants, and the Worshipful Company of World Traders. A glance at the online social calendar for the Worshipful Company of Environmental Cleaners showed that its members were busily engaged in preparations for the annual Inter-Livery Clay Pigeon Shoot, the Inter-Livery Bridge Competition, the Installation of Masters, and the Lord Mayor's Show, in addition to the regular practice sessions of the guild's own Golfing Society.)

The nature of life in medieval times was such that the social, the religious, the economic, and the political spheres were fully mixed. Each guild had its own patron saint and altar. For example, the Fraternity of Pepperers, which begat the Grocers' Company in 1373, which in turn begat the Turkey Company in 1581 and the East India Company in 1600, maintained an altar in the Church of Saint Antonin and paid a priest to pray for the souls of past members. Since London had no police force, guilds also played a role in maintaining public order. As early as the thirteenth century, the guilds controlled the city government of London. They elected the mayor, who was known as the "master of all the companies." But despite their power, the guilds could not always rest secure, because their relationship with the British monarchy was complex and at times tense.

The main reason for that tension was the revenue needs of the throne. By the 1500s, Parliament had gained control over taxation, and the English monarchs were scrambling to develop independent sources of revenue that did not rely on parliamentary approval. One obvious source, especially in time of war, was the wealth of the livery guilds. For example, during the war between England and Spain, it was the Grocers' Company, among others, that financed the ships that defeated the Spanish Armada.

During peacetime, sales of land were a primary avenue of royal revenue, but that source was exhausted by 1685. Another revenue source, employed by both Elizabeth I and James I, was to call in all the guilds' charters for renewal, not because they needed renewal but merely to create an opportunity for collecting fees. Similarly, royal revenue was generated by sales of monopolies, a term that had a somewhat different meaning than it does today. Rather than giving the owner exclusive control over producing a product, a monopoly—also called a "searching and sealing patent"—signified authority over verifying the quality of a certain product. Given the advantages inherent in controlling such a function, it is no wonder that gifts or sales of monopolies to nonguild members provoked bitter opposition from the guilds. In 1580, when Queen Elizabeth attempted to grant a monopoly on the gauging of beer to one of her court favorites, the Brewers' Guild mounted a fierce campaign to dissuade her. Similarly, when one Edward Darcy obtained the right to approve and stamp all skins, his monopoly sparked a rebellion by the Leathersellers.

Despite the objections of the guilds, sales of monopolies became a major source of royal revenues in the sixteenth and seventeenth centuries. In 1623, Parliament passed the Statute of Monopolies, intended to halt the practice, but Charles I exploited loopholes in the act and managed to raise £100,000 per year from selling monopolies. In time, the practice ceased to be an effective source of revenue because there were limits to how far even a king could go in selling off smaller and smaller slices of economic activity.

Meanwhile, as the livery guilds continued to joust with the monarchy over who would ultimately control the innumerable revenue streams produced by the English economy, growing international trade had begun to transform some of the guilds into the first actual business corporations. In 1505, the Mercers' Guild spawned the "Guild or Fraternity of St. Thomas à Becket," also known as the Merchant Adventurers, organized to conduct trade with Holland and Germany. The Merchant Adventurers represented a transitional form; it was still a guild but it was beginning to show a few of the characteristics of the trading companies that would subsequently define the first true corporations. Like a traditional guild, the Merchant Adventurers functioned as an umbrella for a group of independent traders rather than as an organized entity. Financially, each trader operated as a stand-alone entity, raising his own capital and keeping his own separate set of books. But some common operations were beginning to emerge as well. Certain types of infrastructure, such as wharfs, convoys, and overseas embassies, were used by all the members of the Merchant Adventurers, and this shared infrastructure needed to be developed jointly and financed out of pooled capital. This was the starting point for one of the key features that distinguished corporations from guilds: the pooling of capital.

The 1500s and 1600s saw the formation of a number of trading companies (see Table 2.1). For nearby locations such as Spain, the Baltic Sea, and France, the organizational model established by the Merchant Adventurers worked well. Thus, in the Spanish Company, the Eastland Company, and the French Company, each member maintained his own separate capital. But as new geographic discoveries and innovations in shipbuilding and navigation made it possible for voyages to range beyond the coastal areas of Europe to more distant regions, such as Russia, Turkey, West Africa, and China, it became more practical for the merchants to pool their resources.

The typical voyage was unsuccessful, but now and then a ship would return with cargo that generated fabulous returns. Trade was not the only way these expeditions generated revenues—outright piracy was often part of the equation. In 1587, one of Sir Francis Drake's expeditions stumbled on a Portuguese galleon and promptly seized it. The cargo turned out to be worth £100,000, and investor enthusiasm for further expeditions soared.

Table 2.1
Formation of British Trading Companies, 1485–1714

MONARCH (REIGN)	COMPANIES FORMED (YEAR)
Henry VII (1485–1509)	Merchant Adventurers (1505)
Henry VIII (1509–1547)	
Edward VI (1547–1553)	
Mary Tudor (1553–1558)	Russia Company (1553)
Elizabeth I (1558–1603)	Spanish Company (1577) Eastland Company (1579) Turkey Company (1581) Morocco Company (1588) East India Company (1600)
James I (1603–1625)	Virginia Company (1606) French Company (1609)
Charles I (1625–1649)	
Commonwealth and Protectorate (1649–1660)	
Charles II (1660–1685)	Canary Company (1665) Hudson's Bay Company (1670) Royal African Company (1672)
James II (1685–1688)	
William III and Mary II (1689–1702)	Greenland Company (1693)
Anne (1702–1714)	South Sea Company (1711)

Source: Ron Harris, *Industrializing English Law* (Cambridge: Cambridge University Press, 2000), 52.

As in a venture capital fund that finances high-risk opportunities with potentially high returns, the steepness of the "risk-reward curve" made it logical for the financial backers of such voyages to spread their capital across multiple rolls of the dice. To increase their chances of success further, the investor groups sought grants of exclusive access to particular regions, bringing the notion of exclusivity to its apex—the gene of violent organization grafted onto the chromosome of peaceful trade. Inside the boundaries of their designated regions, they deployed private armies and police, waging war against rivals and imprisoning miscreants.

Thus was born the "joint-stock company," the form used by large corporations today. This method of pooling capital was briefly attempted by the Russia Company, which was chartered in 1553, and was also used during the first two decades of the Turkey Company's existence. But it was most fully developed by the British East India Company. Initially, this company raised capital one voyage at a time; next, it tried raising capital for limited periods of eight to fifteen years. In 1613, the company issued its first permanent stock, and by 1650 that method of raising capital became the norm, with profits periodically divided among shareholders.

With pooled capital, the corporation for the first time became a single unified entity rather than a federation of independent merchants. This internal consolidation made the joint-stock corporation ideally suited for the emergence of a key defining principle of the corporate form: the idea that a corporation represents a separate legal identity from its owners. Essentially, a corporation is a deal between the state and a group of people to which the state says: "You can create a separate entity and do business under that name, and the law will deal with the entity rather than with you as individuals." What made the separation even more significant is that shares in joint-stock companies could be sold to third-party investors.

The separation of the legal identity of the corporation from that of its owners had a profound impact in many ways, opening up the possibility of such corporate characteristics as corporate immortality (which doesn't mean, of course, that a corporation is immune from extinction, but merely that it is not constrained by the finite life spans of its mortal owners) and limited liability (the ability of owners to escape responsibility for corporate errors, misdeeds, and debts). Of course, neither immortality nor limited liability were inevitable features of joint-stock companies. Indeed, as we'll see in chapter 5, both of those features were deliberately withheld from corporations in the United States in the decades prior to the Civil War.

BESIDES PIONEERING the use of joint-stock capital and limited liability, the East India Company is historically significant because, quite simply, it was the most powerful corporation that has ever existed. Imagine a

private company so unaccountable that it conducts its own criminal tri-
als and runs its own jails, so dominant that it possesses an army larger
than any other organized force in the world, and so predatory that for
more than two centuries it squeezes the economy of the richest country
in the world until observers report that some regions have been "bled
white." The king is dependent on periodic "loans" from the company. A
third of Parliament owns stock in it, and a tax on its tea constitutes 10 percent of the government's revenues. A 250,000-man army (twice the size
of Britain's) fights the company's wars, and the four out of five soldiers
in that army who are "sepoys"—that is, Indians—are kept in line by such
punishments as "blowing away," strapping an offending soldier across
the mouth of a cannon and then firing the weapon.

At the time of the American Revolution, the British East India Company was nearly two centuries old, having received its charter on December 31, 1600, via a signature by Queen Elizabeth. "The Company of
Merchants of London trading into the East Indies," as it was formally
known—or simply "The Company"—received the largest grant of any
of the trading companies: everything east of the Cape of Good Hope.
Despite the queen's largess, the company's early years were difficult. A
rival group of Dutch investors had gotten a head start and had access to
ten times more capital than the English. In 1623, the Dutch captured ten
employees of the British East India Company in Indonesia, tortured
them on the rack, and executed them. Reluctantly—since Indonesia
(known in those days as *East India*) was considered a more lucrative
source for trade goods than India—the English retreated to the safer
shores of India, whose coastline was large enough to absorb the trading
settlements of multiple European powers.

India in the seventeenth and eighteenth centuries was a patchwork
of small kingdoms engaged in constantly shifting alliances. Officially, the
Mogul empire extended across vast regions, but its actual authority was
tenuous. Within this web of politics and intrigue, the East India Company
sought alliances with various Indian princes and conducted military
campaigns to outflank its European rivals. At the same time, the company's own employees sometimes became the enemy. Consider the case
of Samuel White, who came to India in 1676 at an annual salary of £20.
White developed a colorful side business: using company ships to transport elephants for the king of Siam. Eventually, he added to that the job
of fortifying a port that the king intended to make available for the

French, who happened not only to be allied with Siam but also were perpetual rivals of the British.

Using the small fleet of ships that he had armed for the king of Siam (directly against the interests of the East India Company), White proceeded to betray both of his employers by declaring his own private war on the kingdoms of Burma and Hyderabad. He seized ships belonging to those states and sold their cargoes as his own private property. In a two-year period, White's extracurricular activities earned him over £30,000, a vast fortune for the times.

White was hardly the first employee of the East India Company to engage in the forbidden activity of "free trading." He just happened to be one of the more audacious and successful. Though the local administrators of the company in India tended to overlook such activity as long as it did not interfere too greatly with the company's own revenue streams, the attitude of the central management was considerably harsher, as vividly described by historian Ramkrishna Mukherjee:

> Sir Josiah Child, as Chairman of the Court of Directors, wrote to the Governor of Bombay, to spare no severity to crush their countrymen who invaded the ground of the Company's pretensions in India. The Governor replied, by professing his readiness to omit nothing which lay within the sphere of his power, to satisfy the wishes of the Company; but the laws of England, unhappily, would not let him proceed so far as might otherwise be desirable. Sir Josiah wrote back with anger: That he expected his orders were to be his rules, and not the laws of England, which were a heap of nonsense, compiled by a few ignorant country gentlemen, who hardly knew how to make laws for the good of their own private families, much less for the regulating of companies, and foreign commerce.

Eventually, the company sent a ship to escort White back to the port of Madras, where he would presumably be tried and imprisoned. Under cover of night, he slipped away from the escort and sailed to the Siamese port of Mengui, where he stopped just long enough to inform the Siamese that the escort ship "had come to seize the town." In response, the Siamese attacked the British, killing some eighty Englishmen.

Even more impressive than White's talent for evasion was his sense of timing. By a stroke of luck, the arrival of his renegade ship in London coincided with the flight from the throne of James II, a supporter of the East India Company. His successors, William and Mary, placed more power in Parliament, which at that time was in a mood against the company. Judging the temper of the times to be favorable, White sued the East India Company for £40,000, but his luck had finally run out. Before the case came to trial, he died.

White's story provides a glimpse into an era when corporate enterprise was not yet fully cloaked in legitimacy. If White's behavior was barely a step above piracy, the same could be said for the company itself. Indeed, as the British gradually succeeded in outmaneuvering their opponents and taking over larger and larger portions of the Indian subcontinent, income from trade was dwarfed by revenues gained from taxing crops and local crafts by way of a middle stratum of tax collectors, fee assessors, and mandated buyers of crops and goods.

Far from enhancing the prosperity of areas under its umbrella, *Pax Brittanica,* by all accounts, proved highly ruinous to the unlucky inhabitants of India. In 1773, a parliamentary committee investigating the East India Company wrote, "In the East, the laws of society, the laws of nature have been enormously violated. Oppression in every shape has ground the faces of the poor defenseless natives; and tyranny in her bloodless form has stalked abroad."

In the same year, an anonymous pamphleteer wrote, "Indians tortured to disclose their treasure; cities, towns and villages ransacked, jaghires and provinces purloined: these were the 'delights' and 'religions' of the Directors and their servants."

To guard its own revenues, the East India Company issued edicts prohibiting local trading or the development of local industries. Typically, the extraction of revenues exceeded sustainable levels to the point where entire regions became economically broken and socially ruined—reduced from relative health to destitution.

Table 2.2 shows the devastation suffered by India's manufacturing sector, and the corresponding ascent of Britain's from 1750, shortly before the East India Company extended its control over most of the subcontinent, to 1880, two decades after Parliament finally terminated the company's charter and converted India into a formal colony.

Although the impact of the East India Company on India can generally be compared to a process of slow bleeding, its effect inside England was to create a perpetual struggle that corrupted Parliament and

Table 2.2
British and Indian Shares of World Manufacturing Output,
1750–1880 (in percent)

	1750	1800	1830	1860	1880
Britain	1.9	4.3	9.5	19.9	22.9
India	24.5	19.1	17.6	8.6	2.8

Source: Paul Kennedy, *The Rise and Fall of the Great Powers* (New York: Vintage Books, 1989), 149.

produced fierce conflict in the monied classes. Within months of the first issuing of the East India Company's charter, wealthy interests not included among the two hundred owning families initiated action in Parliament to nullify the franchise. In a pattern that was to repeat itself over the next two centuries, the company's representatives responded by bribing members of Parliament and providing open-ended loans to the monarch. In 1709, the company's rivals finally won out, gaining authorization to replace the East India Company. The British government ordered the old company to relinquish its stations in India to the new company. But the order proved impossible to enforce on the ground. In a standoff, the old company ordered its agents to stay at their posts, and eventually the new franchise had no choice but simply to merge with the old one. It was as though nothing had happened.

As for the other trading companies, they had already begun to collapse, one at a time, unable to ward off the encroachments of independent merchants. In 1606 the Spanish Company vanished; in 1667 the French Company; in 1689 the Eastland Company and the Merchant Adventurers; in 1750 the Royal African Company; in 1752 the Levant Company. The demise of the Royal African Company, whose initials were branded on the chests of thousands of men, women, and children, was typical. Despite government backing and participation by numerous prominent Englishmen, the RAC could not outmaneuver the smaller, family-owned slaving enterprises such as the Browns of Rhode Island and the Hobhouses of Bristol.

The East India Company defied the trend, becoming increasingly wealthy and politically influential throughout the eighteenth century as it gradually assumed control of most of the Indian subcontinent and then began expanding its ambitions even farther, toward China and America. Inevitably, those ambitions led to conflict and even war. The Opium War in China, which led to the acquisition of Hong Kong, was the result of a standoff between the government of China and the East India Company over the company's shipments of opium into southern China. And in the American colonies, as we'll see in chapter 4, an attempt by the East India Company to expand its tea business at the expense of independent American merchants in ports like Boston, Philadelphia, and New York was a principle cause of the merchant-led rebellion known as the Boston Tea Party.

Yet despite the crucial role played by the East India Company in British politics and the events that precipitated the American Revolution, there are other aspects to the story of how British corporations affected the politics and culture of pre-revolutionary America. Of these, the most striking example is the brief and tragic story of the Virginia Company.

CHAPTER THREE

The Ultimate Reality Show

The brutal history of the Virginia Company
(1607–1624)

H OW'S THIS FOR A PRIME-TIME CONCEPT? Take a few dozen British gentlemen, the type who like to search for gold and challenge each other to duels, but who have never done anything useful or practical in their lives. Make sure each brings along one or two footmen to powder his wig, shine his buckles, and prepare his afternoon tea. Add a few specialized workers, such as jewelers and glassmakers, and a few with more down-to-earth skills—but just a few. Then fill up the rest of a ship with half-starved street vagabonds, poor children, the widows of executed thieves, and various petty criminals. Transport the group across the Atlantic Ocean and drop them off on some land under the control of a preexisting nation of indigenous people. Check back in a few years and count how many people are still alive. That, in a nutshell, describes the dismal story of the Jamestown Colony, the one and only business venture of the London-based Virginia Company.

When I began looking into what happened in Virginia, I didn't have to go far. From the coffee table in my living room I picked up a copy of *National Geographic.* The article, "Unsettling Discoveries at Jamestown: Suffering and Surviving in Seventeenth-Century Virginia," described recent excavations on the banks of the James River, sixty miles from the mouth of Chesapeake Bay near the city of Newport News. Here, the first permanent settlement on the Atlantic coast was established in 1607.

In 1992, archeologist William Kelso discovered the site of the original James Fort, and his excavations confirmed in graphic detail the desperate accounts penned by survivors of "the starving time," the winter of 1609–10. The butchered bones of horses, cats, dogs, rats, and snakes indicated the downward spiral that the Virginia settlers found themselves in. There were also many haphazard graves, hastily dug. Some contained multiple human skeletons. Overall, of the 215 settlers who began the winter, only 70 were alive by spring.

Yet even as the first wave of settlers was starving to death, promoters continued to issue breathlessly optimistic new tracts with titles such as "Good News from Virginia." The new land, it was reported, "bringeth foorth all things in aboundance, as in the first creation, without toile or labour." Cedars grew taller than in the Azores. Game was plentiful. And as for grapevines, "in all the world the like abundance is not to be founde." As for the native inhabitants, they were reported to be "most gentle, loving, and faithfull, void of all guile, and treason." Such people, it was thought, would take to the gentle hand of English rule, the "faire and loving meanes suting to our English Natures," as readily as the primitive Britons had taken to the civilizing influence of the Romans.

Excitement about the company ran high and was tinged with the idea of adventure. One did not have to join the expedition to qualify. "Adventurer" included anyone who purchased a £12 share in the company, and the list included not only wealthy aristocrats and merchants but also such notables as William Shakespeare. Members of the Drapers' Guild were especially active. Of course, the organizers were frank about the goal of the company, which was to make a profit, mainly from the discovery of precious metals or minerals, or at least by the production of useful goods like glass, furs, potash, pitch, tar, and sassafras (considered a cure for syphilis). It was also whispered—though officially the idea was a no-no, since King James I had recently made peace with Spain—that the location of the planned settlement would be ideal for launching piracy missions on the rich and poorly guarded Spanish colonies of the West Indies. Some organizers even saw the potential for the English to join forces with rebel Caribbean groups such as the Cimarrons, a group of fugitive slaves, and the Chichimici, a nation of Indians in northern Mexico, and eventually to dislodge the Spanish from their lucrative colonies. If that long-shot scenario came to pass, the Virginia Company might produce returns beyond all imagining.

To its backers, prospects that investing in the Virginia Company would pay off were greatly enhanced by the availability of a virtually unlimited conscript workforce—Britain's dispossessed rural tenants, imprisoned beggars, and petty criminals. Thousands of English people were transported to Jamestown, most against their will. They worked under harsh conditions of forced labor, with poor food and shelter, and brutal punishment. Only one out of five people sent to the colony survived to see the end of their seven-year period of servitude. Among transported children, the survival rate was one in ten.

The Virginia Company's aggressive and careless use of indentured servants had its roots in the conditions of severe stress that characterized English society at the beginning of the seventeenth century. Under feudalism, the nobility had made their earnings on the backs of the peasantry. But in the 1400s and 1500s, many nobles concluded that they could do even better by getting rid of the peasants. The ongoing practice of "enclosure" converted peasant subsistence lands into sheep pastures, driving countless people from the countryside into rural vagabondage or urban destitution. The scope of enclosure was vast: aerial photographs and archeological excavations have revealed more than a thousand deserted settlements, lending support to estimates that nearly a quarter of the land in England was affected by enclosure. Meanwhile, the English conquest of Ireland and the banishment of Gypsies and Africans created further waves of social disruption.

To lose one's land was to become by definition a criminal. Under Henry VIII (1509–1547), vagabonds were whipped, had their ears cut off, or were hanged. During the reign of Edward VI (1547–1553) they were branded on the chest with the letter V. The Beggar Act of 1598 required first-time offenders to be whipped until bloody; repeat offenders were banished to work the oars of galleys or to serve time in the poorhouse.

The organizers of the Virginia Company presented their idea of converting the excess population of England into a new colonial workforce as a neat solution to two challenges: gaining a foothold in the New World and at the same time ridding England of its unwanted populations. Perhaps even more immediate on the minds of British leaders was fear of rebellion. During the Midlands Revolt, a large-scale uprising that took place in 1607, a group of peasants called Levellers took action to fill in (that is, level) the ditches used to enclose and drain peasant fields.

Edward Hakluyt, who spent twenty years promoting the ideas that led to the Virginia Company, was quite frank in calling it a "prison without walls." In 1609 the company applied to the city of London "to ease the city and suburbs of a swarme of unnecessary inmates, as a continual cause of death and famine, and the verey originall cause of all the plagues that happen in this kingdome."

At the request of the company, Parliament in 1618 passed a bill allowing the Virginia Company to capture English and Scottish children as young as eight years of age. John Donne, one of the leaders of the company, promised in 1622 that the Virginia Company "shall sweep your streets, and wash your dores, from idele persons, and the children of idle persons, and imploy them."

Historian John Van der Zee describes children "driven in flocks through the town and confined for shipment in barns." Those who survived the Atlantic passage encountered regimentation and institutionalized cruelty as routine aspects of everyday life. Each person, including children, received a military rank, and those who violated the detailed rules were tied "neck and heels" for the first offense, whipped for the second, and forced to work on a convict galley for the third. Such methods of discipline had been devised by Maurice of Orange for training Dutch soldiers; they were introduced to the Virginia colony by Sir Thomas Gates and Sir Thomas Gale. Even petty crimes were harshly punished. Stealing an ear of corn or a bunch of grapes while weeding a garden was punishable by death. For stealing two or three pints of oatmeal, one worker had a needle thrust through his tongue and was then chained to a tree until he died of starvation.

Speaking out against the leadership of the company earned even worse punishment. For making "base and detracting" statements against the governor, the company managers ordered one servant to have his arms broken, his tongue pierced with an awl, and finally to be beaten by a gauntlet of forty men before being banished from the settlement. For complaining that the company's system of justice was unfair, a man named Thomas Hatch was whipped, placed in the pillory, had an ear cut off, and sentenced to an additional seven years of servitude.

But of all the offenses an employee of the company could commit, the worst—judging by the severity of the punishment—was merely to *quit*. When one group of runaways was found living among the Indians, Governor Dale responded with a frenzy of executions: "Some he appointed to be hanged, some burned, some to be broken upon wheels, others to be staked, and some to be shot to death."

Although some accounts describe the children sent to the Virginia colony as "apprentices," the implication that young people were being educated in a trade in exchange for their uncompensated labor is deceptive. According to historian Edmund S. Morgan, "Almost all servants were

... in a condition resembling that of the least privileged type of English servant, the parish apprentice, a child who (to relieve the community of supporting him) was bound to service by court order, until he was twenty-one or twenty-four, with no obligation on his appointed master's part to teach him a trade or pay him." Ill treatment of children is reflected in the death rate. In 1619, several hundred children between the ages of eight and sixteen were shipped from the London poorhouse to Virginia. Of these, the names of 165 were recorded; six years later, only 12 of the group remained alive.

Degrading treatment of servants appears to have known few if any limits. Elizabeth Abbott was beaten to death by her masters, John and Alice Proctor. A witness counted five hundred lashes inflicted on Abbott prior to her death. A second servant of the Hintons, Elias Hinton, was beaten to death with a rake. It is not recorded what offenses the two had committed.

In some ways, the ill treatment of servants in the Virginia colony merely reflected the harshly enforced class structure that characterized the times. But the corporate organization of the company actually made conditions for servants worse in Virginia than in England, because the absolute power enjoyed by the company's managers over their workers led to the abandonment of English laws and customs that traditionally had given servants at least a small degree of control over their own lives. Buying and selling of servants became a common, even a casual, practice. A Dutch sea captain observed Virginia landowners playing cards, with their servants as gambling stakes. An English sea captain reported seeing servants "sold here upp and downe like horses." In a remarkably short time, the grandees of the Virginia Company had organized "a system of labor that treated men as things."

EXACERBATING THE DIFFICULTIES faced by the Virginia Company was a major dispute among its investors over company strategy. One group, consisting of large merchants, was content to let the company remain unprofitable for a long period. A second group, led by Lord Robert Rich, had obtained privateering commissions from small nation-states such as Savoy and saw the colony as a convenient base for preying on Spanish shipping in the Caribbean. A third group, led by Sir Edwin Sandys, favored more aggressive programs to wring a profit out of the colony.

Finally, the investors managed to unite in support of Sandys' plan, which included creative new incentives for the privileged members of the colony, transporting more servants and laborers, and initiating a diversity of economic projects, including production of lumber, silk, wine, and glass.

As part of the Sandys plan, the company formed a governing body consisting of the governor, his appointed councilors, and twenty-two burgesses elected by the landowning settlers. The Virginia General Assembly convened for the first time in 1619—the same year that African slaves were first brought to the colony. Thus, the Virginia colony, despite its record as a deadly work camp for the English poor and as the starting place for the 244-year holocaust of African slavery, gets credit as the New World's "cradle of democracy" for establishing the first legislative body among Europeans in America. To the north, the Massachusetts Bay Colony similarly spawned a representative legislature among its most privileged members. And as more settlements were organized, the use of legislatures expanded accordingly. New Hampshire, Rhode Island, and Connecticut all modeled themselves after Massachusetts; the southern colonies (except Georgia), after Virginia. Pennsylvania and Delaware, both organized by William Penn, adopted legislatures modeled after that of Virginia. In 1682, the Duke of York, responding to a petition, authorized the governor to call an assembly in New York like those of the New England colonies.

Sandys' plan might be termed the "Enronization" of the Virginia Company because of the way the officers of its spin-off subsidiaries managed to enrich themselves while the company itself collapsed. As described by historian Edmund Morgan:

> The company reserved a "quitrent" of a shilling a year on every fifty acres granted. The amount was small . . . but land was abundant. . . . It would yield a small income in quitrents to the company, increasing with the arrival of every new settler. . . . In order to speed up settlement, [Sandys] induced various members of the company to join in subcorporations or associations to found "particular plantations" peopled by tenants on the same terms. Investors in these associations obtained a hundred acres for every share of stock in the company plus fifty acres for every tenant. . . . In other ways, too, the company encouraged the formation of special-interest groups within itself. . . .

It seems evident that while the Virginia Company was failing in London, a number of its officers in the colony were growing rich. . . . We can see not only the fleeting ugliness of private enterprise operating temporarily without check, not only greed magnified by opportunity, producing fortunes for a few and misery for many.

Eventually, the bitter splits among the Virginia Company's investors led to an outside investigation of the company. A stockholder named Samuel Wrote had made a few calculations. Out of 3,570 people sent to the colony under Sandys, joining 700 people already there, only 900 remained alive just three years later. Approximately 350 people had been killed by Indians—but that left 3,000 deaths unaccounted for. Most, it appeared, had died of starvation, disease, abuse, or simply overwork on the tobacco plantations. "It consequentlie followes that wee had then lost 3,000 persons within those 3 yeares," noted the disgruntled Wrote.

Wrote and others asked the king for an official investigation, and after receiving the commission's findings the king moved quickly in 1624 to revoke the charter of the Virginia Company and place the colony under direct governmental control. Overall, since its founding, 6,000 adults and children had gone to the colony. Of those, an estimated 4,800 had died.

The Virginia colony was not an anomaly but rather just one island of misery in an archipelago that circled the Atlantic rim—from Ireland to West Africa to the Caribbean to the coast of North America. Around this circle, a cross-ethnic culture emerged among the conscript workforces of sailors and plantation workers. News traveled around the circle. Thus, in 1619, a request from the Virginia Company to the London Common Council for a shipment of children from Bridewell prison sparked a revolt among the children. Despite the glowing reports being fed to investors about conditions in the colony, more accurate reports about the deadly conditions in Virginia had apparently reached the inhabitants of Bridewell.

This subculture of resistance resurfaced repeatedly throughout the seventeenth and eighteenth centuries, most dramatically in street battles between sailors and press-gangs. During the Stamp Act protests of 1765, British General Thomas Gage noted that the rebellion was "composed of great numbers of Sailors headed by Captains of Privateers."

By themselves, the indentured servants and conscript sailors who re-belled throughout the eighteenth century in port cities like Boston and New York were not sufficiently organized to pose a serious threat to the established order. As we'll see in the next chapter, the spirit of rebellion that produced the American Revolution did not gain critical mass until it was picked up by more privileged members of society, including intel-lectuals like Tom Paine and merchants like John Hancock. But the debt to these original rebels is undeniable. Groups like Sam Adams' Sons of Liberty, made up of small and well-to-do merchants, consciously mod-eled themselves after the Sons of Neptune, a group of New York sailors. Men with one foot in each world, such as George Hewes, a shoemaker and former sailor who "was mixed up in every street fight, massacre, or tea party that occurred in the Boston of his day," carried the notions of freedom and equality with them as they crossed the boundaries that sep-arated one class from another. There is no doubt that the eloquent ideas that ultimately flowed from the quill of Thomas Jefferson had gestated for generations among indentured servants, plantation workers, and con-scripted sailors. This is the legacy of the men, women, and children who suffered and died of starvation, overwork, and brutal treatment on the to-bacco plantations of the Virginia Company and the ships of the East India Company.

CHAPTER FOUR

Why the Colonists Feared Corporations . . .

*In which the citizens of Boston demonstrate the use
of the hatchet as an anti-monopoly device*
(1770–1773)

A S I PROWLED THE LIBRARY STACKS for books on the history of corporations, I found some of the most entertaining works were those of Roland Marchand, a professor at the University of California and a historian of corporate public relations. Marchand was a collector of images, especially the sort of magazine ads created by corporations to link themselves with patriotic icons such as the Statue of Liberty, the American flag, or the Bill of Rights. These days the blatant imagery of those ads may look campy and nostalgic, but as Marchand argues in books such as *Creating the Corporate Soul* and *Advertising the American Dream*, it was part of a concerted campaign by large corporations throughout the twentieth century to overcome anticorporate sentiments that had old roots in American culture.

At times, those corporate efforts seemed almost transparently opportunistic—any national crisis provided the excuse for more PR. An example is the corporate response to a speech by President Franklin Roosevelt in early 1941 advocating increased American support for Britain against Nazi Germany. To underline his vision of what was at stake, Roosevelt outlined four freedoms: freedom of speech, freedom of religion, freedom from want, and freedom from fear. The speech inspired Norman Rockwell to paint a famous series of illustrations, one for each of the freedoms, and Rockwell's sentimental imagery eventually helped sell over $133 million in U.S. war bonds.

But corporate executives also saw an opportunity to make headway in their private "war within a war" to defeat New Deal interference in the economy and align their interests with the country's aroused patriotic sentiments. Moving quickly in response to Roosevelt's speech, public relations agencies launched an ad campaign that promoted a "fifth freedom"—free enterprise. Armour and Company led the charge with a series of editorials explaining how the "modern corporation works for the nation as a whole—not merely for its own stockholders." According to the ads, such a system "exalts the individual, recognizes that he is created in the image of God, and gives spiritual tone to the American system." Other ads extolled "the simple economics of our American way of life."

Since World War II, this sort of attempt to link corporations with the imagery of American patriotism has become virtually routine. And it has been successful to such an extent that today it almost sounds absurd to say something like, "One of the basic reasons for the American Revolution was colonial opposition to corporate power."

In general, corporate image advertising is softly focused and the political message is subtle. But not always. An example of a not-so-subtle campaign was the $600,000 deal between Philip Morris and the National Archives to celebrate the bicentennial of the Bill of Rights in 1991 with a traveling exhibit that brought one of the original copies of the Bill of Rights to all fifty states. The motivation behind the campaign could not have been more obvious. Faced with mounting restrictions on its ability to advertise its cigarettes, Philip Morris wanted to promote the idea that corporations, just like people, should be entitled to the free speech protections of the Constitution.

But as I read books like Ray Raphael's *A People's History of the American Revolution* and Benjamin Woods Labaree's *The Boston Tea Party,* I found little evidence that defending corporate prerogatives was anywhere to be found among the values and interests that the American rebels were fighting for. Quite the contrary. To a surprising degree, the American Revolution was directly and explicitly an *anticorporate* revolt. Part of the backdrop for that revolt was the long-standing anticorporate sentiment among lower-class people such as indentured servants and conscript sailors. In the eighteenth century, following the legislative suppression of corporate enterprise in Britain after the Bubble Act of 1719, anticorporate views also became common among both French and English intellectuals, and some of those thinkers influenced cosmopolitan Americans such as Benjamin Franklin. Among British and French thinkers, corporate enterprise was considered synonymous with monopoly—a way for privileged elites to profit at the expense of the general public.

This aspect of anticorporate sentiment was a pervasive theme in Adam Smith's *Wealth of Nations*. Smith wrote, "People of the same trade seldom meet together, even for merriment and diversion, but the conversation ends in a conspiracy against the public, or some contrivance to raise prices."

While traveling in England, Benjamin Franklin became friends with Smith, who read to him drafts of *Wealth of Nations*. Smith's objections to corporations also included practical concerns. According to Smith, a core flaw of the corporation as an institutional form was the intrinsic lack of functional accountability caused by separating ownership from management—a problem he famously phrased as that of "other people's money." Smith wrote: "The directors of such companies . . . being the managers rather of other people's money than their own, it cannot well be expected that they should watch over it with the same anxious vigilance with which the partners in a private guild frequently watch over their own. . . . Negligence and profusion, therefore, must always prevail, more or less, in the management of the affairs of such a company."

In support of his opinion, Smith cited a study by French economist André Morellet, who inventoried fifty-five European corporations that had all failed because of mismanagement.

In France, a group of laissez-faire economic thinkers known as the Physiocrats condemned corporations as manifestations of illegitimate royal privilege. So did the influential French economist Jacques Turgot, on similar grounds. During Franklin's stay in France in the 1760s, he visited with both the Physiocrats and Turgot. Franklin's 1769 book *Positions to Be Examined Regarding National Wealth* shows these influences.

But although the anticorporate sentiments of intellectuals and working-class people provided a supportive, and perhaps necessary, context for the American Revolution, neither of those groups was in a position to mount a concerted rebellion of the sort that broke out in Boston, New York, and Philadelphia in 1773. That rebellion required a third group to mobilize: the merchant community.

Merchant resentments about British rule centered on concrete economic issues. As formalized in the Navigation Acts, British law aimed at maintaining the American colonies as producers of raw materials for British manufacturing and as captive markets for British goods. The acts discouraged American manufacturing, prohibiting, for example, the casting of iron pots, as well as the development of infrastructure projects that might enhance any production other than raw materials for export.

Still, despite the unhappiness of the merchants with the subordinate economic role to which they were assigned, it appeared that the British were succeeding at keeping a lid on rebellious spirits. Among historians of the American Revolution, the years 1770 to 1773 are known as the "quiet period." By rescinding all but the tea tax, the British leadership had shrewdly defused popular anger in the colonies caused by a series of taxes levied in 1770. Even the lingering tea tax was largely symbolic, because most tea consumed in the colonies actually arrived via Holland-based smugglers rather than legitimate British traders. Hard-core agitators such as Samuel Adams found themselves stymied. "Taxation without representation" was too abstract an issue to motivate people to rebel when the item being taxed was plentifully available, tax-free. The British, it appeared, had nixed the possibility of a revolt in the American colonies.

And then came the Boston Tea Party, the event that triggered a severe British crackdown, which in turn precipitated the American move to declare independence. The conventional depiction goes something like this: On a dark winter's night in 1773, a band of "Mohawks," decked out in the white man's notion of Native American attire, mounts a mission of creative vandalism, a symbolic protest to dramatize their objection to taxation without representation by a tyrannical king. They board three ships bobbing peacefully at anchor in Boston Harbor. From the hold of each ship, they drag chests of tea onto the deck, chop them open, and unceremoniously toss bales of tea into the harbor.

It's a piece of drama that captures America's characteristic view of itself as a nation of plucky freedom fighters, teasing the arrogant masters into overreacting. Even today, when our military forces encircle the world, we still cast ourselves as the scrappy underdog—the wisecracking GI defying Hitler's war machine, the gladiator leading a slave revolt against Caesar, the towheaded farm boy going one-on-one against Darth Vader. Those are all quintessentially *American* heroes. Even if the movie is set in ancient Rome or in a galaxy "far, far away," the villains are easy to spot by their upper-class British accents.

What's wrong with the conventional story? For starters, there was nothing symbolic about the event. The objective of the "Mohawks" was to destroy tea on a massive scale, and that mission succeeded quite fully. The scope of the destruction far surpassed the level of damage that would have been inflicted if the action had been intended merely to score a political point in theatrical fashion. In a three-hour period, the Bostonians turned some 90,000 pounds of dry tea into "harbor tea." So much was dumped that the tea piled up in the shallow water and threatened to spill back onto the decks. The tea that was destroyed represented about 8 percent of the entire quantity consumed in the tea-happy American colonies per year and as much as a third of the amount normally imported from England rather than smuggled from Holland and elsewhere.

Second, the Boston Tea Party can't be explained merely as an outburst of nationalism. After all, colonial Americans still identified themselves as British. Nor was it an antimonarchal uprising like the French Revolution, at least at the outset. Looking closely at the events that led up to that night, we can see that it was a well-targeted attempt to block the British East India Company from carrying out a specific plan to monopolize American commodities markets, starting with tea. When respectable American businessmen took the uncharacteristically radical action of dressing up in disguise and committing wholesale vandalism, the motivating force was not abstract. It was literally to defend their businesses. In other words, it was a highly pragmatic *economic* rebellion against an overbearing corporation, rather than a *political* rebellion against an oppressive government. Or more accurately, it was a rebellion against a corporation and a government that were thoroughly intertwined.

To UNDERSTAND WHY anticorporate sentiments could run so strong even in the highest stratum of the American business community in 1773, it is important first to note that the corporate form, characterized by a charter and joint-stock ownership, was not how businesses were typically organized in the colonies. Instead, most American businesses were owned by families or partnerships. They had no corporate charters, nor did they need them.

Meanwhile, in the late 1760s, the East India Company entered a period of deepening crisis. During that decade, shareholders twice voted to increase their annual dividend, first from 6 to 10 percent and then from 10 to 12.5 percent. Those increases squeezed profits at an inopportune time, because revenues suddenly came under serious pressure. Because of a famine in Bengal in 1769 and 1770, the company's tax collectors couldn't extract as much revenue as usual from the Bengali peasantry. And in the American colonies, smuggled Dutch tea continued to crowd out English imports.

In 1772 a Europe-wide economic depression caused tea sales on the Continent to plunge. As the company's cash reserves dwindled, various suggestions for dealing with the crisis reached its managers. Among them was a proposal by a stockholder named Robert Herries, who outlined a way for the company to solve two problems at once—both the revenue shortfall and a glut of warehoused tea equal to three years of English domestic consumption. In a nutshell, Herries' idea was that the company should sell tea at drastically reduced prices on the European continent.

After considering the proposal, the managers concluded that tea dumped on the Continent would simply be smuggled back into England, where it would erode domestic prices. They liked the dumping idea, but they had a different destination in mind: the American colonies, where they could undersell the Dutch smugglers. To assist the East India Company with the plan, Parliament agreed to suspend the duties on tea shipments normally collected at the British end, but Foreign Minister North insisted that the colonists still pay the tax collected on the American side.

When news of the plan reached America, there was intense agitation in Boston, New York, and Philadelphia. Pamphleteers brought forth the familiar argument that taxation without representation was fundamentally unjust. Still, the business community, not normally disposed toward any sort of radical action, would not have become involved except for a second aspect of the policy: the plan by the East India Company to sell its tea exclusively through specially commissioned local consignees.

In other words, the East India Company planned to replace independent local merchants with a company-owned distribution system. Today, we would call the approach "vertical integration," whereby the oil company owns the wells, the refineries, and the gas stations. The colonists didn't have such a term, but they readily grasped the implications of the British plan. In Philadelphia, New York, and Boston, pamphleteers laid out the scenario in precise detail, warning that if the British were to succeed in bringing the tea distribution system under the sole control of the East India Company, they would inevitably repeat the same scheme for other imported commodities.

Here was an issue that could move even well-to-do segments of the community to rebel. Furthermore, in selecting the consignees for Boston,

To the Tradesmen, Mechanics, &c. of the Province of Pennsylvania

Hereafter, if they succeed, they will send their own Factors and Creatures, establish Houses amongst us. Ship us all other *East-India* goods; and in order to full freight their Ships, take in other kind of Goods at under Freight, or (more probably) ship them on their own Accounts to their own Factors, and undersell our Merchants, till they monopolize the whole Trade. Thus our Merchants are ruined, Ship Building ceases. They will then sell Goods at any exorbitant price. Our Artificers will be unemployed, and every Tradesman will groan under the dire Oppression.

The *East India Company,* if once they get Footing in this (once) happy country, will leave no Stone unturned to become your Masters. They are an opulent Body, and Money or Credit is not wanting amongst them They have a designing, depraved, and despotic Ministry to assist and support them. They themselves are well versed In TYRANNY, PLUNDER, OPPRESSION and BLOODSHED. Whole Provinces labouring under the Distresses of Oppression, Slavery, Famine, and the Sword, are familiar to them. Thus they have enriched themselves,—thus they are become the most powerful Trading Company in the Universe. . . .

Source: Excerpts from a broadside signed "A Mechanic," distributed in Philadelphia, Dec. 4, 1773. Library of Congress, Printed Ephemera Collection, Portfolio 143, Folder 34d; see http://memory.loc.gov.

Governor Thomas Hutchinson had committed a particularly foolish blunder. Hutchinson had named five men to be the local consignees: two were his own sons, one was his nephew, and the last two were personal friends. Notably absent from the list was John Hancock, the leading merchant in Boston. When Hancock learned that he had been excluded, he patched up a quarrel with Sam Adams and became one of Adams' strongest supporters.

When the cargo ship *Dartmouth* arrived in Boston Harbor, a crowd of over five thousand assembled at the Old South Meetinghouse and voted unanimously in support of the proposition "that the tea should be returned to the place from whence it came." Although the ship's captain agreed to return to England without unloading the tea, British officials refused to issue a pass allowing the ship to leave the harbor. And so, on the night of December 16, 1773, approximately 150 men assembled. They came from a broad range of backgrounds, reflecting the wide spectrum of support for the action—some were apprentices, some were trades-men, and some were wealthy owners of businesses. By dawn, the entire shipment of tea had been destroyed.

WHAT IS PERHAPS most interesting about the incident is the way in which the Boston establishment, which once had taken great pains to keep its distance from the rebellious subculture of indentured servants and conscripted sailors, now embraced that culture—at least in symbolic fashion. For example, in 1770, only three years prior to the Boston Tea Party, John Adams had defended the redcoats who participated in the Boston Massacre against charges that they had committed murder. In court, Adams had appealed to racist prejudices in claiming that the ap-pearance of the Afro-Indian sailor Crispus Attucks "would be enough to terrify any person."

Yet in 1773, when Adams penned a rebellious letter to Governor Hutchinson at the height of the tea crisis, he needed a pseudonym to maintain his anonymity and to signify the determination of the colonists. And the man whose name he selected was the same one he had previously sought to discredit: Crispus Attucks.

The response of the British to the Boston Tea Party was predictable. Provoked and angry, Parliament struck back by passing the Intolerable Acts, a set of bare-knuckled reprisals that closed Boston Harbor and banned the Massachusetts assembly. George III vowed to bring the colonists to their knees. But instead of accomplishing the desired result of isolating and pacifying one radical city, the crackdown generated sym-pathy for Boston and drew the normally fractious colonies into a coor-dinated response.

The American Revolution was under way.

CHAPTER FIVE

. . . And What They Did About It

How the framers of the American system restrained corporate power
(1787–1850)

I hope we shall crush in its birth the aristocracy of our monied corpora-
tions which dare already to challenge our government to a trial of
strength, and bid defiance to the laws of our country. —Thomas Jefferson, 1816

W HEN I FIRST READ this quote by Thomas Jefferson about crushing
"the aristocracy of our monied corporations" in the cradle, I assumed that he was engaging in a mere flight of rhetoric, not literally proposing that corporations be eliminated. Indeed, by 1816 getting rid of the
corporation was no longer a viable political option, but it is worth noting
that a man of Jefferson's political longevity could actually recall a time
when such institutional infanticide would in fact have been quite possible.
Immediately following the revolutionary war, the corporate presence in
America had fallen virtually to nil. At the time of the Constitutional Convention in 1787, only six business corporations other than banks existed in
the United States: one for organizing a fishery in New York, one for conducting trade in Pennsylvania, one for conducting trade in Connecticut,
one for operating a wharf in Connecticut, one for providing fire insurance
in Pennsylvania, and one for operating a pier in Boston.

Although these circumstances provided the opportunity to abolish
the corporation entirely, that was not what the elite American leadership
had in mind. Their idea was to transform the corporate form, not get rid
of it. Their vision was to subordinate corporations to democratic oversight, then make use of this tamed institution as a tool for meeting the
pent-up need for infrastructure such as roads and bridges.

The key political issue, which was debated at the Constitutional Convention, revolved around who would control the authority to issue

corporate charters. The granting of a charter, of course, is what changes an unincorporated business into a corporation. The delegates to the Constitutional Convention recognized the significance of this power. In England, charters had almost always featured some sort of monopoly privilege. But even if a charter did not include such a privilege, it still had value. By incorporating, a business took on a separate legal existence from its owners. This separation made financing easier because it allowed ownership shares to be parceled out to investors in exchange for financing. In addition, it allowed businesses more easily to remain intact through multiple generations of owners. Over time, other advantages would be added to the corporate form, as we'll see in subsequent chapters.

Despite such advantages, incorporation of ordinary businesses was rare in colonial America, since—unlike the building of roads and bridges—most enterprises were modest in size and required little capital. But it was familiar to some of the framers of the new government, including Washington and Franklin. Both men had been shareholders in corporations that received grants of frontier land from the king and that used indentured servants to clear farmsteads and build roads. Franklin was also an advocate of canals, which he saw as a particularly beneficial application of the corporate form. He encouraged canal developer and steamboat pioneer Robert Fulton, who differentiated his efforts from those of the "India or Guinea Company . . . who blindly extirpate one half of the human race to enrich the other."

Believing that corporations could play an important role in building the new country, the framers of the Constitution focused on the issue of how to authorize corporate activity while preventing any single corporation from becoming too large and gaining too much political influence.

At the Constitutional Convention, James Madison twice proposed putting the federal government in charge of corporations "in cases where the public good may require them and the authority of a single state may be incompetent." But among the delegates, a significant contingent had been instructed by their home states to oppose any federal involvement in authorizing corporations, under the belief that granting such powers to a central government created the risk that an American version of the East India Company might come into being. The best preventative against such a development, it was felt, was to keep the power to charter corporations as close to the local level as possible.

Into this standoff, Benjamin Franklin attempted to interject a compromise, a scaled-back version of Madison's idea. Under Franklin's scheme, the federal government would have incorporating powers, but those powers would be limited to authorizing postal roads and interstate canals. The delegates rejected this milder proposal as well: Pennsylvania, Virginia, and Georgia voted aye, New Hampshire, Massachusetts, Connecticut, New Jersey, Delaware, Maryland, North Carolina, and South Carolina voted nay. In the end, the final text of the Constitution contained no mention of corporations whatsoever.

During the next two years, as the states considered whether to ratify the Constitution, five recommended adding an amendment expressly prohibiting the federal government from granting charters that would provide any "exclusive advantages of commerce." For the most part, the states got their wish. Not until the twentieth century did the federal government attempt to issue charters, and even then only for certain quasi-public entities, such as Amtrak. The lone exception prior to the twentieth century was the Bank of the United States, part of a political tug-of-war that went back and forth four times: chartered in 1791, charter revoked in 1811, chartered again in 1816, second charter expired in 1832 and not renewed.

THE SYSTEM THAT EMERGED for chartering corporations in America after the Constitutional Convention flipped the English system upside down. Instead of the monarch using corporate charters to grant special monopoly privileges to men of wealth, the American system placed the chartering function in the hands of the various state legislatures. Furthermore, it put the emphasis on restrictions and accountability measures, rather than on privileges. State constitutions and statutes reinforced the restrictive stance toward corporations. Under this system, charters tended to be granted sparingly, in keeping with the widespread belief that the potential for corporations to accumulate power rendered them inherently dangerous to democracy.

In 1809, an opinion of the Virginia Supreme Court (*Currie's Administrators v. Mutual Assurance Society*) stated that a charter should not be granted if the applicant's "object is merely private or selfish; if it is detrimental to, or not promotive of, the public good." In effect, this meant that most corporate charters were reserved for quasi-public projects like toll roads, bridges, canals, banks, and other sorts of infrastructure. Charters were not issued in situations where nonchartered businesses already operated. Nor were state legislators inclined to grant a corporate charter unless they were convinced that such a measure was necessary. For example, in Pennsylvania in 1833, the legislature split over whether to issue a charter to a coal company. The opposition argued that the coal industry had become sufficiently established to attract private financing without the need for a charter.

According to historian Louis Hartz, public wariness toward corporate entities in the first decades of the nineteenth century was "one of the most powerful, repetitious, and exaggerated themes in popular literature." Note that this anti*corporate* sentiment should not be confused with anti*business* sentiment. In the public mind, the use of the corporate form was associated with monopoly privileges of one sort of another. In 1835, a representative of the National Trades Union wrote:

> We entirely disapprove of the incorporation of Companies, for carrying on manual mechanical business, inasmuch as we believe their tendency is to eventuate in and produce monopolies, thereby crippling the energies of individual enterprise, and invading the rights of smaller capitalists.

Typical of that sort of "invading" was an attempt in 1801 by several of New York's wealthy merchants (including a brother-in-law of Alexander Hamilton named John Church) to get a charter that would allow them the exclusive right to provide bread to the city, hiring previously independent bakers to perform the work. When they caught wind of this bald attempt to drive them out of business, the bakers employed the full force of Jeffersonian rhetoric, arguing that if the legislature granted such a charter "the independent spirit, so distinguished at present in our mechanics, and so useful in republics, will be entirely annihilated."

During the 1820s and 1830s, conflicts over corporate charters became a common occurrence. Beginning in 1827, political parties calling themselves Workingmen's Parties and comprising independent artisans began to rally around the anticorporate theme, only to decline after the mid-1830s as Andrew Jackson's Democrats adopted their ideas. Typical of Democratic Party rhetoric is the following speech by Democratic legislator and journalist Gideon Wells in 1835:

The unobtrusive work-shop of the Mechanic, the residence of free-dom, is beginning to be abandoned, because he cannot compete with incorporated wealth. . . . What encouragement do our laws hold out to the poor but industrious artisan, who enters upon the threshold of manhood with no fortune but his trade, and no resources but his own hands? . . . [Such legislation] paralyzes industry, is unaccompanied by wealth; and it is destroying that equality of condition, which is the parent of independence. Competition on the part of individuals is hopeless, when they find capital entering the field, under privileged laws, and private enterprise is compelled to yield to the unjust influ-ence which partial legislation establishes.

A New Jersey editorialist of the 1830s wrote: "Legislatures ought cau-tiously to refrain from creating the irresponsible power of any existing corporations or chartering new ones. . . . " Otherwise the citizenry would become "mere hewers of wood and drawers of water to jobbers, banks, and stockbrokers."

Legal writers echoed the same themes, as reflected by the words of attorney Theodore Sedgwick in his 1835 book *What Is Monopoly?*

Every corporate grant is directly in the teeth of the doctrine of equal rights, for it gives to one set of men the exercise of privileges which the main body can never enjoy. . . . Every such grant is equally adverse to the fundamental maxim of free trade for it carries on its face that no one but the corporators are free to carry on the trade in question, with the advantages which the charter confers.

The prevalence of such attitudes made it politically feasible to organ-ize opposition to the issuing of new charters, as happened in 1838 when fifty-one journeymen carriagemakers petitioned the Massachusetts leg-islature in opposition to a proposed charter for the Amherst Carriage Company:

We being journeymen at the Coach chaise and harness manufacturing business, do look forward with anticipation to a time when we shall be able to conduct the business upon our own responsibility and receive the profits of our labor, which we now relinquish to others, and we be-lieve that incorporated bodies tend to crush all feable enterprise and compel us to worke out our dayes in the Service of others.

As shown in Table 5.1, charters controlled corporations along all conceivable dimensions.

Table 5.1
Typical Pre–Civil War Controls in Corporate Charters

Activities	Each corporation was limited to performing a specific function, such as operating a school or a bridge.
Life span	Charters of incorporation were issued for terms ranging from twenty to thirty years, after which they would have to be renewed. Banks faced especially tight restrictions (see banking section of table).
Property ownership	Most states limited corporations to owning only property that was directly needed for the authorized activity.
Size	Charters limited the amount of invested capital that an individual corporation could control. Various provisions also had an indirect effect on limiting size, including restrictions on property ownership, the requirement for unanimous shareholder consent in all major decisions, geographic restrictions, and limits on permitted activities.
Geographic scope	Most corporations were not allowed to operate beyond the borders of the state in which they were incorporated. Sometimes they were even restricted to a single county. For example, the 1818 charter for the Main Flour Mills restricted it to owning property in Kennebec County.
Intercompany ownership	As a rule, corporations were not allowed to own stock in other corporations.
Performance criteria	In addition to stating what activities were allowed, charters also frequently specified project completion dates and output requirements. Sometimes the two were combined—for example, an iron company being required to reach a certain tonnage of production within three years.
Profits	Charters sometimes limited the profit a corporation could earn. Many charters also required that profits from a company be used to buy back stock, so that eventually all stockholders would be eliminated and the company would in effect become a public entity under the supervision of the state legislature. Under the Turnpike Corporation Act of 1805, Massachusetts authorized the legislature to dissolve turnpike corporations once their receipts equaled the cost of construction plus 12 percent.

Public privilege	Charters for turnpikes usually exempted farmers, worshippers, and poor people from paying tolls.
Shareholder restrictions and protections for minority owners	In some cases incorporators had to be citizens of the state. Charters also contained a number of specific rules to prevent a single individual from controlling the corporation. Some placed a minimum on the number of shareholders. Some required that the corporation use a voting formula that increased the leverage of small investors. Most stated that certain key decisions, such as issuing new stock or selling the company, required unanimous consent of all shareholders.
Special restrictions on banking	Bank charters were limited to three to ten years. Banks had to get special approval to merge. In some states, they were required to direct their loans to local industries. They were also required to lend money to the state government if requested. Maximum interest rates were designated. Illinois and Indiana banned private banking corporations in their state constitutions; Wisconsin and four other states amended their constitutions to require that all bank charters be approved by popular vote.
Shareholder liability	Limited liability—the principle that shareholders can't be held responsible for judgments against a corporation or for unpaid corporate debts—wasn't a widespread feature of the corporation until about 1875, when unrestricted general incorporation finally eclipsed special charters.
Ultra vires	In addition to other restrictions, corporations were subject to the general ban on activities not expressly permitted in their charter. This doctrine of limited authorization, known as ultra vires, translates as "beyond the powers." Courts would not enforce any contract outside the scope of a corporation's charter.

Of particular note were limits on life span, rejection of liability shields, measures that limited corporate expansion, and enforcement mechanisms.

As the table shows, the charter system took direct aim at the tendency of the corporation to accumulate wealth and power over time by placing restrictions on the term of each charter. Terms of twenty to thirty years were typical for most corporations, after which time the directors would have to seek a new charter. Banks, which were considered the form most subject to abuse, were kept on a tight leash with terms as short as three years.

Limited liability—the doctrine that investors can't be held responsible for debts or settlements against a company—is often mentioned as an essential part of the very definition of the corporation. But limited liability has not always been part of the repertoire of corporate attributes, either in England or America. In England, limited liability was not a consistent feature of corporate law until the late eighteenth century—and wasn't universally available until 1855—although it did appear from time to time. For example, Parliament passed a law in 1662 granting limited liability to "noblemen, gentlemen and persons of quality" in relation to the East India Company, the Guinea Company, or the Royal Fishing Trade. In the United States before the Civil War, state legislatures explicitly rejected limited liability. For example, in 1822 Massachusetts passed a law that read, "Every person who shall become a member of any manufacturing company . . . shall be liable, in his individual capacity, for all debts contracted during the time of his continuing a member of such corporation."

Instead of such "unlimited liability" requirements, most states used a "double liability" formula, which made shareholders liable for twice the value of their investment in the company. Until the end of the 1870s, seven state constitutions applied the principle of double liability to all shareholders in banks. Some states also required that shareholders in manufacturing and utility companies be specifically liable for employee wages.

Perhaps the most significant limitations were those that *restricted corporations from expanding* without specific permission by a state legislature. These worked in various ways:

❖ Corporations were prohibited from engaging in any activities not specified in their charter. Under the legal principle known as *ultra vires,* any contract that dealt with activities beyond a corporation's charter would not be enforced by the courts. For example, the Illinois Supreme Court ordered the Pullman Palace Car Company to divest itself of its company-owned town, Pullman, Illinois, based on the fact that owning a town was not specified among the activities permitted in the corporation's charter.

❖ Corporations could not own stock in other corporations.

❖ Most states placed limitations on the amount of capital a corporation could raise.

❖ Most corporations were not allowed to operate outside their home state, and in some cases outside of their home county.

❖ Corporations were typically forbidden to own property not directly needed for their authorized activities.

Finally, anticorporate sentiment made it possible for state attorneys general to wield the stick of *charter revocation,* the equivalent of a death penalty for errant or scofflaw corporations. For example, in Massachusetts or New York, turnpike corporations could suffer revocation merely for "not keeping their roads in repair." Pennsylvania revoked the charters of ten banks in 1832 alone.

CLEARLY, THE CHARTER SYSTEM reflected an utterly different political consciousness toward corporations than exists today—less cowed, more assertive. Implicit in this approach to dealing with corporations was a different way of drawing the line between public and private than we are now accustomed to. The charter system was an assertion that for democracy to thrive, democratic power must trump corporate power. In other words, democracy should not apply just to public spaces—to spaces not claimed by private interests. If only the sidewalks and not the skyscrapers are considered to lie within the purview of democracy, then democracy is weak indeed.

Although much of the rhetoric surrounding charter fights may create the impression that public attitudes were antibusiness, as noted earlier, this was not the case. It would be more accurate to say that because of the quasi-public nature of the corporation the public believed corporations should be restricted to the building of crucial infrastructure such as canals, wharves, water works, toll roads, banks—and, beginning in the 1840s, railroads. By 1800, there were 335 business corporations in the country. Of these, 76 percent were toll roads, canals, docks, bridges, water supply companies, or other public services; 20 percent were banks or insurance companies. Expansion continued. Pennsylvania alone chartered 2,333 business corporations between 1790 and 1860.

Meanwhile, manufacturing and retailing companies, which tended to organize under noncorporate formats—mainly partnerships—demonstrated dramatic growth. The volume of manufactured goods grew by an average of 59 percent per decade from 1809 to 1839, then by 153 percent in the 1840s and 60 percent in the 1850s. By 1860, America's manufacturing industry had achieved the second highest per capita manufacturing output (after Great Britain) in the world. Clearly, the absence of corporate ownership in manufacturing did not inhibit growth.

For a time, it seemed that America had found a working balance where the corporation was allowed to perform certain functions for which it was well suited, but where corporate political power was kept firmly under the thumb of democracy. Yet as attractive as this finely balanced combination might seem, it was not to last. Beginning in the 1850s, and particularly after the Civil War, legislators sympathetic to the wishes of the rapidly growing railroad corporations effectively dismantled the restrictive features of the charter system, replacing it with a nonrestrictive system of automatic chartering known as "general incorporation." By the 1880s the old system was in near collapse, and by 1900 it had effectively vanished.

A revolution had occurred, a dismantling of a key institutional framework. In its place, a new system was created: a revolutionary reinventing of the corporation. Even today, the impact of this quiet revolution is little appreciated, and the specifics of how it took place are even less understood. Perhaps the reason we fail to appreciate the depth of this transformation is that the role of its leaders is somewhat obscured. Without revolutionaries, we can't see the revolution. And the robber barons—those spoilsmen in black coats and top hats—hardly look like revolutionaries. If they are remembered by history, it is mainly for their energy and unscrupulousness, not as genetic engineers creating a far more virulent strain of an old institution. The next chapter takes a look at one such man and the role he played in the corporate revolution.

CHAPTER SIX

The Genius

The man who reinvented the corporation
(1850–1880)

An electric brain and cool quiet manner.
—Congressman Albert Riddle,
describing Assistant Secretary of War Tom Scott

UNLIKE MANY OF THE OTHER institutions that shape the human world, the modern corporation did not have a charismatic founder or advocate. In contrast to other realms where the signature of a single mind is clearly imprinted, the corporation lacks the mark of any particular historical personality. There was never a Mohammed to take divine dictation, no Saint Paul to journey forth and establish chapters, no Martin Luther to nail a manifesto to the door of the old establishment, no Jefferson to pen an announcement of freedom.

Or was there?

In the decade following the Civil War, three railroads fed into New York City—the Central, the Pennsylvania, and the Erie. The Central was nicknamed "The Empire" because of the autocratic style of its chairman, Cornelius Vanderbilt. The Pennsylvania was known as "The Republic" because of the close ties between its vice president, Tom Scott, and the Pennsylvania legislature. But it was the notorious Erie, run by a pair of brilliant financiers named Jay Gould and "Diamond" Jim Fisk, that captured the attention of the public. Gould and Fisk ran the Erie from offices in New York's Opera House Palace on West Twenty-Third Street, "decorated in Oriental splendor of silken hangings, mirrors, rich rugs, marble statuary and carved oaken furniture" and joined by secret passageways to their private houses and stables. From these opulent quarters they launched operettas and musical revues, in addition to a series of stock frauds, takeover intrigues, and monopolistic predations.

In typical American fashion, the public focused on Gould's and Fisk's personal morality and flamboyant excesses, and on the melodrama of their feuds with other railroad barons. But events of far more significance were occurring behind the scenes, engineered by Tom Scott of the Pennsylvania Railroad. To this day, Scott remains an obscure figure. He rarely spoke in public and left few written records. Though known—and feared—inside the railroad industry in his day, Scott preferred to operate outside the public eye. Perhaps because he never named a university or a foundation after himself, his name has faded into the recesses of nineteenth-century history.

The fact that Scott has been forgotten is not as striking as the fact that the significance of his invention is scarcely recognized. We remember Edison for inventing the electric lightbulb, Whitney for the cotton gin. But in the end, Scott's innovation may outrank any other of the nineteenth century. More than any other person, Scott is responsible for the institution that has increasingly dominated the world since the late 1800s—the corporation in its modern incarnation.

To grasp the importance of Scott's accomplishment, it is worth noting, for starters, that no one saw it coming. Both Adam Smith and Karl Marx failed to predict the reemergence of the corporation as a dominant institution. In *Wealth of Nations,* which Adam Smith wrote in 1776, he saw the corporation as a decrepit and ill-conceived institution, a remnant of medieval privilege that was too prone to mismanagement to be useful for any but a handful of contingencies. In *The Communist Manifesto,* written in 1848, Karl Marx ignored corporations altogether. Both Smith and Marx were influenced mainly by the situation in Britain, where virtually all the giant trading companies had collapsed by the mid-1700s. For the most part, the Industrial Revolution in England flourished under quite simple institutional forms, mainly family-owned enterprises, partnerships, and unincorporated joint-stock companies.

In America the corporation had experienced a revival, but as late as 1850 the charter system appeared to be in good working order. For six decades, that system had functioned as a legal containment vessel preventing the emergence of politically overbearing corporations like the East India Company in England. Yet the system was not getting in the way of rapid economic growth.

The fissures in the containment vessel that ultimately cracked it open originated without notice in the back rooms and committee chambers of state capitols during the early 1850s, as lobbyists for the newly emerging railroad corporations began exacting concessions from state legislatures. Scott, a legislative manipulator without peer, was responsible for one such concession that at the time hardly seemed earth-shattering. It was quite simple: convincing the Pennsylvania legislature to relax the long-standing prohibition against one corporation owning stock in another corporation. Perhaps it is fitting that Scott was a math prodigy in his youth. This inconspicuous change—one corporation owning stock in another—is something like the introduction of the zero by unknown Arab mathematicians—a minimalist placeholder, but nevertheless a monumental invention. As we'll see in this chapter, it proved to be a change of key importance in the evolution of corporate power.

The charter of the Pennsylvania Railroad, which originally was a state-owned enterprise (in the 1830s, the state supplied the locomotives, while private companies supplied the other cars) but later was spun off into private ownership, contained restrictions that were typical of the era. The charter required that the public have access to the records of the railroad, it gave the state the option of buying the railroad entirely if it chose to do so, and it specified that the governance of the corporation would take place via a yearly quasi town meeting of stockholder "citizens." The corporation was prohibited from owning land not directly connected to its business. It was not allowed to conduct any business not specified in the charter—which limited its ability to expand creatively. And every twenty years it had to return to the legislature for charter renewal.

With so many limitations built into its charter, it would have been hard to imagine that the Pennsylvania Railroad might very soon grow into the largest corporation in the world, with transcontinental aspirations. Politically, it faced strong opposition. That opposition came in part from competing transportation interests, especially the immense wagons drawn by six-horse teams that carried goods across the state. Their proprietors held mass meetings along the lines of the turnpikes to protest the introduction of railways, and frequently state legislators were elected solely on the anti-railroad issue. In addition, popular sentiment opposed corporations in principle, traced partially to the failure of numerous chartered banks during the financial panic of 1837 and again during the panic of 1857.

Early hostility toward the Pennsylvania Railroad also rose out of widespread belief that the company had swindled local governments. Some counties had initially helped finance railroad construction by issuing bonds, only to find themselves forced to raise taxes when the Pennsylvania Railroad failed to pay dividends on the bonds. In Allegheny County, the commissioners defied a court order to levy taxes for the payment of interest on the bonds, and the commissioners went to prison for contempt of court.

At the local level, decisions on where to site railroad tracks frequently triggered intense political conflict because it was clear that the location of railroads would determine the survival or extinction of whole communities. In Erie, a two-inch difference in the gauges of two connecting tracks made it necessary for passengers and freight trains to leave one train and board another. The community became divided between the "Shanghais," who favored laying new, standardized tracks, and the "Rippers," so named because of their practice of repeatedly ripping up the new tracks. Members of the factions ceased all social intercourse and refused to attend church services together. According to one historian, "When the contest had reached white heat, the women of the town turned out in a body and burned a railroad bridge."

THIS WAS THE CHARGED CLIMATE into which Tom Scott entered when he became the Pennsylvania Railroad's lobbyist in the state legislature. The son of a tavern keeper at a stagecoach stop, Scott had begun his railroad career in 1850 as a stationmaster. Upon being promoted to the position of lobbyist, his top priority was repealing the tonnage tax levied on the railroad by the state, but his efforts in the legislature were at first unsuccessful. "Public sentiment was so strong against any legislation in favor of corporations that the only reward received was a succession of humiliating defeats," wrote veteran legislator A. K. McClure.

To overcome the opposition, Scott used every tool at his disposal. He began by organizing supporters at the individual county level across the state, and followed up by purchasing advertisements in nearly every Pennsylvania newspaper, whether friendly or unfriendly to the railroad. When the legislature convened, Scott was still far short of majority support in either house, and at that point he began making deals, mainly consisting of promises to build railroad lines to provide service to particular communities in return for the support of the local delegation. The proposed legislation used the ingenious device of allowing the railroad to divert taxes owed to the state to the construction of local spur lines. In this way, Scott turned the railroad's main liability into a political asset.

When the tonnage repeal finally came to a vote, all eyes were on the state senate. Scott personally oversaw the debate from a side room in the senate hall. The measure squeaked by on a close vote, but public reaction was immediate and intense. Revocation of the tonnage tax proved disastrous to the legislators who had supported Scott. Democratic leaders used its repeal as a war cry to recover political power in the state. In the following election, all but one of the legislators outside Philadelphia who had supported the bill were defeated for reelection. But when the next session of the legislature attempted to undo the repeal, they found that the legislation had been written as a contract between the state and the railroad, and that it could not be repealed without consent from both parties. Anticipating just such a backlash, Scott had made sure that the measure was virtually irrevocable.

Outraged legislators opened an investigation into allegations that Scott had used bribes to win the repeal. But Scott's allies in the state senate made it possible for him to personally select five of the seven members of the investigating committee. He also succeeded in ducking every effort of the committee to subpoena him to testify. At one point even Abraham Lincoln became involved in the game of cat and mouse. When Scott's allies told President Lincoln that Scott needed to avoid testifying, Lincoln asked Secretary of War Edwin Stanton to assist Scott, and Stanton complied by ordering Scott on official business out of harm's way until the legislature had adjourned for the year.

With the outbreak of the Civil War, Scott was called to Washington to become assistant secretary of war, and as Washington scrambled to regroup following the North's early losses, his logistical talents proved an exceptional asset. His energies were legendary. On one occasion he worked for thirty-six hours straight "without sleep or rest," personally telegraphing instructions to coordinate the movements of troops on every train of the Pennsylvania Railroad west of Harrisburg. On another occasion, he engineered the movement in record time of twenty-three thousand Union soldiers over twelve hundred miles of rail lines in order to shore up vulnerable frontline positions.

Scott's mastery of the railroad infrastructure was a key part of the North's success in parlaying its coherent system of railroads into a pervasive military advantage against the South, whose fragmented system crippled its ability to supply and deploy its armies. Scott returned to his position at the Pennsylvania Railroad no longer a despised manipulator but as Colonel Scott, war hero. According to Pennsylvania historian McClure, "For nearly twenty years, beginning with 1860, Scott enjoyed the personal confidence of the leaders of State and nation of every political faith, and neither of the two great parties ever nominated an important State ticket without very full conference with Scott."

According to historian Matthew Josephson, Scott's clout in the post–Civil War era grew steadily, allowing him to transform the Pennsylvania Railroad into a political juggernaut, "a single force so formidable that the government became its subject rather than its master."

Scott no longer had to struggle to achieve passage of desired legislation. "At the bidding of the railroad," wrote Josephson, "the Pennsylvania legislature passed necessary measures with reasonable speed. When Mr. Scott, according to legend, had 'no further business' for the legislature, it would promptly adjourn. Thus all the uncertainties and hazards of democratic institutions, such as an imperialistic industrial organization could not have safely endured, were erased."

Having gained an unassailable position in Pennsylvania politics, Scott began to look at wider vistas. The war had given him a panoramic view of both the northern and the southern railroad infrastructures, and after returning to Pennsylvania he began to map the grand vision that was to shape the remainder of his career. The vision was to forge a nationwide railway system running from New York to Washington, D.C., then south into the heart of the old Confederacy, and finally west along the southern tier of states to California.

Scott recognized that the actual building of the railroad lines was not the real problem. Far more difficult would be the highly charged politics surrounding railroad policy in the states of the former Confederacy. The southern railroad lines had originally been built largely by slave laborers under a system where a plantation owner would loan a work group of slaves to a railroad in exchange for a combination of cash and stock. The entire system was a jumble of small, fragmented lines. In contrast to states like Pennsylvania, where railroad interests dominated state governments, economic interests opposed to railroad integration had the upper hand in most southern states. Historian Scott Reynolds Nelson describes the tangled southern transportation hubs:

Well into the 1850s, southern railroads were largely adjuncts to canals, rivers, and sailing ships. Legislators wrote charters that prevented railroad officers from forwarding goods to other railroads or steamships. Many charters allowed city councils to define where railroads had right of way and thus allowed town merchants to choose the location of railroad junctions and company wharves. These charter restrictions ensured that gaps between railroads were large enough for merchants to take advantage of breaks in transit.

In order to consolidate this system into a seamless whole, Scott had to win at a complex political game. He not only had to politically outmaneuver the transport, warehousing, and merchant interests that benefited from the balkanization of the railroads but also had to conceal the hand of the Pennsylvania Railroad. To reveal that a large northern railroad was ultimately behind the consolidation of southern lines would ignite the local suspicions that Yankee capitalists were plotting to colonize the southern economy. And it wouldn't take much for determined opponents to block the takeover of a southern railroad. For example, under North Carolina law and the charter of the North Carolina Railroad, any merger involving that railroad had to be approved by a two-thirds majority of both companies' stockholders *and* a two-thirds majority in each of the state legislatures.

The solution to the problem was a device that Scott had used earlier in Pennsylvania: the holding company. Such a company is formed specifically to own stock in other companies. Intercompany stock ownership was normally prohibited by corporate charters; however, Scott persuaded the Pennsylvania legislature to ease the restriction first for the Pennsylvania Railroad and later for a company he formed to buy up railroad companies in the South.

One of the benefits of a holding company is that it allows one company to control another while owning at most 51 percent of its stock. Indeed, when stock ownership is fragmented, as is frequently the case, a much smaller percentage may be sufficient for the holding company to choose a majority of the directors.

As he sought to expand the Pennsylvania Railroad, Scott purchased controlling interests in smaller railroad companies in western Pennsylvania and Ohio. He could then dictate policies to the companies under his control through their boards of directors, forcing each company to synchronize its rate structures, track specifications, and equipment with the Pennsylvania Railroad. Historians T. Lloyd Benson and Trina Rossman have described this means of expanding the effective scope of the Pennsylvania Railroad as "a complicated spree of leases, stock buyouts, loans, and construction projects involving at least fourteen separate companies. The result was an administrative and financial rat's nest of unparalleled size."

In Pennsylvania Scott used the holding company for business purposes. But as he mapped out his strategy for expanding into the South, it is clear that he envisioned the technique as a political tactic. By using a holding company to buy southern lines, Scott conceived a way of forging an integrated railroad system across multiple southern states without the need to secure charters from potentially hostile southern legislatures.

To lay the groundwork for his southern thrust, Scott sought and received a charter in 1871 from the state of Pennsylvania for a corporation that initially was named the Overland Contract Company. To ensure both secrecy and maximum flexibility, he convinced the legislature to drop the usual requirement that a charter define the specific activities to be undertaken by the company. Instead, the charter of the Overland Contract Company defined it as a general-purpose company with the power to revise its own name and charter as needed. Less than two weeks later the directors of the corporation met in New York City, where they changed the name to the Southern Railway Security Company and configured it as a holding company designed to quietly buy up controlling interests in small railroad companies along the desired route of a future north-south line.

The ruse was only partially successful—Scott's southern-based rivals discovered that, despite the company's name, the true owners of the Southern Railway Security Company were Yankee railroad men and their New York banker partners, and they sought to publicize that information in order to discredit the company and rally southern opposition. Scott responded by literally buying his own sympathetic press—in city after city across the South, he purchased local newspapers and ordered editors to support his plans. After William Johnston, a prominent legislator and former commissary-general of the Confederacy, wrote a circular attacking Scott's scheme ("we shall be unworthy of our sires if we not only quietly submit but seemingly invite the secret power of monopoly to become our master"), Johnston found himself frozen out of newspaper coverage. And when a house committee in Virginia attempted to investigate charges of railroad bribery, even the Richmond press declined to cover the hearings.

Scott responded with similar directness when the Ku Klux Klan began terrorizing crews of black freedmen working to connect the pieces of his railroad system together. Rather than fight the Klan, he simply invited the various wizards and dragons (mainly ex-officers of the Confederate Army) to a lavish oyster dinner, where his lieutenants offered them positions on the boards of various subsidiaries.

To speed up the building of track through the hill country of north Georgia, Scott's managers leased the entire population of the state penitentiary—393 convicts—at no charge. In North Carolina, convicts performed the dangerous work of tunneling through mountain ranges. Many of these workers were former slaves imprisoned for the trumped-up offense known as "theft of services"—that is, not fulfilling one or another of the provisions of their sharecropper contracts.

In the 1870s Scott emerged as a key power broker on the national stage during the crisis that grew out of the disputed presidential election of 1876, in which the candidates were Rutherford Hayes and Samuel Tilden. Although Tilden, the Democratic candidate, appeared to have won by a 250,000-vote margin, the situation in the electoral college was close enough to set off a frenzy of horse-trading for electoral votes.

For months, political and business leaders convened secret meetings as various parties sought to negotiate a complex set of agreements now known as the Compromise of 1877. According to labor historian Philip Foner, Scott himself made the "actual determination" that Rutherford Hayes would be president. On March 2, 1877, Hayes was riding from Columbus, Ohio, to Washington, D.C., in Scott's private luxury railroad car when he received the telegram confirming his selection as president of the United States by a commission of five Supreme Court judges and ten congressmen. The most notorious provision of the deal that put Hayes in the White House was his promise that in return for receiving the votes of southern electors, his administration would withdraw the remaining federal troops from the South. That withdrawal enabled the old southern establishment to reestablish itself, opening the door to the creation of the Jim Crow system of sharecropping, racially separated public facilities and services, and black disenfranchisement. Another tenet of the deal provided that Tom Scott's Texas and Pacific railroad project, connecting the lines of the Southern Railway Security Company to the West Coast, would receive tens of millions of acres of public land and huge federal subsidies.

As it turned out, the federal troops were needed to quell a massive labor uprising in the summer of 1877 that began at the Baltimore & Ohio station in Martinsburg, West Virginia, and quickly spread to the Pennsylvania Railroad. One issue was pay cuts to railroad workers, another was the dangerous use of "doubleheaders"—trains with twice the normal number of cars. The strike spread to numerous cities, involving one hundred thousand workers and shutting down half the nation's railroad capacity. In St. Louis alone, sixty factories were shut down, and the city was run for a period of time by a committee of strikers. Urging that the strikers be given "a rifle diet for a few days and see how they like that kind of bread," Scott repeatedly telegraphed President Hayes for troops. The exact death toll from the suppression of the strike is unknown but is estimated at ninety people or more. In the wake of the strike, armories were built in many cities as forts for the National Guard in any future uprisings.

That a figure such as Scott could amass so much power was precisely what the framers of the American system of government had feared. Scott represented the first generation of a business oligarchy whose power rivaled that of the country's democratically elected leadership. The abolitionist leader Wendell Phillips allegedly said of Scott that when he "trailed his garments across the country, the members of twenty legislatures trembled like dry leaves in a winter's wind."

BUT SCOTT'S PERSONAL POWER is not what makes him an important historical figure. It was his liberation of the corporation from state restrictions—in effect, reinventing the corporation as a far more dynamic entity. Prior to the Civil War, corporations were rooted in place—each was firmly under the control of the state legislature that issued and periodically renewed its charter. No matter what restrictions the state legislature wrote into a corporation's charter, the corporation had to put up with them or face charter termination.

But Tom Scott devised an escape route, one whose seeds had been sown when he had convinced the Pennsylvania legislature to break the long-standing ban forbidding one corporation from owning stock in another corporation. By inventing the holding company, Scott had found the Achilles' heel of state control over corporations. Let's say a company in Missouri didn't like the restrictions contained in its charter. By having its lawyers incorporate a new corporation in New Jersey, and then selling its stock to the New Jersey corporation, the Missouri company could effectively free itself from Missouri's jurisdiction without physically moving.

As mundane as that shift might sound, the impact was profound, because once corporations had the ability to shop for the most sympathetic legal venue, they possessed the ability to exert leverage on state legislatures to ease restrictions of other sorts.

Scott was far ahead of his time. His innovation of the holding company was not yet legal on a general basis in any state. Even in Pennsylvania, he had only been able to set up such an entity because of special action by the compliant legislature. Two decades later, a New York attorney named William Nelson Cromwell succeeded in making Scott's invention a universal option available to any corporation. In the meantime, industrialists such as John D. Rockefeller tried with mixed success to accomplish the same goals using a different mechanism known as the trust. Under this roundabout and legally vulnerable structure, the stockholders of a number of individual corporations exchanged their stock for "trust certificates" controlled by a central board of trustees. The trust allowed a group of companies to operate in concert for purposes of controlling output and setting prices without technically violating the rules against cross-company ownership.

Tom Scott had also experimented with trusts, but he discovered a drawback of that device: the need for *trust,* which, as historian Scott Reynolds Nelson notes, "was no guarantee among capitalists." Nelson recounts Scott's experience creating a trust with Andrew Carnegie, his onetime protégé:

> Only a few months before Scott incorporated the Southern, he had trusted his closest associate, Andrew Carnegie, in a deal that allowed Scott and Carnegie to take over the Union Pacific. This was a deal not protected by a holding company. After the two men became directors, Carnegie saw the price of the stock skyrocket, and he secretly sold the shares that had been entrusted to him by Scott and the Pennsylvania's president. Carnegie had been speculating; he assumed he could buy the stock back before the next election of directors at a lower price and make a healthy profit. But enemies of the Scott

alliance discovered the sale, bought Carnegie's stock, called a special meeting of the Union Pacific board, and deposed Scott and Carnegie. This failure was Tom Scott's most public humiliation.

Another drawback of trusts for businessmen trying to create functional interstate entities was that many states saw the device as a blatant challenge to their authority, and they quickly counterattacked by taking action to dissolve corporations that had joined into trusts. During the 1880s, the attorney general of the state of Louisiana was seeking to revoke the charters of some local cotton oil companies that had put themselves under the control of the Cotton Oil Trust. The main motive of the trust was to gain greater leverage in setting the price for cotton oil, exactly opposite to the interests of Louisiana's cotton farmers.

To defend itself, the Cotton Oil Trust hired Cromwell, who copied Tom Scott's old trick of convincing a willing state—in this case Rhode Island—to make a onetime exemption to the general rule against a corporation in one state holding stock or assets in a corporation located in another. This way, the charters of the local companies participating in the Cotton Oil Trust would no longer be subject to dissolution if attacked by the state of Louisiana. The maneuver engineered by Cromwell used an asset transfer rather than a stock transfer, but the effect of frustrating state regulators was identical. As the confrontation between the Louisiana attorney general and the Cotton Oil Trust drew to a climax, Cromwell quietly transferred all the assets of the Louisiana corporations to a newly minted Rhode Island corporation created solely for that purpose. He then announced to the attorney general that the case was moot because the corporations no longer existed.

The trick worked, but Cromwell didn't stop with this one victory in the Cotton Oil Trust case. Instead, he sent several lawyers connected with his firm to approach the New Jersey legislature; based on their lobbying, the legislature loosened the incorporation statutes so that *any* corporation chartered in New Jersey could hold stock in any other corporation in America.

SCOTT DIED IN 1881, so he did not live to see the legislation that made his innovation of the out-of-state holding company become a routine feature of corporate law. The revision of New Jersey's corporate statutes in 1889 immediately made that state the venue of choice for corporations wishing to escape more restrictive regulation in other states. By 1901, 71 percent of all United States corporations with assets of $25 million or greater were using New Jersey as their home base. According to corporate lawyer Charles Bostwick, "So many Trusts and big corporations were paying tribute to the State of New Jersey that the authorities had become greatly perplexed as to what should be done with [its] surplus revenue."

Other states had two choices: either attempt to compete with New Jersey in a "race to the bottom" or watch locally chartered corporations move their legal home to New Jersey. In 1899, Delaware followed New Jersey, and when Governor Woodrow Wilson tightened the New Jersey law in 1913, Delaware pulled ahead as the corporate venue of choice, a position it retains to this day. A half-dozen other states also relaxed their corporate statutes. Observing the wreckage to state authority over corporations, journalist Lincoln Steffens dubbed New Jersey "the traitor state." By making it easy for corporations to hold stock in other corporations, New Jersey's law opened the door for a huge wave of acquisitions, particularly during the period from 1897 to 1903. During that six-year period, some 2,650 separate firms disappeared into larger entities as industry after industry became dominated by a handful of immense, politically powerful corporations incorporated in states with corporate-friendly statutes. Such entities as International Paper (1898), National Sugar Refining Company (1900), U.S. Steel (1901), and International Harvester (1902) were all formed in this period by merging smaller companies into large corporations. In 1890, the aggregate amount of capital in publicly traded companies was a mere $33 million; in 1903, it surpassed $7 *billion*. Industry after industry had seen a remarkable concentration of market share. U.S. Steel controlled 62 percent of the steel market, International Harvester controlled 85 percent of the agricultural implement market, American Can Company controlled 90 percent of the can market, and so on. By 1903, some 250 large corporations had emerged as dominant, and the structure of the American economy had radically changed.

Sociologists call the 1897–1903 period "the corporate revolution." But, as we have seen, the real corporate revolution took place over a longer period, roughly from 1850 to 1900. During this revolution, larger corporations did not merely come to dominate the American economy. More significantly, the legal structure defining the corporation as an institution was fundamentally altered. A century earlier, the framers of the American system of government had attempted to devise a "containment vessel" for corporate power: the state-issued charter. Now that system was completely disassembled and replaced with another whose goals were the exact opposite—as though the steel bars that had formed a cage were melted down, recycled, and used to create a suit of protective armor instead. Rather than protect democracy from corporate power, the legal system increasingly shielded corporations from legislative power.

Just as the legal system was bent, little by little, to accommodate the needs of the corporation, American culture shifted as well, in ways that often seemed perfectly harmless but that affected the most fundamental gestures and rhythms of daily life. Consider this: even the standardized time by which we set our clocks is a corporate product, created in 1883. Prior to that year, every city and town in the United States established its own time. Meanwhile, every railroad company internally synchronized its own train schedules. As historian Alan Trachtenberg described the situation, "By early 1883 there were about fifty such distinct universes of time, each streaming on wheels through the countryside, oblivious of the others."

Standardization into four continental time zones came neither from an act of Congress nor from an executive order by the president, but rather from a joint decision of the country's railroad corporations. Precisely at noon on November 18, 1883, synchronized by telegraph, all the railroad stations in the country set their clocks according to four standardized zones. There was scattered resistance—especially, for reasons unknown, among the clergy. One minister exhorted his congregation to follow "God's time—not Vanderbilt's." In Tennessee a preacher punctuated that point by taking out a hammer and smashing his watch on the pulpit. But most people accepted the change quite readily, setting their clocks by railroad time and going on with their lives.

Time zones, of course, are harmless. Yet the episode feels vaguely creepy—or maybe funny, it's hard to tell—a sort of dadaist coup. The message seems to be: "You can keep your silly democracy. But don't forget—we own the clocks!"

CHAPTER SEVEN

Superpowers

The corporation acquires nine powerful attributes
(1860–1900)

FOR BETTER OR FOR WORSE, we human beings are stuck with the attributes that nature gave us. That doesn't mean we can't imagine new ones—after all, isn't that what comic books are all about? Consider the following top ten items from a Web site entitled "The Top 47 Super Powers You Wish You Had" (www.keepersoflists.org):

1. X-ray vision
2. Invisibility
3. Telepathy
4. Ability to mute people on command
5. Ability to teleport
6. Power to freeze time
7. Ability to fly
8. Superstrength
9. Ability to change the weather
10. Power to make telemarketers quit calling my house

But corporations aren't like us. Because their powers are determined by laws, not by nature, it is possible to engineer them with all sorts of qualities, including some attributes outside the realm of human possibility. In theory, that programming can go either way: society can make corporations stronger by removing restraints and adding new legal powers, or it can make them weaker by doing the reverse. The key lesson is this: corporations are only as powerful as they are legally designed to be.

As the previous chapters described, the engineers of the American political system deliberately created a framework of laws to keep corporations politically weak. That framework was subsequently undermined by the ingenious maneuvers of Tom Scott and other businessmen, lawyers, and sympathetic legislators. So extensive were the changes in the legal framework that the corporation of 1900 was quite different from the corporation of 1860. This chapter summarizes that transformation. As shorthand, I'll call the corporate institution that existed before the Civil War the *classic corporation*. And I'll call the corporation that emerged by the end of the nineteenth century the *modern corporation*. Table 7.1 compares these two institutional forms.

Table 7.1

Differences Between the Classic Corporation (Before 1860)
and the Modern Corporation (After 1900)

ATTRIBUTE	CLASSIC CORPORATION	MODERN CORPORATION
Birth	Difficult: requires a custom charter issued by a state legislature	Easy: general incorporation allows automatic chartering
Life span	Limited terms	No limits
"Shape-shifting"	Corporations not allowed to own stock in other companies; restricted to activities specified in charter	Corporations free to pursue acquisitions and spin-offs
Mobility	Usually restricted to home state	No restrictions
Adaptability	Restricted to activities specified in charter	Allowed to pursue multiple lines of business and initiate or acquire new ones at company's discretion
"Conscience"	Actions constrained by shareholder liability and by threat of charter revocation	Fewer constraints due to limited liability, disuse of charter revocation, and tort reforms
"Will"	Managerial action hampered by legal status of minority shareholders and of corporate agents	Legal revisions enable consolidation of management's power
Size	Limited by charter restrictions	Asset limits removed; antitrust laws generally not effective
Constitutional rights	Functional only	Steady acquisition of constitutional rights

As the table shows, the differences are extensive and highly significant. Indeed, they may be likened to the differences between *Star Wars'* C-3PO, the fussy, awkward, highly specialized droid who possesses excellent manners but little else, and Arnold Schwarzenegger's *Terminator*, a more robust, more focused, faster, more adaptable being.

Change #1: Creating Corporations Gets Easier

By 1902, anyone in the United States could receive a corporate charter merely by filing some papers with the state. The new system was a dramatic change from the incorporation system that existed prior to the Civil War, when charters required specific legislative approval and many contained special provisions unique to that entity.

This new system of automatic approval for new corporate charters, known as *general incorporation,* had actually first been introduced in the late 1700s as a means to allow churches to receive charters without the need to seek specific approval from the state legislature. The goal was to let churches enjoy the functional benefits provided by corporate ownership of land and property while at the same time avoiding the potential impingement on religious freedom that might have resulted if church charters were subject to the political process.

In 1811, the first general incorporation statute was passed by the state of New York for certain types of business corporations, including manufacturing, textiles, glass, metals, and paint. It allowed companies with capital of up to $100,000 to be automatically incorporated for a life span of up to twenty years. In 1846, New York offered general incorporation to all companies. (See Table 7.2.) But for decades, charters issued under general incorporation laws continued to contain a variety of restrictive clauses, which explains why corporations in states such as New York began fleeing to New Jersey in the 1890s, even though both had general incorporation standards. Though New York began offering general incorporation much earlier, New Jersey was quicker to drop most restrictive features from its law. Only when truly modern-style general incorporation, with no restrictions, was introduced by New Jersey and then by Delaware, West Virginia, and other states, did it become impossible for states to control corporations in the way they had when a customized charter was required for each new corporation.

Table 7.2
The Spread of General Incorporation Requirements
in State Constitutions

1846	New York	1864	Nevada	1875	Maryland
1846	Iowa	1864	Louisiana	1876	Colorado
1848	Illinois	1865	Missouri	1876	Texas
1848	Wisconsin	1866	Nebraska	1889	Idaho
1849	California	1867	Alabama	1889	North Dakota
1850	Michigan	1868	North Carolina	1889	South Dakota
1851	Ohio	1868	Georgia	1889	Montana
1851	Maryland	1870	Tennessee	1889	Washington
1851	Indiana	1871	Arkansas	1890	Mississippi
1855	Kansas	1872	West Virginia	1895	Utah
1857	Minnesota	1874	Pennsylvania	1897	Delaware
1857	Oregon	1875	New Jersey	1902	Virginia

Source: *Liggett v. Lee* (1933).

Change #2: Corporations Acquire an Unlimited Life Span

The classic corporation was chartered for a limited term and had to apply periodically to have its charter extended—every six to fifty years, depending on the type of business. After the advent of general incorporation statutes, states gradually began to replace limited terms with perpetual terms; almost half had done so by 1903. Thus, a key difference between the classic corporation and the modern corporation is that the latter, at least in theory, enjoys an unlimited life span. This does not mean that modern corporations can never go bankrupt, or that one corporation can't absorb another. According to a study by Royal Dutch/Shell Group, the average Fortune 500 company survives about forty to fifty years before it vanishes, sometimes due to bankruptcy but more often because it is swallowed up by a bigger fish. If we consider the acquisition of one company by another to be a continuation of both companies' lives, the estimates of corporate life spans become significantly longer, especially for the largest corporations. Among the top twenty-five corporations on the *Financial Times* Global 500 list for 2002, the median age is 113 years. Only six companies among the top twenty-five are younger than 50 (Microsoft, Wal-Mart, Intel, Vodafone Group, Cisco, and Home Depot).

From a social and legal perspective, perpetual existence creates tremendous difficulties in holding corporations accountable for criminal behavior; in addition, it allows corporations to benefit indefinitely from behavior that once was legal but now is not. For example, despite the destruction of the Nazi and the Japanese fascist regimes, a number of German, Japanese, and even American corporations that benefited from the use of slave labor in the 1930s and 1940s can be found on today's Global 500 list, including IBM (#12), Siemens (#57), Daimler-Chrysler (#81), Deutsche Bank (#100), Ford (#157), BMW (#167), Bayer (#175), BASF (#187), Volkswagen (#211), General Motors (#308), Mitsubishi (#380), and Mitsui (#472). IBM bears a particularly heavy historical burden; evidence uncovered by historian Edwin Black describes how IBM's data processing technology helped the Nazi regime implement its genocidal policies.

With many corporations having roots extending back earlier than the American Civil War, it is not surprising that at least one Canadian and seven American companies on the Global 500 list also benefited from the use of slave labor prior to 1865, including American International Group (#11), JP MorganChase (#44), FleetBoston (#109), Lehman Brothers (#283), Union Pacific (#285), Gannett (#212), and Tribune (#327).

The point here is not that corporations that engaged in murderous practices in the past deserve to be smeared by the broad brush of history. Rather, the point is that the legal attribute of indefinite existence makes the corporation truly a different sort of social actor than you or me. For example, when evidence emerged that Kurt Waldheim, former U.N. secretary-general and then president of Austria, had played a leadership role in military units responsible for World War II atrocities, much of the world responded by ostracizing him, and he did not run for a second presidential term in 1992. In contrast, a corporation such as IBM, whose close involvement with the Nazi regime produced suffering on a vastly larger scale than anything Waldheim could have done, has experienced no lingering reproach other than calls for reparations.

Although perpetual existence allows corporations to outlive their own crimes and atrocities, it also has a very practical benefit in ordinary political and legal affairs. Consider, for example, the antitrust litigation against Microsoft initiated by the United States Justice Department under the administration of Bill Clinton. Such cases usually last at least a decade, often longer, and this gives companies such as Microsoft the chance to roll the dice with a new administration. In Microsoft's case, the Bush administration arrived in time to apply a more lenient philosophy to the case—and the company slipped the noose.

Change #3: Corporations Learn to Shape-Shift

As useful as it is, corporate immortality becomes even more potent when used in combination with the modern corporation's ability to morph dramatically in any number of ways. Corporate governance expert Ralph Estes has termed this morphing ability "indefinite entity," which he describes as "the ability to disguise itself, to run and to hide, or to reorganize into a whole new entity... sell off divisions and subsidiaries, be taken over and absorbed into a different company, or . . . rename itself and emerge as, seemingly, a completely different company." Estes cites the example of Drexel Burnham Lambert:

> Its image befouled with six felonies plus the legacy of junk bond king Michael Milkin, Drexel used a tax loophole to give itself a whole new identity as the spanking clean New Street Capital Corporation. Drexel, with its felonies, couldn't get a license to run a gambling casino in Puerto Rico it wanted to take over. New Street could—even though it emerged out of Drexel's hide.

Prior to the Civil War the sort of maneuvering described by Estes would have been beyond the capacities of any company. Under the charter system, a classic corporation was not allowed to own stock in another, so both hostile takeovers and spin-offs from one corporation to another were ruled out. Charters tended to be quite specific about the activities that a given corporation was allowed to undertake. In order to go beyond the terms of its charter, a corporation had to return to the state legislature and receive approval for a charter amendment.

By 1900, all those restrictions had vanished. As noted in the previous chapter, the key changes that undermined the antebellum charter system were Tom Scott's innovation of the holding company as a political tool in Pennsylvania in 1871, and the 1889 legislative change in New Jersey that made the holding company an option for any corporation chartered in that state.

By loosening their corporate statutes, New Jersey and the states that mimicked it created a new environment in which, according to historian Lawrence Friedman, "the corporation had torn free of its past—it could be formed almost at will, could do business as it wished, could expand, contract, dissolve."

Change #4: Corporations Gain Mobility

A key feature of the classic corporation was its firm link to the chartering state. That connection was reinforced by a number of factors, including a prohibition on one corporation owning stock in another, and *ultra vires*, a legal doctrine under which any contract outside the activities permitted in a corporation's charter was considered null and void by the courts. Although *ultra vires* lingered in theory into the 1930s, judges had mainly abandoned attempting to enforce it by 1900. Of course, once a corporation could both act beyond the legal definitions of its charter and change its legal location to a venue far removed from the communities where it conducted its operations, the ability of states to hold corporations accountable was greatly diminished. Indeed, the ability of corporations to go "venue shopping" encouraged states to compete with each other to create the most permissive corporate atmosphere. For example, when Connecticut's legislatures held the line with strict corporate rules, including a provision requiring that a majority of the board of directors of any company be Connecticut residents, the state "drove from her borders not only foreign enterprises but also her own industries." New Jersey, with a combination of low taxes and loose statutes, became "the favorite state for incorporations." Another corporate favorite was West Virginia, a "Snug Harbor for roaming and piratical corporations," the "tramp and bubble companies of the country."

Change #5: Corporations Become More Adaptable

Charters issued by legislatures prior to the Civil War were quite specific about the activities that a corporation could pursue. Just as states restricted the mobility of corporations, they also made it illegal for a corporation to alter its activities without seeking a change in its charter. After the Civil War, those restrictions were lifted, often a decade or two after the change from special chartering to general incorporation. For example, New York switched fully to general incorporation in 1844, but the statutory change that permitted incorporation "for any lawful purpose" came in 1866. Illinois made the conversion to "any lawful purpose" in 1872, Massachusetts in 1874, Maine in 1876. Other states followed shortly.

The removal of clauses that defined and limited what a company was permitted to do, combined with new rules permitting holding companies, opened the door to the creation of two kinds of corporations that were not permitted under the classic corporation system. One was the conglomerate—a holding company that owns a diversity of companies. The other was the vertically integrated company, which attempts to control the entire life span of a certain product group from production through distribution and retail. Both approaches led to immense, potentially monopolistic corporations.

Change #6: Corporations Shed Their "Conscience" Mechanisms

Science fiction writers who have imagined the introduction of intelligent automatons into society have recognized the need for building at least a rudimentary "conscience" mechanism into robots and androids. Isaac Asimov imagined a solution in which robots were programmed with simple rules, such as, "A robot may not injure a human being, or, through inaction, allow a human being to come to harm."

Because corporations are complex systems, in which large numbers of people and machines interact with the real world in myriad ways, it is a difficult challenge to program into them a "conscience"—that is, mechanisms to ensure that human beings aren't trampled. But that does not mean it is impossible, and indeed a major preoccupation of the law is to develop various ways to protect people from being harmed not just by corporations but by institutions in general.

Much of this sort of programming is simply an extension of the legal provisions that protect humans from hurting each other, such as civil and criminal laws. Of course, criminal law never had any teeth in the first place when it came to corporations because of the obvious uselessness of the corporal disincentives that the law has traditionally relied on—flogging, imprisonment, and so forth. Instead, the designers of the classic corporation relied on the limitations contained in corporate charters and on the ultimate sanction of charter revocation. But by around 1875, general incorporation had largely replaced the system of individually issued charters, and charters ceased to provide a means for controlling corporate behavior.

The end of the charter system also marked the full arrival of the doctrine of limited liability, which ended any legal incentive for corporate shareholders to concern themselves with the behavior of the businesses in which they owned an interest. As described in chapter 5, investors in some British corporations had enjoyed limited liability as early as the 1660s, but limited liability protection as a universal feature did not occur in Britain until 1855. Even then, Parliament required that a company "announce its members' irresponsibility" by appending the phrase "LLC" (limited liability company) to its official name. In America, limited liability was highly controversial prior to the Civil War. For example, in Maine, the law changed back and forth nine times between 1823 and 1857—between no liability and full liability, depending on whether the Whigs or the Democrats had a majority of the legislature. Between about 1810 and 1860, judges began to develop a doctrine that conferred limited liability on shareholders in the absence of any charter provision to the contrary. Usually, however, charters were not silent. Some required that shareholders be exposed to unlimited liability for debts or legal settlements against a corporation; others required "double liability," which meant that shareholders' exposure was limited to twice the amount of their investment.

Of course, the ultimate effect of shielding stockholders from risk is to shift potential losses onto society at large. Such a shift also occurred in areas of civil law such as the law of torts, as summarized by political scientist Arthur S. Miller:

> As with constitutional law, so with the private law of contracts, of property, and of torts. Judge-made rules in those fundamental categories had the result of transferring the social costs of private

enterprise from the enterprise itself to the workingman or to society at large. Tort law provides apt illustration. Under its doctrines, a person who willfully or negligently harms another's person or property must answer by paying money damages. The analogue of contract, which is a consensual obligation, a tort is a nonconsensual legal obligation. Who, then, bore the costs, in accidents and in deaths, of the new industrialism? Not the businessman. Not the corporation. The worker himself. (Often those workers were children.) And who bore the costs of pollution and other social costs? Society at large. How did this come about? In tort law judges created doctrines of "contributory negligence," "assumption of risk," and the "fellow servant rule," all of which served to insulate the enterprise from liability. By "freely" taking a job, said the judges, the workers "assumed the risk" of any accident that might occur.

Change #7: Unleashing the Corporate Will

In the context of corporate law, legal scholar Paul Vinogradoff has defined will as "the faculty of taking resolves in the midst of conflicting motives; a governing brain and nerves, in the shape of institutions and agents; a capacity for the promotion and the defense of interests by holding property, performing acts in law, and exercising rights of action in courts."

One of the least noted differences between the legal framework of the classic corporation and that of the modern corporation is the relative status of shareholder and management. According to legal historian Gregory Mark, shareholders played a dominant role in the classic corporation, but in the modern corporation a clear trend developed toward managerial supremacy. With managers winning the role of "governing brain," decision making became far more streamlined and definitive, and managers could undertake strategic maneuvers such as mergers and acquisitions without fear of being blocked by a small minority of balking shareholders.

The elevation of the power of management occurred as a result of a variety of legal changes. In 1890, New York became the first state (followed by New Jersey in 1896 and Delaware in 1899) to rescind the common law doctrine known as "the rule of unanimous consent." According to that doctrine, any fundamental change of corporate purposes, especially the sale of corporate assets, required unanimous approval by the shareholders. In practice, the rule of unanimous consent significantly hampered the creation of large corporate conglomerates, at least in cases where ownership of a corporation whose assets were being acquired were widely dispersed. Combined with the removal of restrictions that had been built into the charters of the classic corporation, the elimination of unanimous consent allowed the modern corporation a new degree of nimbleness, even though the size of the largest corporations at the end of the nineteenth century was far beyond that of earlier firms.

Court decisions also served to make shareholders subordinate to managers. A key case was the 1884 decision by the federal district court in St. Louis involving Jay Gould's Wabash, St. Louis, and Pacific Railway. Setting a new precedent that dramatically increased the powers of management over shareholders, the court agreed to Gould's request that his representatives be appointed receivers for the railroad company. Prior to that time, prevailing doctrine gave control over bankruptcy proceedings to impartial receivers, who were to balance the interests of stockholders, workers, and creditors. The St. Louis court's decision, however, affirmed and legally reinforced the control of management over a corporation's fate.

Change #8: Removing Restrictions on Size

In many cases the charters of the classic corporation placed explicit limits on size. For example, the 1818 charter of a Massachusetts company, the Main Flour Mills, limited the total property the corporation might hold to $50,000, of which the land could not exceed $30,000 in value. Most state constitutions also featured limits on the amount of investment capital that a single corporation could control, as shown in Table 7.3.

As we've already seen, many common charter provisions also indirectly limited the size of corporations. Such provisions included restrictions on the activities that a particular corporation could pursue; prohibitions against owning land not directly connected to a company's activities; prohibitions against owning stock in other corporations; geographic restrictions; requirements in some states that excess profits be used to buy back stock, so that eventually stockholders would be eliminated and a corporation in effect would return to public ownership. In addition, the doctrine of unanimous shareholder consent for major

Table 7.3
Nineteenth-Century Statutory Limits on Amount of Invested Capital a Single Corporation Could Control

New York until 1881	$2,000,000	Maine 1867–1876	$200,000
New York 1881–1890	$5,000,000	Maine 1876–1883	$500,000
Pennsylvania until 1863	$500,000	Maine 1883–1891	$2,000,000
Pennsylvania after 1863	$5,000,000	Maine after 1891	$10,000,000
Alabama until 1876	$200,000	Vermont	$1,000,000
Alabama 1876–1896	$1,000,000	New Hampshire	$1,000,000
Arizona after 1864	$5,000,000	Massachusetts 1851–1855	$200,000
Illinois 1852–1857	$300,000	Massachusetts after 1855	$500,000
Illinois after 1857	$1,000,000	Michigan 1846–1885	$100,000
Maine 1862–1867	$50,000	Michigan after 1885	$5,000,000

Source: Liggett v. Lee (1933).

decisions such as acquisitions or asset sales provided a brake on rapid conglomeration, because it allowed a small minority of dissident shareholders to block such action. With the modern corporation, all those constraints were lifted, opening the door to the wave of mergers around 1900 described earlier.

It might be argued that the framework of antitrust laws—beginning with the Sherman Antitrust Act in 1890 and followed by the Clayton Antitrust Act in 1914 and the Celler-Kefauver Act in 1950—functions to place a ceiling on size. And antitrust legislation has indeed produced occasional results, most notably the breakup of Standard Oil in 1911, American Tobacco, also in 1911, and AT&T in 1982. Of course, to deal with the complexity of business, such legislation must be written in broad terms, which means that enforcement and judicial interpretation are both highly subject to political ideology. Under Chief Justice Earl Warren in the 1960s, the Supreme Court viewed the intent of antitrust legislation as incorporating broad goals. These included the traditional goal of curbing monopoly pricing power, but also two key social goals: concern for the viability of locally controlled industries and small businesses, and other social effects, such as undue political influence. Thus, the Warren Court in the 1962 Brown Shoe case blocked the merger of two shoe companies, Brown and Kinney, even though the merger would have given Brown only 5.5 percent of total U.S. shoe production and allowed Brown to move from fourth to third among U.S. shoe companies.

With the arrival of the Burger Court in 1974, followed by the Reagan administration in 1981, judicial and executive antitrust philosophy shifted dramatically. In 1982, the Justice Department relaxed the standards for mergers, citing the need to allow American corporations to compete internationally, especially against large Japanese companies. The head of the Anti-Trust Division, William F. Baxter, rejected the idea that large corporations "by virtue of their size have something called economic power."

The result of this more lenient policy on mergers has been a rapidly accelerating trend to concentration. In 1980, there were only three acquisitions larger than $1 billion in value. In 1986, there were thirty-four such mergers. As late as 1992, total U.S. merger activity remained under $100 billion. But in the late 1990s, acquisitions exploded, topping $1 trillion in 1998. In 2000, a single merger—the $166 billion acquisition of Time-Warner by America Online—was larger than the *combined value* of all mergers and acquisitions in the United States from 1970 through 1977.

By any measure, corporations dominate the world economy, and among the largest corporations, an overwhelming majority are based in Japan and the United States. According to Martin Wolf, chief economics commentator at the *Financial Times,* thirty-seven of the top one hundred economies in the world, measured on a value-added basis, are corporations. That analysis, however, may understate their economic clout. A different comparison—of the revenues of corporations and the budgets of governments—finds that sixty-six of the one hundred largest economic entities in the world are corporations; only thirty-four are governments. In 1999, among the top two hundred companies, ranked by sales, fifty-eight Japanese firms accounted for 39 percent of total sales, while fifty-nine U.S. firms accounted for 28 percent of sales. Ranked by market value, however, nineteen of the top twenty-five firms worldwide in 2002 were U.S.-based. (See Table 7.4.)

Table 7.4
The Top Twenty-Five Corporations in the World, Ranked by Market Value

RANK	COMPANY	COUNTRY	MARKET VALUE ($ BILLIONS)
1	General Electric	U.S.	372
2	Microsoft	U.S.	327
3	ExxonMobil	U.S.	300
4	Wal-Mart	U.S.	273
5	Citigroup	U.S.	255
6	Pfizer	U.S.	249
7	Intel	U.S.	204
8	British Petroleum	United Kingdom	201
9	Johnson & Johnson	U.S.	198
10	Royal Dutch/Shell	Netherlands/ United Kingdom	190
11	AIG	U.S.	188
12	IBM	U.S.	179
13	GlaxoSmithKline	United Kingdom	145
14	NTT DoCoMo	Japan	138
15	Merck	U.S.	131
16	Coca-Cola	U.S.	130
17	Vodafone Group	U.S.	127
18	SBC	U.S.	125
19	Verizon	U.S.	125
20	Cisco Systems	U.S.	124
21	Procter & Gamble	U.S.	117
22	Novartis	Switzerland	114
23	Home Depot	U.S.	114
24	Philip Morris	U.S.	113
25	Total Fina Elf	France	109

Source: Global 2002 list, *Financial Times,* May 13, 2002.

Change #9: Corporations Win Constitutional Rights

There can be no doubt that the changes from classic corporation to modern corporation allowed greater business flexibility. For example, as described by historians John Mickelthwait and Adrian Wooldridge,

"Nowadays, nobody finds it odd that, a century after its foundation, the Minnesota Mining and Manufacturing Company makes Post-it notes, or that the world's biggest mobile-phone company, Nokia, used to be in the paper business."

But the same changes that made corporations more flexible in their business operations also made them a far more potent force in the political realm. To make sure that this growing corporate power did not overwhelm the ability of state legislatures to control corporations, it would have made sense in the late nineteenth century for courts to affirm the constitutional authority of those legislatures to regulate corporations as they saw fit. Instead, the opposite took place, as courts systematically developed doctrines that allowed corporations to block unwelcome state laws and taxes.

In England, corporations had never been protected from state action, even when that action was of a highly arbitrary nature. Centuries of English legal tradition had established firmly the principle that corporate charters were revocable and alterable at any time. As described by Ron Harris, a historian of English constitutional law:

> The larger the corporation and the more consequential the effects of its activities, the more likely was the State to interfere in its business at one point or another. Incorporation itself was not considered a protectable property right. The State could, at will, withhold an incorporation franchise which, in many cases, was of limited duration. Such withdrawal was not common, but it conformed to the Stuart conception of the constitution, which held that granting and revoking incorporation charters lay within the King's prerogative and discretion. It also conformed to the post-1689 constitutional settlement which made the Parliament supreme and, as such, free to enact and repeal incorporation acts, according to changing circumstances or majorities.

Although 1886 is universally considered the year in which corporations won their first constitutional right—in the *Santa Clara* decision, already mentioned in chapter 1—as early as 1819 the Supreme Court had begun to establish a legal status for corporations in America that exceeded the traditional legal status enjoyed by corporations in England. The case that marked the first departure from the principle of corporate subordination to the will of the state was the 1819 case *Dartmouth College v. New Hampshire.* Encouraged by Thomas Jefferson, among others, New Hampshire had enacted legislation converting Dartmouth College from a private college into a public one. Jefferson had written to the governor, "The idea that institutions, established for the use of the nation, cannot be touched or modified . . . may perhaps be a salutory provision against the abuses of a monarch, but it is most absurd against the nation itself." To make a corporate charter sacrosanct, said Jefferson, would amount to a belief that "the earth belongs to the dead, and not to the living."

Seeking to block New Hampshire from making the college public, Dartmouth's trustees went to court, arguing that the 1769 charter between the college and King George qualified as a contract entitled to protection under the contract clause of the Constitution (Article 1, Section 10), which prohibits states from "impairing the obligations of contracts." The New Hampshire Superior Court agreed with the state. "These trustees are the servants of the public," declared the court, "and the servant is not to resist the will of his master, in a matter that concerns that master alone."

The trustees then appealed to the U.S. Supreme Court, where they had better luck. They were represented by the most renowned attorney of the day, Daniel Webster, a moving speaker. Though it was not recorded, Webster's oratory—"It is . . . a small college, and yet there are those who love it"—aroused such emotion that some members of the audience were said to have fainted, and Chief Justice John Marshall openly wept.

In its decision, the Court agreed with the trustees of Dartmouth that the charter they had received from King George in 1769 should be considered a contract protected by the Constitution. This decision, Justice Story later wrote, was intended to protect the rights of property owners against "the passions of the popular doctrines of the day."

Dartmouth cut two ways. In practical terms, legislatures quickly figured out how to get around the problem. They added a new clause to charters stating that the state reserved the right of revocation. Moreover, the ruling included a clear statement by Justice Marshall that corporations remained subordinate to state power. Marshall wrote that the corporation is an "artificial being, invisible, intangible and existing only in contemplation of law." On the other hand, the case marked the beginning of a long process by which the Supreme Court steadily elevated the legal status of corporations above anything that had previously existed in Anglo-American law. Thus, it opened the door for a steady erosion of state sovereignty over corporations, allowing them to begin to carve out a legal zone of immunity from state legislatures.

By 1860, that process was still in its infancy. Most notably, corporations failed to win protection as "citizens" under the Comity Clause (Article IV, Section 2), which states: "The Citizens of each State shall be entitled to all Privileges and Immunities of Citizens in the several States." That strategy was turned down by the Supreme Court in the 1839 *Bank of Augusta* decision. The 1844 *Louisville, Cincinnati* decision did give corporations the right to seek review of state laws in federal courts. But until the late 1870s, the attitudes of judges toward corporations remained consistent with revolutionary era wariness of corporate power.

By 1900, the prevailing judicial philosophy had shifted dramatically. A new generation of judges had embraced the corporation as the engine of American economic progress, and a series of cases had been decided giving corporations the right to challenge state legislation under the Fourteenth Amendment and federal legislation under the Fifth Amendment. The following chapters examine this shift, including the role played by Supreme Court Justice Stephen Field, and they look more closely at the twists and turns of the *Santa Clara* decision, the strange case that gave corporations their first constitutional right.

CHAPTER EIGHT

The Judge

Stephen Field and the politics of personhood
(1868–1885)

Whenever he has a case before him in which the community and the corporations are arrayed against each other, his lights always lead him to discover points against the people. —San Francisco Chronicle, September 28, 1882

Indeed, there is nothing which is lawful to be done to feed and clothe our people, to beautify and adorn their dwellings, to relieve the sick, to help the needy, and to enrich and ennoble humanity, which is not to a great extent done through the instrumentalities of corporations. —Justice Stephen Field, circuit court opinion, September 25, 1882

IN 1834, A YOUNG MAN moved from Missouri to Illinois, where he fell in love with a woman named Harriet and married her in 1836 at the Fort Snelling military post. Two years later, while the family was traveling on the Mississippi River on the steamboat *Gipsey*, Harriet gave birth to their first child, whom they named Eliza. Seven years after Eliza, a second baby girl was born. They named her Lizzie.

It is not known when Lizzie began to hear about her parents' lawsuit against a man named John Sanford. She probably was too young to remember the hours she spent sitting in the heat and humidity of the first-floor courtroom of the federal courthouse in St. Louis, which had to be divided into two rooms when it was discovered that an architectural flaw threatened to cause the collapse of the ceiling of the west wing.

By the time the United States Supreme Court issued its decision, Lizzie was eighteen years old, and the case had undoubtedly come to dominate her consciousness, simply because the stakes were so high. If her family won, they could walk out of the court in freedom; if they lost, they would be doomed—all four would lose their freedom for the rest of their lives.

The lawsuit filed in federal court by Lizzie's father, Dred Scott, charged that a man named John Sanford had "laid his hands" on Scott, Scott's wife Harriet, and Eliza, and had therefore assaulted them. Sanford frankly admitted the charge, but he asserted that he was only exercising appropriate control over items of property that he had lawfully acquired, and furthermore that, as property, Dred Scott and his family had no right to take him to court. According to Sanford's lawyers, the critical fact in the case was that Sanford's ancestors were European, whereas Scott's were African.

By a margin of seven to two, the Supreme Court voted in 1857 to deny Lizzie, Eliza, Harriet, and Dred any right to bring their case to court. In the majority decision, Chief Justice Taney wrote that the framers of the Constitution clearly considered anyone whose ancestors had come from Africa to be "a subordinate and inferior class of beings . . . [who] had no rights which the white man was bound to respect."

Four years later, the United States went to war against itself, and at the end of that war two new amendments were added to the Constitution. The Thirteenth Amendment abolished slavery outright. The Fourteenth Amendment, which guaranteed all persons "due process" and "equal protection of law," sought to protect the rights of freed slaves:

> All persons born or naturalized in the United States and subject to the jurisdiction thereof, are citizens of the United States and of the State wherein they reside. No State shall make or enforce any law which shall abridge the privileges or immunities of citizens of the United States; nor shall any State deprive any person of life, liberty, or property, without due process of law; nor deny to any person within its jurisdiction the equal protection of the laws.

But the most profound effect of the Fourteenth Amendment on the American political system was neither anticipated nor intended when it was enacted in 1868—namely, the empowerment of the corporation. And the person who did more than anyone else to bring about this empowerment was Supreme Court Justice Stephen J. Field.

The son of a New England Congregational minister, Stephen Field was strongly influenced by two of his brothers who also achieved prominence during the Gilded Age. Younger brother Cyrus was the promoter of the first transatlantic cable. Older brother David was an eminent attorney who pioneered the codification movement for organizing American law, and also served as counsel for the notorious railroad barons Jay Gould and Jim Fisk.

After graduating from law school and clerking in his older brother's firm, Stephen Field traveled to Europe in 1848, a time of major uprisings and the publication of the *Communist Manifesto*. In December, he read President Polk's announcement of the discovery of gold in California, and in 1849 he joined the California gold rush. Arriving in the newly organized settlement known as Marysville, he was elected alcalde (mayor) on his third day.

In the fall of 1850, Field was elected to the state legislature, and his political career advanced quickly. His life in Marysville gives no particular clues of his future as railroad point man on the United States Supreme Court. Instead, the biographical vignettes from those years are like episodes from the old TV show *Gunsmoke:* confrontations with lynch mobs, personal disputes settled at knifepoint, courtroom scenes with drawn pistols, debts paid in gold dust, elections bought with whisky and cigars. Volatile and domineering, Field was better at picking fights than settling conflicts—hardly a model of judicial temperament. Nevertheless, in 1857 he was elected to the California Supreme Court, and in 1859 he became chief justice. When Congress passed an act in 1863 creating a new federal court of appeals for the Pacific region, Field was an obvious candidate. At that time, the head of each circuit court also served as a U.S. Supreme Court justice. Governor Leland Stanford of California personally recommended Stephen Field for the position, as did Field's older brother David, a Lincoln partisan. Lincoln nominated Field for the Supreme Court. After joining the Court, Field remained closely associated with Leland Stanford, who went on to lead the Sacramento "Big Four"—Stanford, Collis Huntington, Mark Hopkins, and Charles Crocker—the organizers of the Central Pacific Railroad and later the Southern Pacific Railroad. Field socialized with the railroad men, and when Leland Stanford organized Stanford University he appointed Field as a trustee.

Field's sympathies for the railroads and his personal ties to the Central Pacific leadership quickly became notorious both in California and in Washington. Although there is no evidence of any direct financial gain by Field (at the time of his death, his estate was valued at $65,000, a pittance by robber baron standards), his efforts on behalf of his railroad friends embarrassed more circumspect members of the Court, including Chief Justice Waite, himself a former railroad attorney. In 1875, Waite angered Field by refusing his requests to write the majority decisions in the case of *United States v. Union Pacific.* In a note to Field, Waite wrote:

> It seems to me . . . to be specially important that the opinion should come from one . . . who would not be known as the personal friend of the parties representing these railroad interests. There was no doubt of your intimate personal relations with the managers of the Central Pacific, and naturally you, more than any one else in the court, realize the vast importance of the great work that has been done.

Waite was right in his assessment of Field's bias. Letters between Field and his friend, Professor John Norton Pomeroy, show that Field secured a lucrative position for Pomeroy as legal consultant to the Central Pacific, then secretly provided Pomeroy with internal Court memoranda. As for the feelings of the railroaders for Field, a revealing exchange of letters leaked to the *San Francisco Chronicle* in 1878 showed railroad executives discussing among themselves how best to strategically deploy Field in a crucial upcoming case. In one letter, David Colton of the Central Pacific wrote: "Judge Field will not sit in the Gallatin Case [in the U.S. district court], but instead will reserve his best efforts (I have no doubt) for the final termination of the case at Washington before the full bench."

Even more indicative of Field's relation with the railroad barons is a remarkable exchange of letters between Republican presidential candidate James Garfield and Whitelaw Reid. In the letters, Reid spoke on behalf of railroad baron Jay Gould, who sought guarantees that in return for a large contribution, he would be allowed to control the appointment of three new justices to the Supreme Court. On August 31, 1880, Reid wrote to Garfield:

Your visit to my house was good, and at least stopped the headway the other side was making. The real anxiety of these people [Jay Gould and his attorney William Phelps] is with reference to the Supreme Court. The next President will almost certainly have the appointment of three new Judges—even if a great enlargement of the court should not be ordered. All monied men, and especially all corporations, regarded the course of the Supreme Court in the Granger cases and in the Pacific R.R. case as bad law and bad faith. I believe that you sympathize with the general view of the law taken by Judge Field and his associates in the minority. . . . These people hesitate because they say they are unwilling to elect a President unless they are sure that he disapproves what they call the revolutionary course of the majority of the court. If they could be satisfied on this point, I know we could make a big demonstration at once, and probably settle things beyond a peradventure.

Two days later Garfield responded to Reid with vague assurances that he would "refrain from adopting any policy which would prevent capitalists from extending our great railroad system." Reid, however, was not satisfied, and on September 6 he wrote: "Yours of the 2nd inst. is at hand. It is scarcely so precise on the point of the decisions of Judge Field as wd. be desired by some of the gentlemen concerned." Garfield responded, again failing to make the exact guarantees that the railroaders were looking for, and so Reid continued to press. Finally, on September 23, Garfield caved, providing the promise Reid wanted:

I have stated to you, fully, my well considered views of the Constitution in reference to the sanctity of Contracts and of vested rights— Under no circumstances would I entrust the high functions of a Justice of the Supreme Court, to any person whom I did not believe to be entirely sound on those questions. I should insist upon evidence which would be satisfactory to you as well as to me.

A week later Reid replied: "It has all worked out right." Jay Gould wrote a check for $150,000, which proved to be a crucial contribution, since Garfield was forced to spend $100,000 in the final week of the campaign to save Indiana for the Republicans. At a high-spirited victory dinner, vice president-elect Chester Arthur told the tipsy crowd how he and Garfield had won the state:

Indiana was really, I suppose, a Democratic State. It had been put down on the books always as a State that might be carried by close and perfect organization and a great deal of — [laughter]. I see the reporters are present, therefore I will simply say that everybody showed a great deal of interest in the occasion and distributed tracts and political documents all through the State.

True to his word, as one of his first acts of office, Garfield nominated Stanley Matthews, formerly Jay Gould's chief attorney in the Midwest, to the Supreme Court. Matthews, who had previously been nominated and rejected during the Hayes administration for a position on the Court, had also served as attorney for the Louisville and Nashville Railroads, the Springfield and Mansfield Railroad, and other railroads, and was a director of the Knoxville and Ohio Railroad. It is clear that the railroaders felt he would be a significant asset on the Court.

The ties between Matthews and the railroads were so blatant that large segments of the business community joined in opposing his nomination, as shown by the following telegram received on February 7, 1881:

> To the Judiciary Committee of the United States Senate, The Hon. A. G. Thurman, Chairman.
>
> In behalf of 800 business firms of the New York Board of Trade and Transportation, we respectfully but earnestly protest against the confirmation of the Hon. Stanley Matthews as judge of the Supreme Court of the United States for the following reasons:
>
> We are informed and believe that the great railroad corporations of the country are endeavoring to obtain control of this Court of last resort, which has heretofore been the most important bulwark in defending the public interests against the encroachments of corporations; that Mr. Matthews has been educated as a railroad attorney, and views railroad questions from a railroad standpoint; that his actions while in the United States Senate prove this, and in this important respect render him unfit for a Justice of the Supreme Court.
>
> Ambrose Snow, President
> Darwin R. James, Secretary

Despite the furor, Matthews was confirmed. Yet in the end, the attempts by Jay Gould and the other railroad barons to pack the Supreme Court under the Garfield administration were unsuccessful. Although everything about Matthews' background made it appear that he would be the perfect pro-railroad justice, once on the Court he proved more independent than expected and failed to ally himself closely with Justice Field and the railroad agenda. Garfield was assassinated before being able to make any more nominations, and it wasn't until 1896 that Field's positions enjoyed an ironclad majority on the Court.

WHY WAS CONTROL of the Supreme Court so important to railroad corporations in the 1870s and 1880s? After all, in the years following the Civil War, the railroads seemed to have little trouble manipulating Congress to do their bidding. Bribery by railroad lobbyists was rampant among senators and congressmen. For example, between 1875 and 1885 the Central Pacific spent $500,000 yearly on graft; in a single year, the LaCrosse and Milwaukee Railroad spent $872,000 for influence, including $50,000 for a governor, $10,000 for a state controller, $125,000 for thirteen legislators, and so on. Among the fruits of these expenditures by railroad interests were immense land grants. Ultimately, they acquired two hundred million acres of land—a tenth of the area of the entire country.

But at the state level the railroad barons *did* need help from a Supreme Court—one willing to throw thunderbolts from Washington invalidating state legislation on constitutionality grounds. Such help was not required in every state. It wasn't needed in Pennsylvania, for example, which, as described in chapter 6, was firmly under the control of Tom Scott of the Pennsylvania Railroad after the Civil War. But in the Midwest and the West, railroad corporations repeatedly found themselves ambushed and outgunned by agricultural and labor movements that seemed to come out of nowhere. Such movements often succeeded in enacting regulatory legislation and taxes aimed directly at the railroads.

The first post–Civil War threat to the railroads was the Order of the Patrons of Husbandry, more commonly known as the Grange. The Grange was conceived in the 1860s by a Minnesota farmer and journalist named Oliver Hudson Kelley, who envisioned it as a secret society complete with rituals, handshakes, and passwords. The movement sought the full voting involvement of both women and men, and its ambitions ranged from breaking the social isolation of farm life to initiating a number of self-help projects such as cooperative stores and grain elevators. By 1875, the Grange claimed 850,000 members in 21,000 chapters, enough to make it a powerful force in several states. Grange ideology was militant, and that militancy was shared by other farm organizations. For example, the Illinois State Farmers Association passed a resolution in 1873 that read as follows:

> Resolved, that the railways of the road, except in those countries where they have been held under the strict regulation and supervision of the government, have proved themselves arbitrary, extortionate, and as opposed to free institutions and free commerce between states as were the feudal barons of the middle ages.

On the issue of passing regulatory statutes that would prevent rate-gouging by railroads and grain elevators, the Grangers were supported by small-town merchants, and the result in Illinois was the creation of a state regulatory commission armed with broad powers.

Corporate interests challenged the Granger laws in court, claiming that the regulation of railroad and grain elevator rates by Illinois officials violated the Fourteenth Amendment's due process requirement. In 1877, a key case known as *Munn v. Illinois* came before the U.S. Supreme Court, and in the decision on the case the Supreme Court ruled, in a vote of seven to two, that such regulation was acceptable for businesses under the principle articulated two centuries earlier by Lord Hale that when private property is "affected with a public interest, it ceases to be *juris privati* only."

In JUSTICE FIELD'S DISSENT in the *Munn* case, Field proposed a new interpretation of the Fourteenth Amendment—not as a protective shield for freed slaves in the South, but rather as a protective shield for corporate and property interests. Field took aim at the idea that property "affected with a public interest" is fair game for regulation:

> If this be sound law, if there be no protection, either in the principles upon which our republican government is founded, or in the

prohibitions of the Constitution against such invasion of private rights, all property and all business in the State are held at the mercy of a majority of its legislature.

Prior to the *Munn* case, Field had made similar arguments in his dissent in the 1873 *Slaughter-House* cases. Together, Field's dissents in *Slaughter-House* and *Munn* set the stage for the aggressive antiregulatory doctrine known as *substantive due process,* which finally won the support of a majority of the Court in the late 1880s. We'll look at substantive due process in more detail in chapter 11. Meanwhile, Field's views were also being shaped by events in his adopted state of California, which was the scene of sharp clashes between railroad interests and an emerging populist movement throughout the 1870s. California populism had an ugly side: virulent anti-Chinese agitation. Both the railroad issue and the Chinese issue proved potent rallying cries among white voters worried about economic threats posed by low-wage immigrants and by powerful corporations.

In typical fashion, Field saw the Chinese issue through the eyes of the railroads, which used immigrant workers for their dirtiest, most hazardous jobs. During construction of its line across the Sierra Nevada mountains, the Central Pacific railroad had been stymied until it brought in some eight thousand to fourteen thousand Chinese laborers, mostly recruited by agents of the railroad directly from the coastal villages of Guangdong Province. Enduring grueling conditions and suffering heavy loss of life, the Chinese broke the back of the mountains for the Central Pacific.

Unfortunately for the railroads, the populist movement was surging, and in 1879 that movement succeeded in writing a number of anti-Chinese and anticorporate provisions into the new California constitution, including a ban against any employment of Chinese workers by corporations. Field's advocacy for Chinese immigrant rights was hardly based on his human rights views. He wrote to Professor Pomeroy: "You know I belong to the class, who repudiate the doctrine that this country was made for the people of all races. On the contrary, I think it is for our race—the Caucasian race."

But if Field believed that the United States was made for Caucasians, he believed even more strongly that the railroads had the right to employ cheap immigrant labor. And so he worked diligently to overturn the anti-immigrant rules. Field's post as lead judge on the federal ninth circuit court—as already noted, a job he performed concurrently with his position on the U.S. Supreme Court—gave him a judicial arena where his fellow justices shared his antiregulatory philosophy. In his ninth circuit court decisions, Field made no effort to disguise his support for railroad interests, and it was in solving various of the railroads' tricky problems that he created the procorporate interpretation of the Fourteenth Amendment that came to be known as "Ninth Circuit Law." That development was aided by the fact that most employment cases considered by the ninth circuit belonged to a class of cases that could not be appealed to the Supreme Court. Between 1868 and 1885, Congress withdrew the Supreme Court's appellate jurisdiction in all *habeus corpus* cases—that is, cases having to do with the legitimacy of a person's arrest or detention. Most Chinese immigrant cases were *habeus corpus* cases, so Field could issue ninth circuit court opinions in these cases that the Supreme Court could not overrule.

One such case, *In Re Ah Fong* (1874), involved a Chinese citizen who was being prevented from entering California because of California's anti-Chinese laws. Among other arguments, Field supported Ah Fong's claim on the basis that the Fourteenth Amendment had guaranteed equal treatment of all persons.

Field's strategy had two pieces: first, to undermine the idea that the Fourteenth Amendment was intended only to help the emancipated slaves, and second, to assert that corporations were entitled to Fourteenth Amendment protection. Field's decisions in cases such as *In Re Ah Fong* advanced the first piece of the strategy. To accomplish the second piece, Field ingeniously utilized a case that involved *both* Chinese rights and corporate rights. The case, *In Re Parrott,* came before the ninth circuit court and was ruled on by two of Field's close allies, Judge Hoffman and Judge Sawyer. But Field's fingerprints are clearly present.

The case involved a corporation owned by a man named Tiburchio Parrott, who was arrested for hiring a Chinese worker. In their decision, Hoffman and Sawyer echoed Field's ruling in *Ah Fong,* deciding in favor of Parrott on the basis that his equal protection rights had been violated.

By the early 1880s, Field's Fourteenth Amendment doctrine was ready to be applied to the cases that mattered most to the railroads: state taxes. Big money was at stake. Under the 1879 California constitution, the system for assessing taxes from railroads had been consolidated and placed under the control of a democratically elected body known as the State Board of Equalization. The board proved to be the railroads' worst nightmare. Unlike the poorly trained local tax authorities that the railroads had found easy to manipulate, both the counties and the state now had top-flight legal and accounting talent at their disposal.

At issue was how to value land for tax purposes. In assessments of individual property, any outstanding mortgage on the property was subtracted from its value. For example, a farmer would only be taxed on the proportion of his land that he owned free and clear. For railroads, applying this method would have resulted in the deletion of all state property taxes, because the railroads could point to bonds valued far beyond the value of the land.

In other words, valuing individual property and railroad property was a case of comparing apples to oranges, and state law recognized that reality. Nevertheless, the case went to court, and among the arguments of the railroads was the assertion that the difference in the assessment methods violated the Fourteenth Amendment requirement of "equal protection" for all persons.

In 1882 and 1883, two tax cases with essentially the same set of facts reached Stephen Field's ninth circuit court. The first was *San Mateo County v. Southern Pacific Railroad,* the second was *Santa Clara County v. Southern Pacific Railroad.*

In the ninth circuit's *San Mateo* decision, both Justice Field and Justice Sawyer ruled in favor of the corporation on the grounds that the California tax laws violated the Fourteenth Amendment's guarantee of "equal protection" to all persons. However, the two judges differed significantly on the interpretation of the word "person." Sawyer's view was simply that a corporation is a legal person—period. But Field knew there was little constitutional support for such a position. After all, the meaning of the word "person" as it had been applied to corporations both in England and the United States had always been much more limited. What personhood had always meant was the functional ability to make contracts and to own property, and to use the courts to enforce contracts and property claims. The notion that this restricted sort of legal personhood entitled corporations to a broader set of rights had previously been rejected by the courts, as Field was well aware. So in attempting to justify why the railroad corporations ought to be afforded "equal protection" under California law, Field used a more restrained line of argument than Sawyer. Instead of saying that *corporations* were persons, he argued that it was the Fourteenth Amendment "personhood" rights of *stockholders* that were violated when the counties taxed the corporation in a discriminatory way.

Had it been adopted by the Supreme Court, the rationale Field used in his circuit court decision would have strengthened the position of the corporation. It would have given corporate property the benefit of Fourteenth Amendment protection. But the basis of corporate empowerment would have been more specific and limited, and it would have been harder to parlay it into other rights. For example, it would have been hard to use Field's rationale as an argument for giving corporations First Amendment free speech rights, since limiting the free speech of a corporation does not limit the free speech of its stockholders.

In his circuit court opinion in the second, and historically more crucial case, *Santa Clara,* Field used the same rationale as in the *San Mateo* opinion for giving Fourteenth Amendment protections to corporations:

> Surely these great constitutional provisions, which have been, not inaptly, termed a new *Magna Charta,* cannot be made to read as counsel contend, "nor shall any state deprive any person of life, liberty, or property without due process of law, *unless he be associated with others in a corporation,* nor deny to any person within its jurisdiction the equal protection of the laws, *unless he be a member of the corporation."* How petty and narrow would provisions thus limited appear in the fundamental law of a great people! [italics in the original]

Although in his personal relations Field was known for being temperamental, his legal style showed care and strategy as he advanced his doctrine of corporate empowerment in small, deliberate steps. His "shareholder rights" rationale provided a neater, more focused way of applying Fourteenth Amendment protections to corporations than a blanket assertion that corporations are persons.

Field's view coincided closely with that of his friend John Pomeroy. To Pomeroy, the critical idea was that courts should "look past" the corporate veil and recognize that state actions that affect a corporation's property also affect the owners of the property. Pomeroy wrote:

> The truth cannot be evaded that, *for the purpose of protecting rights, the property of all business and trading corporations* IS *the property of the individual corporators.* A state act depriving a business corporation of its property without due process of law, does in fact *deprive the individual corporators of their property.* In this sense, and within the scope of these grand safeguards of private rights, there is no real distinction between artificial persons or corporations, and natural persons.

As simple and logical as this argument sounds, it represented a significant departure from established court doctrine, which had always made a distinction between corporate property and individual property. The most crucial distinction is that owning shares in a company allows a person to own property without being subject to the sort of accountability to the community that normally attends the ownership of property. For that reason, courts had never assumed that shareholders in a corporation should expect equal rights; on the contrary, the enjoyment by corporate shareholders of privileges such as limited liability justified applying special restrictions to corporations and their owners. Legal scholar Gregory Mark describes the trade-off like this:

> Because an individual corporator could neither use corporate property as a personal asset, nor generally be held responsible for corporate debts, the usual linkage of ownership and control did not exist. . . . For example, the power to sue a corporation in which one held stock would be senseless if the corporation were a mere convenience for arranging one's own property. Control differentiated co-ownership and corporate ownership. The shareholder renounced control over his property and freed himself from responsibility for the consequences of how control was exercised. . . . Modern theories of property began with the assumption that a person's control over and interest in property should be concurrent.

THE REASONING IN FIELD'S DECISIONS makes it clear that his relationship with the founders of the Central Pacific Railroad not only influenced his sentiments but also his basic conception of what a corporation actually is. To Field, the founders, owners, and managers of a corporation are all one and the same. Indeed, he saw these entrepreneurs as tinged with an almost halo-like glow. In his September 25, 1882, circuit court opinion in the railroad tax cases, Field wrote:

> As a matter of fact, nearly all enterprises in this state, requiring for their execution an expenditure of large capital, are undertaken by corporations. They engage in commerce; they build and sail ships; they cover our navigable streams with steamers; they construct houses; they bring the products of earth and sea to market; they light our streets and buildings; they open and work mines; they carry water into our cities; they build railroads, and cross mountains and deserts with them; they erect churches, colleges, lyceums, and theaters; they set up manufactories, and keep the spindle and shuttle in motion; they establish banks for savings; they insure against accidents on land and sea; they give policies on life; they make money exchanges with all parts of the world; they publish newspapers and books, and send news by lightning across the continent and under the ocean. Indeed, there is nothing which is lawful to be done to feed and clothe our people, to beautify and adorn their dwellings, to relieve the sick, to help the needy, and to enrich and ennoble humanity, which is not to a great extent done through the instrumentalities of corporations.

To Field, there was no basic difference between a corporation, no matter how large, and a small, closely held, unincorporated business such as a partnership. But as the nineteenth century drew to a close, big business was already moving rapidly away from that simple model. As Gregory Mark writes:

> In the publicly held industrial corporations that were created in the 1890s and after, . . . the shareholders were more properly viewed as creations of managements seeking capital for a variety of purposes. The reality of the corporation apart from its members was becoming clearer as the relationship of the shareholders to the operations of the business became increasingly distant. Neither the corporation nor the shareholders could be taken as agents for the other; the actions of the one only rarely put the other at legal risk. The life of the corporation could no longer be identified with that of the corporators.

Corporations had become complex creatures indeed, matrices within which the interests of stockholders, managers, employees, consumers, and the greater "public good" both conflicted and intertwined. The fact that shareholders could sue the corporation was proof that the corporation and the shareholders were not one and the same. To state that a tax on the corporation was equivalent to a tax on the shareholders—especially when the continual buying and selling of stocks meant that such a group was in a state of perpetual flux—was to talk about a world that did not exist.

What did exist was the smoky, industrial, frenetic, ruthless world of contradictions that we call the Gilded Age. Capital was on the move, not just figuratively in the sense of economic growth, but quite literally in the geographic expansion that was under way. When Field joined the U.S. Supreme Court in the early 1860s, he traveled each year via long ship journey to conduct his summer circuit court in California. But with the completion of the transcontinental railroad, he could ride back and forth between Washington and California in style and luxury by Pullman car.

And so, having developed a new theory of the Fourteenth Amendment in his circuit court decisions on the *San Mateo* and *Santa Clara* cases, Justice Field traveled to Washington to take part in what he obviously hoped would be the culmination of his careful preparation—the ratification by the United States Supreme Court of his new doctrine of corporate constitutional empowerment.

CHAPTER NINE

The Court Reporter

Who really decided the Supreme Court's
most important corporate case?
(1886)

ALTHOUGH BOTH REACHED the Supreme Court, the two nearly identical cases that Justice Field had pinned his hopes on for extending
the Fourteenth Amendment to corporations suffered different fates. *San
Mateo* was quickly withdrawn from consideration and faded into obscurity. *Santa Clara* was decided by the Supreme Court in favor of the railroad, and it gained mythic status in American political culture as the
decision by which corporations won personhood status under the Fourteenth Amendment.

But there's a big problem with the traditional view of the *Santa
Clara* case when it reached the Supreme Court. In fact, the ruling issued
by the Court in the case didn't say anything at all about corporate personhood. The circumstances under which *Santa Clara* came to be regarded as such a precedent are extremely odd, and they deserve a full
explanation.

If you go to a law library and read the *Santa Clara* decision in
Supreme Court Reporter, Vol. 6 (1886), you will not find anything about
corporate personhood. The decision, written by Justice Harlan and announced on May 10, 1886, includes a lengthy discussion of fences and
mortgages, and a final conclusion that those technical factors fall in favor
of the railroad. That's about it.

So where does the idea come from that the *Santa Clara* decision established corporate constitutional personhood? If you go back to the library and ask for a different compilation of Supreme Court decisions,
United States Reports, Vol. 118, J. C. Bancroft Davis, Reporter (1886), you'll
find in that version the following paragraph inserted in a section prefac-
ing Justice Harlan's decision entitled "Statement of Facts":

One of the points made and discussed at length in the brief of counsel for defendants in error was that "Corporations are persons within
the meaning of the Fourteenth Amendment to the Constitution of
the United States." Before argument Mr. Chief Justice Waite said: The
Court does not wish to hear argument on the question whether the
provision in the Fourteenth Amendment to the Constitution, which
forbids a State to deny to any person within its jurisdiction the equal
protection of the laws, applies to these corporations. We are all of
opinion that it does.

Another reference to personhood appears in the "Syllabus" or "Headnotes" to the case—that is, the annotations prepared by the court reporter to summarize the opinion. The first sentence of these headnotes
is as follows:

The defendant Corporations are persons within the intent of the
clause in section I of the Fourteenth Amendment to the Constitution
of the United States, which forbids a State to deny to any person within
its jurisdiction the equal protection of the laws.

In other words, even though the written decision made no mention
of the notion that corporations deserve Fourteenth Amendment equal
protection rights, Chief Justice Morrison Waite made a comment from
the bench that seemed to endorse the view that corporations are persons for purposes of the amendment. The court reporter, J. C. Bancroft
Davis, incorporated those verbal comments into the statement of facts.
And in the syllabus (the court reporter's summary of the case), he highlighted Waite's verbal "personhood" comment as the main point of the
case.

The unusual way in which the verbal statement of Chief Justice Waite
made it into the record and subsequently became the basis for an entirely new doctrine of corporate rights leads to a number of questions,
which we'll consider in turn.

First, how did all this come to light? Do historians agree on the facts?
In 1960, the following exchange of notes between court reporter Bancroft Davis and Chief Justice Waite was discovered by Fourteenth Amend-

ment scholar Howard Graham, and also by Waite's biographer, C. Peter Magrath. The first note is from court reporter J. C. Bancroft Davis to Chief Justice Waite, exactly four months (September 10, 1886) after the announcement of the *Santa Clara* decision:

> I have a memorandum in the California Cases, *Santa Clara County v. Southern Pacific*, as follows:
>
> In opening the Court stated that it did not wish to hear argument on the question whether the Fourteenth Amendment applies to such corporations as are parties in these suits. All the Judges were of opinion that it does.
>
> Please let me know whether I correctly caught your words and oblige.

The second note is Chief Justice Waite's response to the court reporter, five days later:

> I think your mem. in the California Railroad Tax cases expresses with sufficient accuracy what was said before the argument began. I leave it with you to determine whether anything need be said about it in the report inasmuch as we avoided meeting the constitutional question in the decision.

The fact that these notes had escaped previous discovery is not surprising, since the Library of Congress alone maintains a collection of twenty thousand items related to Justice Waite—and that does not include the papers that were kept by family members in Cincinnati and Ann Arbor, and by libraries in Toledo, New York, and Chicago. The exchange of notes was first discussed in print in 1963 by Magrath in *Morrison R. Waite: The Triumph of Character*. It was mentioned in 1986 by David O'Brien in *Storm Center: The Supreme Court in American Politics*. Most recently it was highlighted by Thom Hartmann in *Unequal Protection: The Rise of Corporate Dominance and the Theft of Human Rights*.

Although both Magrath and Graham felt the finding of these notes was significant, there are several reasons why it escaped wide recognition in the early 1960s. Most important was the timing. As will be seen later in this book, the era in which the Supreme Court used the Fourteenth Amendment aggressively to block state regulation of corporations came to an end in 1937. In the early 1960s, when Graham discovered the Waite-Davis notes, the whole issue of corporate personhood was seen as more a matter of historical interest than of political importance. Few people anticipated that a new expansion in corporate rights would soon be under way.

Other circumstances also contributed to the obscurity of the finding. Graham was shy, deaf, and nearing the end of his career—hardly in a position to trumpet his discovery. Although corporate empowerment had been the primary focus of his Fourteenth Amendment research in the 1930s, by the 1950s his interest had shifted somewhat to the Civil Rights aspects of the amendment.

A final reason why these Waite-Davis notes escaped wider attention was that a dense thicket of related historical controversy already surrounded the Waite Court and the Fourteenth Amendment. At the time of the discovery of the Waite notes, the facts surrounding another Fourteenth Amendment intrigue—the "Conkling deception" about congressional intent—were still being settled (discussed in chapter 10). This older controversy overshadowed the new one.

Did Chief Justice Waite intend his verbal comments to set a precedent establishing corporate personhood under the Fourteenth Amendment?

It is not certain why Waite made his verbal comment supporting corporate personhood, but his note to court reporter J. C. Bancroft Davis makes it clear that he did not intend to set a corporations-are-persons precedent. The notes show Waite taking a fairly casual attitude toward whether the court reporter includes the comments made from the bench in the report on the case. The reason is clear: Waite did not think the decision in the case had broken any new constitutional ground.

If Chief Justice Waite did not intend to set a precedent, why did he make the comments supporting corporate personhood?

The reason Waite stopped oral argument on the issue of corporate personhood is probably because the Supreme Court had recently heard such arguments in the *San Mateo* case. Moreover, it is likely that Waite believed that the *Santa Clara* case could be decided on simpler, more technical grounds, without resorting to a new interpretation of the Fourteenth Amendment. In general, the Supreme Court avoids breaking new constitutional ground when cases are not really ripe for it. There can be little doubt that a chief justice wishing to issue dictum would do so as a concurrence and would include a rationale. According to Waite's biographer C. Peter Magrath, "It seems almost inconceivable that he would have delegated the announcement of a major constitutional doctrine to the court reporter."

As for Waite's statement—as set down by Bancroft in his memo—that the judges were "of the opinion that it does," the meaning is clear. Several years earlier, Roscoe Conkling, a member of the congressional committee that wrote the Fourteenth Amendment, had provided detailed testimony that the intent of Congress had been to include corporations as "persons" within the meaning of the amendment. Apparently, Waite had found that testimony convincing and believed that the other justices had as well. As we will see in the next chapter, historians now believe Conkling's testimony was not only incorrect but intentionally deceptive.

Did other justices at the time believe that a "personhood" precedent had been established?

On the same day that the Court's opinion in the *Santa Clara* case was announced, the Court also announced its opinion in the case of *County of San Bernardino v. Southern Pacific Railroad*. In a concurrence to that opinion, Justice Field—the leading advocate of corporate personhood on the Court, as we have already seen—expressed disappointment with *Santa Clara*, complaining that the Court had not done

> its duty to decide the important constitutional questions involved.... The question is of transcendent importance, and it will come here and continue to come until it is authoritatively decided in harmony with the great constitutional amendment which insures to every person, whatever his position or association, the equal protection of the laws; and that necessarily implies freedom from the imposition of unequal burdens under the same conditions.... Much as I regret that the question could not now be decided, I recognize fully the wisdom of the rule that the constitutionality of State legislation will not be considered by the court unless by the case presented its consideration is imperatively required.

*Did the court reporter inappropriately play up the
chief justice's comment?*

There is no doubt that he did. Waite's note to him had been clear: the
Court did not intend to address any constitutional issues in the *Santa
Clara* case.

Why would a court reporter "spin" a decision?

The issue of J. C. Bancroft Davis's motivation was explored recently by
Thom Hartmann in *Unequal Protection.* Hartmann notes that the position
of chief court reporter in the late nineteenth century held much more status and responsibility than that of an ordinary transcriber, which makes
Davis's autonomous action more comprehensible. According to Hartmann's account, Davis was actually something of a political player: he had
previously served as assistant secretary of state under two presidents, as
acting secretary of state, as a minister to the German empire, and as a
court of claims judge. Davis's own political views are hard to guess, since
he not only was involved with the international socialist movement but
served on a railroad board as well. An acquaintance of Karl Marx, Davis
reported from the socialist reunion at Gotha, Germany, in May 1875. He
also served as president of the board of directors of the Newburgh and
New York Railroad Company. Davis's personal views on the legal issue of
corporate personhood are unknown, but he was certainly aware of the
political significance of the issue, and his ties to railroad interests are at
least suggestive of why he might want to empower the railroads.

When did subsequent opinions begin treating
Santa Clara *as a "personhood" precedent?*

Five months after the *Santa Clara* decision was announced, and two
months after the exchange of notes between Bancroft Davis and Chief
Justice Waite, the notion that *Santa Clara* established that corporations
are persons under the Fourteenth Amendment received its first citation
by a Supreme Court justice. In his dissent in the case of *Philadelphia Fire
Association v. New York,* decided on November 15, 1886, Justice Harlan
wrote the following:

> At the last term of this court, when counsel was about to enter upon
> the argument in the case of *Santa Clara County v. Southern Pacific
> Railroad,* 118 U. S. 394, 396—involving the validity of a system devised

by one of the States for the taxation of railroad corporations of a certain class—the Chief Justice observed: "The Court does not wish to hear argument on the question whether the provision in the Fourteenth Amendment to the Constitution, which forbids a State to deny to any person within its jurisdiction the equal protection of the laws, applies to these corporations. We are all of opinion that it does." This, it is true, was said in regard to corporations of the particular State whose legislation was assailed as unconstitutional; but it is equally clear that a corporation of one State, doing business in another State by her consent, is to be deemed, at least in respect to that business, a "person" within the jurisdiction of the latter State, in the meaning of the Fourteenth Amendment."

What is the legal status of headnotes and statements of fact?
According to Supreme Court historian David M. O'Brien, the status of headnotes was decided by the 1905 case of *United States v. Detroit Lumber Co*, where the Court ruled that headnotes are not part of a decision of the Court. Since *Santa Clara* predates *Detroit Lumber,* the legal status of headnotes was not yet formally determined in 1886. Regarding *Santa Clara,* O'Brien notes:

> There is perhaps no better illustration of the consequence of a headnote than in *Santa Clara County v. Southern Pacific Railroad Company* (1886). There, after consulting Chief Justice Waite, the Reporter at his own discretion decided to note in an otherwise uninteresting tax case that the Court considered corporations "legal persons" entitled to protection under the Fourteenth Amendment. Corporations, like individual citizens, could thereafter challenge the constitutionality of congressional and state legislation impinging on their interests.

Is the Santa Clara decision valid?
The passage of time has a way of validating Supreme Court decisions, even those that are clearly wrong. Even though the exchange of notes between Davis and Waite has been on the historic record for forty years and clearly showed that Waite did not intend to set a personhood precedent in *Santa Clara,* there are other indications in the record that the justices did in fact agree with the statement; these include Justice Harlan's quote of Waite's

statement in his dissent later that same year. Also, subsequent Court decisions readily cited *Santa Clara* and cited the "personhood" formulation as a precedent.

What are the wider consequences of what happened in 1886?

The most unfortunate outcome of the *Santa Clara* case is not that corporations were declared to be persons. Given the steady ascendancy of the stridently procorporate Field faction on the Court, that result would have come inevitably within the following decade—certainly no later than 1895. But interestingly enough, Field's doctrine of personhood, as articulated in his circuit court opinions in the *San Mateo* and *Santa Clara* cases, was actually a good deal more circumscribed than the blanket "corporations are persons" doctrine that came to be ascribed to *Santa Clara*. As noted in chapter 8, Field based his doctrine of corporate rights on the notion that an unfair tax on corporate property amounted to a violation of stockholder rights. If this rationale had been articulated clearly by the Court in *Santa Clara*, the precedent would have been a much narrower one than it turned out to be, and it would have been much easier eventually to reverse.

Instead, the muddled and confusing circumstances behind the *Santa Clara* decision, combined with the lack of any stated rationale for it, served the interests of those seeking the broadest possible interpretation of the decision as a basis for corporate empowerment. That confusion was no accident—it was deliberately produced through the artful deception of one well-placed, highly skilled, unscrupulous man, former U.S. senator Roscoe Conkling. This feat of deception is the subject of the next chapter.

CHAPTER TEN

The Lavender-Vested
Turkey Gobbler

How a "majestic, super-eminent" lawyer
deceived the Supreme Court
(1883)

A s DESCRIBED IN THE PREVIOUS CHAPTER, historians have known
since 1963 that the "corporations are persons" formulation frequently cited in reference to the *Santa Clara* decision was not actually
part of the opinion of the Supreme Court but rather an insertion of
words by chief court reporter J. C. Bancroft Davis based on a comment
made from the bench by Chief Justice Morrison Waite. After this reve-
lation, the legitimacy of *Santa Clara* as a basis for corporate rights would
seem to be in tatters.

But we have one more mystery to clear up—namely, why Waite expressed his verbal opinion in the first place, and why the Supreme Court,
despite the quirkiness of the *Santa Clara* decision, acquiesced to the use
of that decision as a personhood precedent.

The "conversion" of the Court to the idea that Congress intended the
Fourteenth Amendment to include corporations can be traced to a day in
December 1882, two years prior to the *Santa Clara* decision, when a former
senator named Roscoe Conkling argued the issue before the Supreme
Court in a case very similar to *Santa Clara*. As we've seen, that case, *San
Mateo County v. Southern Pacific Railroad*, was withdrawn before it was actually decided. However, it is clear that the oral testimony of Conkling was
sufficiently convincing to cause Chief Justice Waite to announce from the
bench, three years later, prior to announcing the Court's *Santa Clara* decision, "The Court does not wish to hear argument on the question whether
... the Fourteenth Amendment ... applies to these corporations. We are all
of the opinion that it does."

How did Conkling succeed so completely with his argument? It could not have been on the basis of his personal charisma. Even by the puffed-up standards of the times, Conkling was considered unbearably pompous. Described as "the great egoist, hater, and cynic of a mediocre Senate," he was notable for "his haughty disdain, his grandiloquent swell, his majestic, super-eminent, overpowering, turkey gobbler strut." Conkling was the epitome of the Gilded Age politician. During his career he had done it all: Congress, the Senate, leader of the Republican Party in New York, not one but two attempts by presidents to nominate him for the Supreme Court. Chief Justice Waite owed his position to the fact that Conkling had declined President Grant's attempt to make him chief justice; Justice Blatchford owed Conkling his job as well, because Chester Arthur had appointed him associate justice after Conkling declined that appointment.

At the time he presented his oral argument to the Court, Conkling was dealing with something of a setback. A year earlier, he had resigned from the Senate in a huff over President Chester Arthur's refusal to give him patronage control over government jobs in New York. Conkling had expected to be reelected, but the New York legislature took the opportunity to dump him. (Prior to the adoption of the Seventeenth Amendment in 1913, senators were picked by state legislatures rather than by popular vote.) He then suffered additional humiliation when the loopy assassin Charles Guiteau, an avowed supporter of Conkling's faction of the Republican Party, shot and killed President Garfield.

After the fiasco that cost him his Senate seat, Conkling found financial solace in the Southern Pacific Railroad, which happily signed him onto its all-star legal team, alongside Silas Sanderson (formerly chief justice of the California Supreme Court). Conkling's job on that dream team really boiled down to one simple task: to convince the Supreme Court that the congressional intent of the Fourteenth Amendment was that corporations be considered "persons" under the amendment.

Conkling's usefulness to the railroads had little to do with his rhetorical skills, his senatorial bearing, or his connections on the Supreme Court. Although Field and Conkling were friendly with each other, Chief Justice Waite was definitely not a Conkling fan. Waite's biographer notes that the possibility that Conkling might become an associate justice led Amelia Waite to write to her husband, "I have been afraid it would get you ill." To which Waite replied, "I can stand him if necessary, but it will be a grind unless he changes his manner towards me."

Rather than resting on any of those factors, Conkling's value to the Southern Pacific Railroad lay in his irrefutable claim to inside knowledge about the true congressional intent of the Fourteenth Amendment, because *Conkling had been a member of the committee that wrote it*—the Joint Committee of Fifteen on Reconstruction. Of course, the intent of the committee had never been previously revealed, either during the open debates by the full Congress on the amendment in 1866 or during the subsequent debates in the various state legislatures. But Conkling had a piece of documentary evidence to support his assertion—*a secret journal.* Just in case any of the justices were inclined to doubt his credibility or his memory nearly two decades later, Conkling brought along a previously unknown journal of the committee's deliberations, and on the day of the oral arguments before the Supreme Court he quoted liberally from that journal to support his claims about the committee's intent.

For Charles and Mary Beard, two influential radical historians, Conkling's account of a secret intent among the members of the Joint Committee of Fifteen on Reconstruction to empower corporations provided a rare glimpse into the ways in which economic interests have shaped and controlled the political process in the United States since its inception. Charles Beard's *An Economic Interpretation of the Constitution of the United States* had documented the property and class status of the men who drafted the Constitution, attempting to show how those economic interests influenced the shaping of that document. In 1927 the Beards published *The Rise of American Civilization,* which repeated Conkling's assertion that the committee that drafted the Fourteenth Amendment had deliberately worded it in a way that would protect corporations.

The publication of *The Rise of American Civilization* was blessed by timing. Two years later came the stock market crash of 1929, and Americans began searching to understand the roots of corporate empowerment. Even before the crash, the book had been a best-seller, and the story of how, as a favor to their businessmen cronies, Conkling and the other members of the Joint Committee on Reconstruction had slipped a powerful "capitalist joker" into the Constitution was widely repeated.

A few skeptical commentators doubted the whole affair. Why, they wondered, would Conkling willingly expose his own backroom machinations to the Supreme Court? Historian Walter Hamilton wrote that the theory "endows the captains of a rising industry with a capacity for forward plan and deep plot which they are not usually understood to possess." Moreover, as Justice Hugo Black pointed out in 1938, the entire notion of a "secret congressional intent" is essentially oxymoronic: "a secret purpose on the part of the members of the committee, even if such be the fact, . . . would not be sufficient to justify any such construction." But for most people, Conkling's brazenness seemed perfectly in tune with the shaky ethical standards of the Gilded Age. They saw the incident as an illustration of how the Establishment at times must scramble to get its various parts to synchronize: one smoke-filled room (the Joint Committee on Reconstruction) communicating with another smoke-filled room (the United States Supreme Court).

If you accept this way of looking at history, you can easily imagine the power brokers at work. First, the conversations in the cloakrooms of Congress: *See, if we use the word "person" here instead of "citizen," we can later tell the courts that we meant to include corporations under the Fourteenth Amendment.* Then Conkling goes to the Supreme Court and says, in essence: *Hey, get with the program—Congress wanted to give corporations more rights. How clearly do I have to spell it out to you?* Then Chief Justice Waite, team player that he is, dutifully tells the assembled justices, "The Court does not wish to hear argument. . . . We are all of the opinion that it is."

This is the sort of incident a radical historian dreams of: the operations of the smoke-filled room caught by stroboscopic flash and photographed. A rare snapshot of how things really work. But is the photo too perfect? What about that line where it looks like one guy's head has been glued onto another guy's body?

In reality, things were a little different. Corporate lawyers were indeed trying to make inroads into the Constitution. That had been going on even before the Civil War, as shown in cases stretching back to the 1819 *Dartmouth* decision and in various legislative maneuvers at both the state and federal levels. Many of these bids for power ended up in front of the Supreme Court. But the particular conspiracy that the Beards fingered— the Committee on Reconstruction plotting to use the word *persons* in a particular way that would later allow corporations to claim coverage under the Fourteenth Amendment—actually appears to have been a fabrication. The evidence, as it turns out, says it didn't happen.

But what about the documentary evidence—specifically, the journal quoted by Conkling? Misplaced for three decades after Conkling appeared before the Court, the *Journal of the Joint Committee of Fifteen on Reconstruction* was finally located and published in 1914 by Princeton professor Benjamin Kendrick. No one actually sat down to compare the journal, word by word, with the quotations from it that Conkling had used in his arguments before the Court. It was generally assumed that the discovery of the journal confirmed what Conkling had said.

Finally, twenty years after the journal was made public, a Stanford University law librarian named Howard Graham took the time to study it closely. Graham did not initially set out to disprove the Conkling-Beard claim that Congress secretly intended the Fourteenth Amendment to include corporations. But as he began routinely checking the quotes cited by Conkling in his Supreme Court testimony against the journal uncovered by Professor Kendrick, Graham made an interesting discovery. Roscoe Conkling, it appeared, had deceived the Supreme Court, deliberately switching key words here and there to "prove" his point about the intent of the committee that drafted the Fourteenth Amendment.

Conkling's main fabrication was his claim that in drafting the Fourteenth Amendment, the Joint Committee on Reconstruction had gone back and forth between using the word *person* and using the word *citizen,* settling finally on the word *person* because the broader legal meaning of that word could include corporations. Conkling walked the Justices through the wording of three successive drafts of the amendment, discussed in committee on three successive weeks. According to Conkling, the first version, considered by the committee on January 12, 1866, was as follows:

> The Congress shall have power to make all laws necessary and proper to secure to all *persons* in every State within this Union equal protection in their rights of life, liberty, and property.

A week later, according to Conkling, the committee revised the amendment, adopting the following wording:

> Congress shall have power to make all laws necessary and proper to secure to all *citizens* of the United States, in every State, the same

political rights and privileges; and to all citizens in every State equal
protection in the enjoyment of life, liberty, and property.

Finally, according to Conkling's version of events, Congressman Bing-
ham proposed the following amendment, reinserting the word *persons* in
place of the word *citizens:*

> Congress shall have power to make all laws necessary and proper to
> secure to all *persons* in every State full protection in the enjoyment of
> life, liberty and property; and to all citizens of the United States in any
> State the same immunities and also equal political rights and privileges.

According to Conkling, concerns that corporations would not be protected if the word *citizen* were used caused the committee to change the
word *citizen* back to *person* in the final version.

As presented by Conkling, the story was plausible. But, in fact, as Graham discovered when he read Conkling's "secret journal," the switch from
persons to *citizens* and back to *persons* had not actually occurred. All drafts
of the amendment had used the word *person* consistently. In his argument to the Supreme Court, Conkling had made a great show of em-
phasizing the switch, first to *citizen* and then back to *person.* To Graham,
the evidence was clear that Conkling's argument was not only wrong but
was intended deliberately to deceive the Court.

In 1938, Graham published an article debunking the Conkling-Beard
thesis in the *Yale Law Journal,* entitled "The 'Conspiracy Theory' of the
Fourteenth Amendment." Later that year, Graham published a second
conspiracy theory article in order to tie up a few loose ends. His perfec-
tionist impulses kept him pursuing minor but telling details literally for
decades. He published more updates in 1943, in 1950, and in 1952—eventually eight detailed elaborations on the origins of the Fourteenth Amendment over a total of twenty-six years. In 1968 the entire collection was
gathered into a book entitled *Everyman's Constitution,* which stands as the
definitive work on the subject. His final verdict, supported not only by his
revelations about Conkling but by a convergence of additional evidence,
was that the Joint Committee on Reconstruction never intended to include corporations as "persons" protected by the Fourteenth Amendment.

Where, then, does this leave the Beards' theory of a corporate conspiracy in which members of the Joint Committee on Reconstruction

deliberately inserted a "capitalist wildcard" into the Fourteenth Amendment? As described earlier, it's not that the Beards were wrong in thinking that corporate attorneys were intent on making the Fourteenth Amendment into a tool for their clients. The forces of corporate empowerment were certainly converging on the Fourteenth Amendment—just not as early nor in quite the way Roscoe Conkling had claimed. Basically, the Beards' mistake was to overestimate the foresight of the corporate legal strategists. In short, they looked in the wrong smoke-filled room. If they had enjoyed the benefit of Howard Graham's twenty-six years of meticulous digging, of Peter Magrath's explorations into the twenty-thousand-item collection of Chief Justice Waite's papers, of various equally extensive biographies of Stephen Field, they would have seen a number of players acting toward the same end, though not necessarily in coordinated fashion, the overall picture becoming discernable only in retrospect.

They would have seen Roscoe Conkling, eager to earn his $10,000 retainer from the Southern Pacific Railroad, sitting up late at night preparing his oral testimony and cleverly planning how to twist an old transcript to "prove" his arguments.

They would have seen Stephen Field, sympathetic to railroad interests but working relentlessly to build a new body of constitutional law based on the Fourteenth Amendment, although using a somewhat different angle than Conkling.

They would have seen Chief Justice Waite, health failing yet reluctant to move Court doctrine at the pace demanded by Field. Unable to refute the claims of Conkling, he acknowledges them verbally but resists writing them into a precedent-setting decision.

They would have seen a court reporter with a mind of his own. Despite his allegiance and personal ties to Waite, J. C. Bancroft Davis seems more sympathetic to Field's aggressive pace than to Waite's. So he plays up Waite's verbal statements in his notes accompanying the written record of the case.

And finally, they would have seen Justice Harlan playing an enigmatic role. In May 1886, he writes an opinion that uses a technical argument to decide the *Santa Clara* case, declining to use the "personhood" rationale. But in November of the same year, we see him citing *Santa Clara* as a personhood precedent. The particular reasons for his change are unknown.

Paradoxically, this more complex view of events does not so much refute the Beards' vision of corporate forces seizing the law as refine and deepen it. Capital may not be as clever a plotter as Charles and Mary Beard supposed it to be. The capture of the Fourteenth Amendment was not the result of clever plotting in 1868, but rather of a more opportunistic process that did not take place until the 1870s and 1880s. Still, the sense of a tidal inevitability in all this is inescapable: if *Santa Clara* had not made corporations into persons, it seems that some other set of events would have.

But wait a minute—by adopting this point of view, aren't we falling back into the fallacy of seeing corporate power as an inevitable fact, rather than as the result of a specific series of historical events? Perhaps the lesson is that *both* are true: the tidal forces of history are undeniable, but timing and other particulars are important too. As we'll see in the next chapter, the final decades of the nineteenth century were not only a period of rising corporate power but also of rising social movements contesting that power. Often, conflicts between the two that arose in factory strikes or legislative battles were settled in the courtroom. During this critical period, a significant delay in the push by corporations to win constitutional rights would have allowed corporate opponents, such as the California and southern populists, the socialists, the Grangers, the Knights of Labor, and other progressives and social reformers, a chance to regroup and resist the corporate juggernaut. Had things gone differently in 1886 with the *Santa Clara* decision, who can say how history would have unfolded?

CHAPTER ELEVEN

Survival of the Fittest

"People power" versus a social Darwinist agenda
(1886–1937)

CHARLES DARWIN DID NOT actually coin the term "survival of the fittest." That distinction goes to the English philosopher Herbert Spencer, himself a survivor of tragedy. Following his birth in 1820 to a Methodist schoolteacher and his wife, all eight of the couple's subsequent children died in infancy.

One can only speculate at the effect of such overwhelming and relentless familial loss on the surviving child. What we do know is that Spencer had already formed the cold core of his philosophy at a precocious age. At sixteen, he published his first essay attacking laws intended to protect the poor. The lazy and the foolish, wrote young Herbert, should not prosper at the expense of the diligent and the thrifty. Spencer managed to find Scripture citations to support his beliefs. Later, the supporting rationales shifted away from religious reasoning to the quasi-scientific justification known as *social Darwinism,* but the point of the argument remained fixed. Spencer believed that, contrary to the intentions of those who promote them, measures aimed at assisting the weak or the vulnerable are actually shortsighted and even cruel because they run counter to nature's fundamental order. He wrote that "the average vigour of any race would be diminished did the diseased and feeble habitually survive and propagate; and that the destruction of such, through failure to fulfill some of the conditions to life, leaves behind those who are able to fulfill the conditions to life, and thus keeps up the average fitness to the conditions of life."

Of all the intellectual influences on the Supreme Court over the past two centuries, few can claim the impact of Spencer's laissez-faire ideas, which shaped constitutional doctrine for roughly fifty years—from the 1880s to the 1930s. During the closing decades of the nineteenth century, his books sold a phenomenal 350,000 copies in the United States. At a time when the canyon between rich and poor was widening, Spencer's "synthetic philosophy," especially as articulated in his most popular book, *Social Statics,* proved immensely popular among American elites.

With Spencer as moral coach, a judge could crush a piece of social legislation in the morning and go home that night thinking of himself as a humanitarian—after all, the central point of Spencer's philosophy was that trying to legislate the human condition into a kinder form only made matters worse. In *Social Statics,* he wrote:

> Pervading all nature we may see at work a stern discipline, which is a little cruel that it may be very kind.... It seems hard that a labourer incapacitated by sickness from competing with his stronger fellows, should have to bear the resulting privations. It seems hard that widows and orphans should be left to struggle for life or death. Nevertheless, when regarded not separately, but in connection with the interests of universal humanity, these harsh fatalities are seen to be full of the highest beneficence—the same beneficence which brings to early graves the children of diseased parents, and singles out the low-spirited, the intemperate, and the debilitated as the victims of an epidemic.

A KEY ASSUMPTION behind the laissez-faire ideal was that every person is the master of his or her own fate. In Spencer's view, what that person does with this gift of freedom is not the responsibility of society or the state, even if the person suffers from disabilities entirely not of his or her own making.

Of course, there was a problem with all this, and that problem was simply that many people in the nineteenth century weren't really free at all. Long after the ratification of the U.S. Constitution and the adoption of the Bill of Rights, most aspects of employer-employee relations continued to be regulated by a common law legal structure that enforced principles of privilege and hierarchy derived from the feudal society of the late Middle Ages. As explained by political scientist and historian Karen Orren, "The original, mainly landholding, masters had long since been overtaken by business owners and managers; however, their privileges remained, passed on to their successors largely intact."

This system of workplace regulation, also known as the "law of master and servant," was similar to that applied to husband and wife, parent and child, and guardian and ward. The power of employers over their workers was considered a *private* relationship, where normal constitutional rights did not necessarily apply. Thus, common law permitted measures of enforcement that were unacceptable in other social realms. For example, it was not until 1843 that American courts stopped permitting employers to beat their employees.

Industrial relations in the United States were rooted in their English antecedents. In England, the Industrial Revolution of the previous century had introduced a system of labor organization in which workers were controlled not only for the duration of an eighty-hour week but for the remainder of their waking hours as well. Historian Charles Perrow describes how even religious instruction served to reinforce the totalitarian society in a typical English iron factory of the early eighteenth century that employed more than a thousand workers and provided a doctor, a minister, and three teachers:

> By his instructions, the clergyman Crowley attempted to dominate the spiritual life of his flock, and to make them willing and obedient cogs in his machine. It was his express intention that their whole life, including even their sparse spare time (the normal working week being eighty hours) should revolve around the task of making the works profitable.

Such accounts lead to an obvious question: Why would workers voluntarily submit to such a confining and claustrophobic system? In many cases they didn't. Sidney Pollard explains:

> There were few areas of the country in which modern industries, particularly the textiles, if carried on in large buildings, were not associated with prisons, workhouses, and orphanages. This connection is usually underrated, particularly by those historians who assume that the new works recruited free labour only.

Such was the pattern in England from which relations between factory and employee were formed at an early stage, and as the first factories appeared in America in the early nineteenth century, a similar pattern of exploiting the most vulnerable segments in society was similarly applied. When Samuel Slater, an English immigrant, set up the first mechanized textile factory in America, his first employees were nine children ages seven to eleven. According to historian Jack Beatty, "As the first workers in the first American factories, women and children were the pioneers of the industrial revolution in America."

Even "free white men" weren't necessarily free. Many industries, including textiles and mines, maintained blacklists of workers who attempted to leave. And by being required to buy necessities, at inflated prices, at company stores, workers remained in perpetual debt and could be imprisoned for those debts if they left the company. Yet another control mechanism was the fact that "crimes of status"—crimes that result not from a person's action, but simply from his or her circumstances—continued to be enforced in nineteenth-century America. Writes Karen Orren, "In every jurisdiction in the United States, not to work or be seeking work, if one was an able-bodied person without other visible means of support, was a crime, punishable by fine or imprisonment."

Another feature of common law was the principle that labor was "entire." What this meant was that a worker was not entitled to wages until the term of employment was finished. This naturally gave employers tremendous power over employees, who could be discharged at any time and find the recovery of their unpaid compensation virtually impossible.

For all these reasons, social historians describe the condition of workers in nineteenth-century America as one of *relative liberty*: "Whatever the public rights and private aspirations of the worker, he or she was in reality a free person against everyone except his or her employer."

Of course, this dual reality of American life—rights and freedoms in the public sphere, lack of freedom in the workplace—remains largely true today, more so for those in the lowest-paid, most regimented jobs, but true in many respects for most corporate office workers. In 2002, author Barbara Ehrenreich described working conditions at maid-service companies where she did stints as a domestic worker in order to write her book *Nickel and Dimed:*

> You have rules such as no talking to your fellow employees . . . you're subject to surveillance; you have no privacy whatsoever. . . . The workplace, especially the low-wage workplace (but it extends to a lot of mid-level people, too) is more like a dictatorship. You really check your civil rights at the door.

In 1842 Charles Dickens toured the famous Lowell mills, each of which, he told his English readers, "belongs to what we should term a Company of Proprietors, but what they call in America a Corporation." These mills were operated by Francis Cabot Lodge and the Boston Associates, who had recruited a workforce consisting mainly of New England farmers' daughters. Typically, the young women worked only a few years in the mills prior to marrying or returning to their families. Because the young women were not absolutely dependent on working in the mills, the Boston Associates took pains to create a relatively pleasant environment.

Dickens praised the Lowell mills as a marked contrast to those of England: "In the windows of some, there were green plants, which were trained to shade the glass; in all there was as much fresh air, cleanliness, and comfort, as the nature of the occupation would possibly admit of." He noted in particular the cultural amenities provided in the workers' quarters. The farmers' daughters labored twelve-hour days, but they subscribed to circulating libraries, published a periodical known as *The Lowell Offering* with funds provided by the company, and played music on "joint stock pianos."

However, what sociologist Charles Perrow calls the "benign phase" of the Lowell mills did not last long. As impoverished Irish and French Canadian immigrants offered mill owners a cheaper, more vulnerable workforce, the amenities quickly disappeared. This new workforce did not have the option of going home to their families. Instead, they were trapped in a cycle of poverty, with wages declining as profits boomed, amid assembly-line speedups. Increasingly, the workforce in the factories was made up of children—45 percent of the workforce by 1865.

In Manayunk, Pennsylvania, state investigators found children working days as long as thirteen hours and forty minutes. Nine-year-old children carried heavy boxes up and down stairs for as many as twelve hours. The investigators asked for the imposition of a ten-hour day for children, but were rebuffed.

LABOR ORGANIZING had begun during the Civil War, and in its wake the effort to shorten the working day became a primary focus. Initial progress was rapid. By 1868, eight-hour statutes had been enacted in Illinois,

Wisconsin, Missouri, Connecticut, New York, and Pennsylvania. Success with the eight-hour issue quickly led to new organizing efforts and more ambitious demands. From 1868 to 1873 fourteen new unions emerged. These included the National Labor Union, which openly proposed destroying the power of large corporations and giving workers a greater share of national wealth.

But the initial success of the eight-hour movement proved ephemeral. Although laws had been passed, most lacked penalties or enforcement provisions. In addition, eight-hour laws provided a "free-contract" exception, allowing employers to come up with different arrangements if agreed to by workers. Thus, decades after workers had "won" the eight-hour day, most were required to work much longer hours. Samuel Gompers, leader of the American Federation of Labor, concluded that seeking legislative reforms was a pointless exercise. Only collective bargaining, he believed, could produce real improvements in working conditions.

Collective bargaining itself, however, faced an uphill battle because of a growing wave of repression against labor organizers by corporate security agencies, local police forces, and state militias. The Paris Commune of 1871 was one trigger for the crackdown. The Commune was the first major event to be communicated instantly by transatlantic cable, and it produced profound fear among American elites. During the uprising, thousands of workers and soldiers took control of Paris, elected their own government, reopened shuttered factories as cooperatives, burned the guillotine, and decreed separation of church and state. After two months, Paris was reoccupied by the French army, who killed some thirty thousand people. The movement roused American workers, who held meetings to raise money for the French revolutionaries. An Englishman who was acquainted with a number of rich Americans wrote that they shared "an uneasy feeling that they were living over a mine of social and industrial discontent . . . and that some day this mine would explode and blow society into the air."

In the wake of the Paris Commune, repression of labor organizing intensified, and "communist" became an all-purpose epithet. One seminary professor wrote that "today there is not in our language, nor in any language a more hateful word than communism." A prominent businessman vowed, "Every lamp-post in Chicago will be decorated with a communistic carcass if necessary to prevent wholesale incendiarism."

In 1873, a financial panic disrupted the economy, and it was followed by five years of economic depression and widespread unemployment. As in the Great Depression of the 1930s, those without work roamed the country, established makeshift camps, and held demonstrations demanding relief. In St. Louis, New York, Chicago, and other cities, crowds of people who gathered to demand relief were attacked by mounted police. Legislators advocated feeding tramps with poisoned food. Labor conflict was particularly harsh in the Pennsylvania mine fields, where a Pinkerton security agent infiltrated and crushed a secret society known as the Molly Maguires. Nineteen men were identified as ringleaders and hanged.

In the 1880s, the labor movement experienced a new wave of hopeful expansion followed by repression and collapse. In 1881, a formerly secret organization called the Knights of Labor unveiled itself to the world, issuing a Declaration of Principles that roundly condemned the power of corporations in American society:

> The alarming development and aggressiveness of great capitalists and corporations, unless checked, will inevitably lead to the pauperization and hopeless degradation of the toiling masses. It is imperative, if we desire to enjoy the full blessings of life, that a check be placed on the unjust accumulation, and the power of evil of aggregated wealth.

After going public, the membership of the Knights of Labor exploded, from 43,000 in 1882 to 730,000 at the movement's peak in 1886, organized into fifteen thousand locals across the country. The Knights were open to both men and women workers, regardless of occupation, race, or nationality. In 1886, a strike by members of the union against Jay Gould's railroads in the Southwest was crushed by force, with seven workers killed by company deputies in East St. Louis, Illinois. On May 1, 1886, the union sponsored a nationwide strike in support of the eight-hour day, with 350,000 workers at more than eleven thousand establishments walking off the job. In Chicago, police fired into a group of picketers and killed four people. At a meeting in Haymarket Square to protest the shootings, someone threw a bomb that killed one policeman and wounded sixty-six others. The Haymarket incident led to an intense crackdown. Eight anarchist leaders were put on trial, and prosecutors stated openly that they had been selected not for their role in the bombing but simply because of their role as movement leaders. The state's attorney told the jury, "Gentlemen of the jury: convict these men, make examples of them, hang them and you save our institutions, our society." The jury convicted all eight. In prison, one committed suicide, four were hanged, and three received reduced sentences. The incident spelled the downfall of the Knights of Labor.

The cycle of a labor upsurge followed by repression and union collapse was again repeated in the 1890s. Increasingly, repressive efforts included the use of injunctions by the courts. In 1894, Eugene V. Debs, the leader of the American Railway Union, organized a sympathy strike in support of workers locked out after striking against the Pullman Palace Car Company. U.S. Attorney General Richard Olney met with Charles Walker, the attorney for the railroad industry's General Managers' Association. Walker recommended that Olney seek an injunction against the strike under the terms of the Sherman Antitrust Act of 1890, which had been intended to be used against corporate monopolies. In a precedent-setting decision, the federal district court in Chicago granted an injunction ordering Debs to stop the strike, citing conspiracy to disrupt postal service and damage to the "general welfare" caused by the disruption to interstate commerce. On appeal, the U.S. Supreme Court's 1895 *In Re Debs* decision supported the district court's decision.

The use of injunctions to stop strikes was attractive to corporations for several reasons. With an injunction, there was no need to make a case to a jury—an impediment in communities sympathetic to strikers. Moreover, an injunction provided judges with the power to imprison union leaders for "contempt of court" if the strike went forward.

During the period from 1880 to 1930, courts issued over four thousand injunctions against strike efforts: 105 in the 1880s, 410 in the 1890s, 850 in the 1900s, 835 in the 1910s, and 2,130 in the 1920s. After *In Re Debs,* the Supreme Court issued additional decisions strengthening the injunction. *In Re Lennon* (1897) allowed blanket injunctions, which applied to anyone who had notice of them, whether or not specifically named in the injunction.

IN NEW YORK, where new workweek legislation *with* penalties passed in 1895, a famous constitutional showdown between business and reformers came about in the case of *Lochner v. New York*. In this 1905 case, the Supreme Court overturned the New York statute mandating a sixty-hour week in baking establishments, ruling that the statute violated the Four-teenth Amendment due process and the Constitution's freedom of con-tract provisions. The decision of the Supreme Court in *Lochner* represents the high-water mark of social Darwinist philosophy, engineered into a complex legal doctrine known as "substantive due process" under the leadership of Justice Stephen Field. But the case is far more famous for the arguments of the losers than of the winners, because ultimately the los-ing side—the position articulated by Justice Oliver Wendell Holmes—was to succeed in defeating the social Darwinist doctrine.

To understand the *Lochner* decision, it is helpful to start by looking at the facts on the ground—or more accurately *under the ground*. In the 1890s, most bakers worked in low-ceilinged, poorly lit cellars, "exposed to flour dust, gas fumes, dampness, and extremes of hot and cold," writes historian Paul Kens. But a bigger complaint among bakers than physical conditions was the length of the normal shift, which made marriage and family life difficult at best. Typically a baker would have to go to work sometime between 8:00 P.M. and midnight. He would work all night, re-turn home around lunchtime, and spend the afternoon sleeping. Then he would have a few hours free for supper and family life before returning to work. The weekly schedule was either six or seven days, and some bak-ers actually were required to work a 24-hour shift on Thursdays. Work-weeks as long as 114 or even 126 hours were reported. Under those conditions, merely gaining a 12-hour day would represent a significant improvement, and as late as 1881 bakers in New York City went on strike to achieve that goal.

In 1895, a coalition of reformers succeeded in passing the New York Bakeshop Act. The reformers were led by Henry Weismann, a German immigrant who headed the Journeymen Bakers' and Confectioners' In-ternational Union of America (small and understaffed, despite its im-pressive-sounding name); Cyrus Edson, New York City's health commissioner; and Edward Marshall, the Sunday editor of the *New York Press*. Spurred by an exposé on bakery conditions published by the *Press*, numerous middle-class and upper-class citizens wrote letters advocating bakeshop regulations. Many of these supporters explicitly rejected the philosophy of social Darwinism, noting that "men are not equally able to protect their interests." Some of them argued in favor of moderate re-form as a way of immunizing society against more radical upheavals. One such leader was the Reverend William S. Rainsford, pastor of

St. George's Episcopal Church. He wrote to the bakers union: "I congratulate you on the moderation of your demands and also on the moderate manner and wise methods which you use in presenting them."

In the never-ending power struggle between corporations and workers, Rainsford and Spencer represent two classic alternatives: on the one hand, a "kinder, gentler" approach, aimed at placating workers; on the other hand, a tough approach that emphasizes the rights of employers. In *Lochner,* the two approaches collided head-on, and "kinder, gentler" took a serious beating.

The facts of the case were simple and uncontested. In 1901, a bakery owner named Joseph Lochner was arrested and charged with the misdemeanor of requiring a baker named Aman Schmitter to work for more than sixty hours in one week. Lochner was convicted and fined $50, and his case eventually reached the Supreme Court, which decided in his favor.

THE COURT'S DECISION in *Lochner,* though it came a full decade after Justice Stephen Field's retirement from the Supreme Court, was the epitome of the legal doctrine of substantive due process that Field had developed, beginning with his dissent in the 1873 *Slaughter-House* case, the 1877 *Munn* case, and the Chinese laborer cases (see chapter 8). In those cases, Field had first articulated a new interpretation of the Fourteenth Amendment phrase "nor shall any State deprive any person of life, liberty, or property, without due process of law."

Field's formulation owes much to University of Michigan law professor and state supreme court justice Thomas McIntyre Cooley. In 1868, Cooley published *A Treatise on the Constitutional Limitations Which Rest Upon the Legislative Powers of the States of the American Union,* in which he advanced the argument that due process essentially prohibited state legislatures from enacting any legislation that would deprive a person of his or her rightful property.

Normally, the requirement of due process means merely that governmental decisions must be enacted and enforced by means of rational, orderly measures—as opposed to arbitrary and capricious ones. But Cooley's *substantive* due process notion implied a far more expansive interpretation, applying not merely to the application of laws but to their creation as well. It claimed for the Supreme Court the authority to overturn state laws not only if they failed to meet the requirement of rational, orderly procedure but also if the Court viewed them as impinging on federal constitutional rights, including the right to make and enforce contracts and the rather vague right of "liberty." The term *substantive* indicated that the Court might review not only the procedural aspects of a piece of legislation but also its content or substance.

In order to give corporations protection under the substantive due process doctrine, a new set of precedents was needed that would allow corporations to claim that the due process provision of the Fourteenth Amendment applied to them. By affording corporations Fourteenth Amendment equal protection, the 1886 *Santa Clara* decision had set the stage, although another decision would still be needed before corporations could also claim due process protection. Two cases filled the gap: *Minneapolis & Saint Louis Railway v. Beckwith* (1889) and *Chicago, Milwaukee and St. Paul Railway v. Minnesota* (1890). In *Minneapolis & Saint Louis,* the Supreme Court upheld an Iowa law that required corporations to compensate ranchers for livestock killed by trains, but the decision made it clear that the Court now considered corporations to be fully protected by the due process language of the Fourteenth Amendment. In *Chicago, Milwaukee,* the Court ruled that a Minnesota rate-setting commission had to allow railroads to appeal its decisions on the grounds that the railroads enjoyed due process protection under the Fourteenth Amendment.

With those precedents secured, Field was ready to begin applying his substantive due process doctrine on a wide basis. To do so, he needed more allies on the Court. Following the death of Justice Waite in 1888, the allies began to arrive, including Melvin Fuller in 1888 and David Brewer (the son of Stephen Field's missionary sister Emilia) in 1890. With the arrival of arch-conservative Rufus Peckham in 1896, the Field faction gained full control of the Court.

The *Lochner* decision, which overturned the New York Bakeshop Act, made it clear that the Supreme Court subscribed fully to the Spencerian notion that employees and employers had the constitutional right to enter into any sort of contract they wished, unless that contract posed an overt threat to "morals, health, safety, peace, and good order." Such freedom of contract was seen as a clear example of the "liberty" guaranteed to all persons by the Fourteenth Amendment: "Nor shall any State deprive any person of life, liberty, or property, without due process of law; nor deny to any person within its jurisdiction the equal protection of the laws."

Although the *Lochner* case did not actually involve a corporation—since the bakery which objected to the maximum workweek was unincorporated—the Fourteenth Amendment corporate personhood precedents (in *Santa Clara, Minneapolis & Saint Louis Railway,* and *Chicago, Milwaukee*) extended the decision to relations between corporations and their employees.

Lochner remains famous as the epitome of the Court's aggressive embrace of laissez-faire, but a minority of the Court retained a far different view, as expressed by Justice Oliver Wendell Holmes's famous dissent in the case. At the time of *Lochner,* Holmes was sixty-five years old. He had been on Court for only five years but had long since established himself as the preeminent legal mind of his day. He had published his masterpiece, *The Common Law,* before his fortieth birthday, and he had served three decades on the Massachusetts Supreme Court.

In contrast to Field's procorporate fervor and in-your-face social Darwinism, Holmes was a skeptic of doctrines and ideologies. During the Civil War, Holmes had witnessed firsthand the appalling slaughter at Antietam, where he was shot and left for dead behind enemy lines. He blamed the war on the American tendency toward ideological certainty, systematically destroyed all his youthful letters advocating abolition, and for the rest of his life sought to undermine fervent ideologies of all stripes.

Holmes's dissent in the *Lochner* case expresses that skeptical cast of mind:

> This case is decided upon an economic theory which a large part of the country does not entertain. If it were a question whether I agreed with that theory, I should desire to study it further and long before making up my mind. But I do not conceive that to be my duty, because I strongly believe that my agreement or disagreement has nothing to do with the right of the majority to embody their opinions in law. . . . The 14th Amendment does not enact Mr. Herbert Spencer's *Social Statics.*

Despite Holmes's eloquent opposition, the Court remained on its social Darwinist streak until the late 1930s. Central to the Court's prevailing ideology during this period was an almost religious worship of the sanctity of contracts, the notion that no truer expression of liberty exists than an agreement entered into by two citizens for their mutual benefit. Of course, making this idealized model the central concept of employee-employer relations requires that one ignore the reality that a huge corporation and an individual worker don't enjoy anything even roughly resembling equivalent negotiating power. As Franklin Roosevelt once remarked, "Necessitous men are not free men." Similarly, Alexander Hamilton wrote, "The power over a man's subsistence amounts to a power over his will." For the Supreme Court to invalidate legislation that attempted to address such obvious real-world power imbalances showed just how radically pro-corporate the Court had become.

Unable to dissuade his colleagues, Holmes watched the substantive due process doctrine develop into such a potent weapon that by the mid-1930s, the Supreme Court had used it to invalidate approximately two hundred statutes, including child labor laws, laws limiting the length of the workweek, safety standards, worker injury compensation funds, and other legislation. As for the original intent of the Fourteenth Amendment, that of protecting freed blacks from repressive laws, Justice Hugo Black later observed that in the first fifty years after the amendment was adopted, "less than one-half of 1 percent" of the cases in which it was invoked had to do with protection of African Americans, whereas 50 percent involved corporations.

While the substantive due process doctrine smothered hundreds of laws enacted by state legislatures, the use of the labor injunction reached a crescendo during the 1920s under Chief Justice William Howard Taft, an avowed foe of organized labor who once said, "We have to hit [labor] hard every little while, because they are continually violating the law and depending on threats and violence to accomplish their purposes."

Prior to the Taft Court, two earlier cases, *Gompers v. Bucks Stove and Range Company* (1908) and *Loewe v. Lawlor* (1908), had already outlawed the use of boycotts as a pressure tactic by unions. Now in *Duplex Printing Co. v. Deering* (1921), the Supreme Court outlawed secondary boycotts—that is, boycotts in support of a strike. Even worse for union organizers, *Hitchman Coal & Coke Co. v. Mitchell* (1917), allowed courts to issue injunctions against unions that attempted to organize workers who had signed "yellow-dog" contracts—that is, company contracts in which workers promised not to join a union. With the aid of *Hitchman* a judge could shut down an entire region to union organizing, as in 1927, when a single injunction barred the United Mine Workers from organizing in 316 Appalachian coal companies with over forty thousand workers.

Other anti-labor decisions of the Taft Court included *American Steel Foundries v. Tri-City Central Trades Council* (1921), which limited picketing to one picket per plant gate; *Truax v. Corrigan* (1921), which declared Arizona's antilabor injunction law unconstitutional; and the *Coronado Coal* cases (1925), which prohibited unions under the Sherman Anti-Trust Act from striking in order to organize the unorganized segment of an industry.

IT SEEMS FITTING that a doctrine based on social Darwinism would itself be made extinct by more powerful forces. With its 1937 decision in *West Coast Hotel Company v. Parrish,* the Court abandoned substantive due process and began to uphold the same sorts of social legislation it had previously tended to invalidate. In that decision, the Court upheld the constitutionality of a Washington State law fixing minimum wages for women and children.

The dynamics behind the Court's abandonment of the doctrine of substantive due process speak volumes about the effect of political pressure on a body that is supposedly divorced from political considerations. By 1933, the Great Depression had brought the United States economy to its knees: industrial production was down by 50 percent; unemployment reached 25 percent. Two million people wandered the country looking for work. Over twenty-five thousand veterans and their families marched on Washington to demand early payment on bonus certificates. Rather than leave the city, the veterans built semipermanent encampments, published their own newspaper, set up a library, and staged vaudeville shows where they performed such songs as "My Bonus Lies Over the Ocean." Eventually, President Hoover, having been given reports from the FBI that the "bonus army" was communist-led and might trigger uprisings around the country, decided to attack the veterans. Under the leadership of General Douglas MacArthur, tanks rolled through the streets of the capital for the first time in the nation's history. Military units used tear gas to clear the encampments, then razed the shanties.

Around the country, there were similar episodes of social unrest. Wildcat strikes were becoming ubiquitous, with workers often defying their own union leadership and engaging in rioting and factory occupations. Seeing organized unions as preferable to anarchy, Congress passed the Norris-LaGuardia Act, which outlawed the labor injunction. During the same year, Franklin Roosevelt campaigned against Herbert Hoover on populist themes, taking aim at corporate power. On September 23, 1932, in San Francisco, he noted that six hundred companies controlled two-thirds of American industry: "If the process of concentration goes on at the same rate, at the end of another century we shall have all American industry controlled by a dozen corporations, and run by perhaps a hundred men. Put plainly, we are steering a steady course toward economic oligarchy, if we are not there already."

When the votes were counted, Roosevelt had defeated Hoover by seven million votes. Once in office, he quickly pushed Congress to enact an intense flurry of legislative initiatives aimed at jump-starting the economy.

As Roosevelt's initiatives were enacted by Congress, the Supreme Court responded by striking them down one after another. On February 5, 1937, the president turned up the pressure on the Court by asking Congress for the authority to appoint an additional judge to the Supreme Court for every judge who was over seventy and had not retired. This would have allowed Roosevelt to add six new justices. Roosevelt's plan to pack the Court died when it was rejected by the Senate Judiciary Committee. Nevertheless, historians generally credit the initiative with causing the Court finally to budge.

But according to Justice Owen J. Roberts, the member of the Supreme Court whose defection to the pro-Roosevelt faction on the Court gave it a one-vote majority, Roosevelt's pressure tactics were of less influence than were the conditions of social unrest that prevailed across the country. In his memoirs, Justice Roberts wrote that his decision to support federal intervention in the affairs of private corporations was the result of his desire to preempt "even more radical changes." Like many other conservative and liberal leaders, Roberts feared that if liberalizing reforms continued to be blocked, an increasingly mobilized public would challenge the system itself. It was people power—tremendous political pressure rising from the grassroots—that compelled Roberts to change his position.

With the defection of Justice Roberts, the decades of the substantive due process doctrine came to an end. In a series of pro-Roosevelt decisions, the Court signaled that it would no longer block government intervention in the economy, including greater regulation of corporations.

Indeed, for a time it seemed that the Court was moving toward reversing the *Santa Clara* decision as well, under the prodding of two New

Deal justices, William O. Douglas and Hugo Black. Both wrote eloquent dissents criticizing *Santa Clara* and decrying the tendency to grant large corporations a growing number of constitutional rights. But even though Douglas and Black could not persuade the rest of the Court to reverse *Santa Clara,* the general sentiment of the Court resisted any further expansions in corporate rights. During the fifty-year period from 1922 to 1970, only one Supreme Court decision expanded the inventory of corporate rights. In a relatively obscure opinion known as *Fong Foo,* the Court gave corporations the Fifth Amendment protection against being tried twice for the same offense.

DURING HIS LAST TERM IN OFFICE Roosevelt proposed a "second Bill of Rights" that would address issues of economic fairness and security. It would guarantee the right of all workers to employment at an adequate wage, the right of farmers to a decent return on their products, the right of small businessmen to protection from monopolies and unfair competition, the right of all families to a home, the right of everyone to education and medical care, and the right of the aged, the disabled, and the unemployed to economic security.

Roosevelt's wider vision of rights was the natural culmination of a movement that had begun in the 1600s and 1700s to elevate the status of *individuals*, particularly in relation to powerful institutions. In the late 1600s John Locke established the philosophical foundation for human rights by articulating the idea that political authority derives not from divine right but from the "consent of the governed." Locke's notions were elaborated into specific rights and freedoms by writers such as Rousseau (the right not to be enslaved), Voltaire (freedom of the press), and Beccaria (freedom from cruel punishment). The late 1700s saw the first actualization of these ideas as direct political statements. Thomas Jefferson composed America's Declaration of Independence (1776) with the assistance of Tom Paine; later Jefferson spent time in Paris helping Lafayette write France's Declaration of the Rights of Man and the Citizen (1789). In 1791 the Bill of Rights was added to the American Constitution as the first ten amendments, modeled after similar bills in Massachusetts and other colonies.

After a long period of dormancy, interest in human rights began to revive in the years leading up to World War II. In 1940 British science fiction author H. G. Wells penned a modern updating of Jefferson, Lafayette, and Paine. In the midst of the war, Penguin's publication *H. G. Wells on the Rights of Man* sold thousands of copies and was translated into thirty languages. Wells had worked out many of his ideas in conversation with a circle of socialist and pacifist friends that included A. A. Milne, creator of Winnie the Pooh. His justification for human rights was a simple one: "Since a man comes into this world through no fault of his own he is entitled to certain basic rights."

The rights advocated by Wells ranged from the civic (freedom of speech and assembly) to the cardigan-sweater homey ("a man's private house or apartment or reasonably limited garden enclosure is his castle"). Although these ideas rested firmly in the traditions of the seventeenth-century philosophers and eighteenth-century revolutionaries, his sympathetic and concrete vision of human needs suggested an easy bridge to a much wider vision of rights.

After her husband's death, Eleanor Roosevelt served as chair of a United Nations committee that drafted the Universal Declaration of Human Rights. Adopted in 1948, it combined the "first-generation" rights typical of the eighteenth century with "second-generation" economic security rights similar to those proposed by President Roosevelt before his death.

Because it lacks any enforcement mechanism, the Universal Declaration of Human Rights plays a somewhat different role than does a set of baseline legal guarantees like the U.S. Bill of Rights. It provides a humanistic way of measuring the march of civilization, suggesting that progress is not to be counted by heroic monuments, dazzling cities, and enormous factories—and certainly not by the grandiose and ugly visions of fascists and militarists—but rather by the success of society in creating and protecting *human-scale* spaces of safety, freedom, and sustenance. Although still unachieved, its adoption must be included among the milestones of Western civilization.

As for President Roosevelt's impact on American society, historians have differing perspectives. One angle is that he was the champion of the working man, the leader whose expansion of big government lifted the country out of the grinding poverty of the Great Depression. Another perspective is that Roosevelt was an innovative patrician in rocky times who preserved the capitalist system by knowing just how much ground to give up.

Both outlooks are essentially correct. But one thing is indisputable. Just as Justice Roberts's decision in *West Coast Hotel Company v. Parrish* extinguished the doctrine of laissez-faire on the Supreme Court, Roosevelt banished from the public discourse the social Darwinist vision. His genius was in devising the win-win solution: the idea that a well-paid, socially secure workforce was entirely compatible with a huge expansion in corporate activity and profits. Under the approach created by Roosevelt and adhered to by both Democratic and Republican administrations for the next three decades, corporate growth remained brisk and expansion continued at the same time that the distribution of wealth in the United States became far more evenly distributed than before the Great Depression. Thus, while the share of wealth owned by the top 1 percent of the population was nearly 45 percent in 1929, it had fallen to 20 percent by 1971.

THE PERIOD FROM the inauguration of Franklin Roosevelt in 1932 to the 1970s can hardly be characterized as a tranquil one in American history. From Pearl Harbor to Vietnam, America was repeatedly at war, and McCarthyism, the civil rights movement, and the movement to end the Vietnam War all produced tension and upheaval. But in contrast to the intense power struggles between workers and large corporations that had periodically flared up from the Gilded Age to the Depression, the reforms begun in the 1930s ushered in an era when those struggles were remarkably subdued.

To liberals like economist John Kenneth Galbraith, it looked as though the win-win policies of the New Deal had permanently exorcized the Progressive-era fears of looming corporate domination. Violent labor uprisings such as the Homestead Strike and the Ludlow Massacre were largely a thing of the past. Labor was now part of the American establishment. A social contract that allowed factory workers health insurance and other middle-class benefits seemed secure. Galbraith announced that the Progressives had been wrong to worry so much about corporate power. He postulated a new self-adjusting social physics—the idea that corporate power automatically produces an equal and opposite reaction. "Private economic power," wrote Galbraith, "is held in check by the countervailing power of those who are subject to it." Under Galbraith's countervailing power theory, a system of offsetting forces exists in American society, with the power of corporations limited by labor unions, governmental regulatory bodies, and a range of civic institutions.

Not everyone subscribed to Galbraith's sanguine theory, however. On the surface, it did appear that business was content to share power with labor unions and federal regulators. But what would happen if business were sufficiently provoked—either by the encroachment of working-class incomes on profits or by the encroachment of government regulations on corporate prerogatives? If big business made a concerted effort to flex its political muscle, would "countervailing power" really keep that effort in check? As we will see in the next chapter, the events that have unfolded from 1971 to the present show clearly that the answer is *no*.

CHAPTER TWELVE

The Revolt of the Bosses

The new mobilization of corporate political power
(1971–2002)

I N AUGUST 1971, TWO NEIGHBORS in Richmond, Virginia, happened to have a little chat. One was Eugene B. Sydnor, Jr., a department store owner who had recently been appointed chairman of the U.S. Chamber of Commerce's Education Committee. The other was Lewis Powell, Jr., one of the most well-connected corporate attorneys in the country and a director on eleven corporate boards. The two talked about politics, and Sydnor was so intrigued by Powell's ideas that he asked Powell to put them in a memo to the Chamber of Commerce committee.

The late 1960s and early 1970s weren't the best of times for men like Sydnor and Powell. Public attitudes toward businessmen were in a free fall. From 1968 to 1977, the percentage of Americans who agreed that "business tries to strike a fair balance between profits and the interests of the public" dropped from 70 percent to 15 percent. The country was experiencing the biggest social upheaval since the Great Depression, and much of what was going on seemed aggravating if not downright frightening to big business. Writes one political scientist, "Order seemed to be unraveling: massive antiwar protests on the mall; a half-million-troop war effort bogged down and hemorrhaging in the mud of Southeast Asia; economic stagnation and declining profit rates; and in the cities, skyrocketing crime coupled with some of the most violent riots since the Civil War."

At the center of the turbulence was President Richard Nixon, who had built his career as a Red-baiting politician but whose actual style of governing, once in office, involved an eclectic mixture of conservative and liberal positions, flavored with a strong dose of old-fashioned corruption. Nixon supported a number of measures opposed by business: a repeal of the Kennedy-era investment tax credit, an increase in the capital gains tax, limits on the use of tax shelters, a strengthened occupational safety and health bill, and tough new regulations on air pollution.

By 1971, it was clear that both the consumer and the environmental movements, which had barely existed five years earlier, were forces to be reckoned with. Seven major environmental and consumer groups were established in 1969 and 1970 alone: Friends of the Earth, the Natural Resources Defense Council, Public Citizen, Common Cause, Environmental Action, the Center for Law and Social Policy, and the Consumer Federation of America. Caught flat-footed by this grassroots mobilization, corporations were unable to mount enough opposition to stop such legislation as the National Environmental Protection Act (1969), the Clean Air Act Amendments (1970), a ban on all cigarette commercials from radio and television (1970), and the cancellation of funding for the Supersonic Transport Plane (1970). Thus it was Richard Nixon who presided over one of the greatest expansions in the regulatory scope of the federal government, including creation of the Environmental Protection Agency, the Occupational Safety and Health Administration, and the Consumer Product Safety Commission.

Perhaps it could have been foreseen that the successes of the environmental and consumer movements would trigger some sort of backlash by big business, but the scale of the corporate political mobilization proved to be unprecedented. Even more improbable was the man whom many credit with inspiring that mobilization, sixty-four-year-old Lewis J. Powell, Jr.

A few days after his conversation with Sydnor, Powell called in his secretary to take dictation and composed a memorandum describing his view on the malaise afflicting corporate America and the steps he felt the U.S. Chamber of Commerce should take to reverse the slide in the political fortunes of big business. The memorandum was marked "Confidential" and was distributed as a special issue of the Chamber of Commerce's periodical *Washington Report* to top business leaders. Titled "Attack on American Free Enterprise System," it is a remarkable document, forming the seminal plan for one of the most successful political counterattacks in American history. But the memorandum is also remarkable for another reason. Two months after writing it, Lewis Powell was nominated to the Supreme Court by President Nixon, placing him in an incomparable strategic position to advance the goals expressed in the memo. Thus, the memorandum written by Powell is worth reading, not just as a rallying cry directed toward business in general but as a way of understanding the pro-corporate constitutional shift that occurred in the Supreme Court under his leadership.

Like Justice Stephen Field a century earlier, Lewis Powell was a conservative Democrat appointed to the Supreme Court by a Republican president. Like Field, Powell identified closely with the goals of big business, both ideologically and personally. As already noted, he had spent his career as a corporate lawyer, and he eventually rose to the presidency of the American Bar Association.

From today's perspective, the Powell memorandum paints a rather surprising portrait of attitudes among corporate leaders just thirty years ago, a time when such men actually saw themselves as a despised, downtrodden, "impotent" element in American society. Free enterprise, wrote Powell, was under "massive assault," not just by "extremists of the left" but from "perfectly respectable elements of society: from the college campus, the pulpit, the media, the intellectual and literary journals, the arts and sciences, and from politicians." He warned that the problem could not be dismissed as a temporary phenomenon: "It has gradually evolved over the past two decades, barely perceptible in its origins and benefiting from a gradualism that provoked little awareness." Unfortunately, business was proving sluggish in waking to the situation. Spurred by "the hostility of respectable liberals and social reformers," the growing force of antibusiness sentiments "could indeed fatally weaken or destroy the system." Most dangerous, according to Powell, was one man, Ralph Nader, "a legend in his own time and an idol of millions of Americans." Quoting *Fortune* magazine, the memo described Nader as ruthless, implacable, and frighteningly powerful:

> The passion that rules in him—and he is a passionate man—is aimed at smashing utterly the target of his hatred, which is corporate power. He thinks, and says quite bluntly, that a great many corporate executives belong in prison—for defrauding the consumer with shoddy merchandise, poisoning the food supply with chemical additives, and willfully manufacturing unsafe products that will maim or kill the buyer. He emphasizes that he is not talking just about "fly-by-night hucksters" but the top management of blue chip businesses.

The memo made it clear that Nader was not alone. A "wide public following" had steadily emerged in support of the idea that "the 'capitalist' countries are controlled by big business." Such a notion, wrote Powell, could not be further from the truth:

> As every business executive knows, few elements of American society today have as little influence in government as American business, the corporation, or even the millions of corporate stockholders. . . . One does not exaggerate to say that, in terms of political influence with respect to the course of legislation and government action, the business executive is truly the "forgotten man."

Though Powell's memo pointed to many causes of the problems facing corporate America, he identified college campuses as "the single most dynamic source," noting that the "social science faculties usually include members who are unsympathetic to the enterprise system," including outright socialists as well as "the ambivalent liberal critic who finds more to condemn than to commend":

> They are often personally attractive and magnetic; they are stimulating teachers and their controversy attracts student following; they are prolific writers and lecturers; they author many textbooks, and they exert enormous influence—far out of proportion to their numbers—on their colleagues and in the academic world.

The notion of charismatic social science professors threatening the power of the Fortune 500 may sound overblown, but there is no doubt that Powell was correct in his general assertion that corporate America—at least for the moment—was experiencing a rare feeling of political helplessness. During a series of private meetings for CEOs sponsored in 1974 and 1975 by the Conference Board, a New York–based research group, executives expressed fear that the very survival of the free enterprise system was at risk. At the meetings, 35 percent of the participants stated that "government" was the most serious problem facing business in general. One participant said that "the American capitalist system is confronting its darkest hour." Another noted, "At this rate business can soon expect support from the environmentalists. We can get them to put the corporation on the endangered species list."

Of course, federal regulation of business was hardly something new—in fact, the creation of much of it had been sponsored or supported by corporations themselves. The first regulatory body was the Interstate Commerce Commission, created in 1886. Internal correspondence among railroad executives indicates that they saw it as a boon rather than an impediment. The Pure Food and Drug Act and the Meat Inspection Act of 1906 created product standards supported by manufacturers. In 1911, the National Association of Manufacturers wrote a model workers' compensation law that was adopted by twenty-five states over the next three years. The Federal Reserve System, created in 1913, was strongly supported by bankers. Businesses initiated and supported the establishment of the Federal Trade Commission in 1914. In the 1930s, more regulatory agencies were added, including the Securities and Exchange Commission, the National Labor Relations Board, the Federal Communications Commission, and the Civil Aeronautics Authority. And during the industrial drive to support military action in World War II, big government and big business became even more interconnected.

Those previous regulatory waves had largely been welcomed by corporations because they found the supervision of federal agencies useful for such purposes as maintaining price floors, excluding potential competitors from entering their markets, performing research and marketing, and organizing subsidies.

In contrast to this old-style regulation, the new wave of consumer and environmental regulation was by nature more intrusive and adversarial, and consequently far less palatable to corporate America. How, then, to fight back? Obviously, business would have to organize. New strategies and tactics were needed.

In the past, most business political activity had centered around industry-specific trade groups, though occasionally larger coalitions would form to deal with a specific issue. For example, prior to World War I a number of corporations, led by liquor and including textiles, mining, and railroads, had joined forces to block women's suffrage. The liquor industry feared women's support for Prohibition; other industries worried that giving women the vote would add momentum to such "home-and-hearth" issues as higher wages and stronger social benefits. But on the whole, sustained political cooperation among large corporations was more the exception than the rule. Even in the 1930s, when CEOs like Alfred Sloan of General Motors and advertising executives like Bruce Barton cajoled their colleagues to become more active in counteracting the public's negative perceptions of big business, most companies or trade groups mounted independent publicity efforts.

Lewis Powell realized that sporadic or half-hearted organizing would not work. It was time, he wrote in his memorandum, for corporate America to get as serious about politics as it was about business:

> Strength lies in organization, in careful long-range planning and implementation, in consistency of action over an indefinite period of years, in the scale of financing available only through joint effort, and in the political power available through united action and national organizations.

The key phrases here—"long-range planning," "consistency of action," "indefinite period of years"—set the Powell memorandum apart from the usual call to the barricades. Enthusiasm, mobilization, and commitment were all fine, but something more was needed. Executives would have to apply to politics the same methodical execution that they applied to business in general. To truly succeed in resetting the terms of American politics, corporations needed to systematize their approach, creating new institutions and giving those institutions their sustained support.

According to Powell, the resources needed for such an effort could only come by securing a new level of committed involvement among those at the top of the corporate hierarchy: "The day is long past when the chief executive officer of a major corporation discharges his responsibility by maintaining a satisfactory growth of profits. . . . If our system is to survive, top management must be equally concerned with protecting and preserving the system itself."

As though in direct answer to Powell's rallying cry, an unprecedented wave of political organizing began among business executives soon after the publication of the memo. The most important development came in 1972, when Frederick Borch of General Electric and John Harper of Alcoa spearheaded the formation of the Business Roundtable, an organization made up exclusively of CEOs from the top two hundred financial, industrial, and service corporations.

Because of the composition of its membership, the Business Roundtable occupied a position of unique prestige and leverage. It functioned as a sort of senate for the corporate elite, allowing big business as a whole to set priorities and deploy its resources in a more effective way than ever before. For example, in 1977, major corporations found themselves divided over a union-backed legislative proposal to reform and strengthen federal labor law and repeal the right-to-work provisions of the Taft-Hartley Act. Some members of the Roundtable, such as Sears Roebuck, strongly opposed the legislation because they believed it would provide leverage to their low-paid workforces to unionize. On the other hand, members whose workforces had already unionized, such as General Motors and General Electric, saw no need to oppose the legislation. However, after the Roundtable's policy committee voted to oppose the legislation, all the members of the organization joined in the lobbying efforts. Political scientists mark the defeat of that proposed legislation as a watershed.

Alongside and in the wake of the Roundtable, the 1970s saw the creation of a constellation of institutions to support the corporate agenda, including foundations, think tanks, litigation centers, publications, and increasingly sophisticated public relations and lobbying agencies. According to Lee Edwards, official historian of the Heritage Foundation, wealthy brewer Joseph Coors was moved by Powell's memo to donate $250,000 to the Analysis and Research Association, the original name of the Heritage Foundation. Other contributors followed his example. Powell also inspired an initiative by the California Chamber of Commerce that led to the formation of the Pacific Legal Foundation, the first of eight conservative litigation centers. Former secretary of the treasury William Simon, head of the Olin Foundation and one of the engineers and funders of this effort, described its goal as the creation of a "counterintelligentsia" that would help business regain its ideological footing.

While the Business Roundtable pursued a highly public approach to corporate advocacy at the federal level, another group pursued an "under the radar" approach at the state level. Founded by conservative leader Paul Weyrich in 1973, the American Legislative Exchange Council originally focused on right-wing causes such as abortion and school prayer. But as numerous corporations began contributing to the council in the 1980s the emphasis shifted to business-oriented issues. Eventually, the number of corporations involved in funding the council grew to over three hundred. ALEC now presented itself as a nonpartisan provider of technical services to chronically understaffed state legislators. Its forte was the drafting of model bills with beguiling titles such as "The Environmental Good Samaritan Act" or the "Private Property Protection Act." The approach proved to be highly successful, especially in complex areas such as electricity deregulation, where state legislators leaned on the group's technical expertise. On such issues, the combination of ALEC's seemingly neutral model bills and the active lobbying of its members, such as Enron CEO Kenneth Lay, proved highly effective. During the 1999–2000 legislative cycle, legislators belonging to ALEC introduced more than 3,100 bills based on the organization's model bills. Of these, 450 were enacted.

At the national level, the permanent organizations that made up the corporate political infrastructure would assemble short-term coalitions as needed to wage particular battles. These coalitions often combined the prestige, financial resources, and Washington clout of the Business Roundtable with the ability of industry-specific groups to mobilize large numbers of people. Some coalitions such as USA*NAFTA lasted only as long as needed to pass or defeat a particular piece of legislation. Others became long-standing fixtures in the Washington landscape.

Typical of such coalitions were the Center for Tobacco Research, described by the *Wall Street Journal* in 1993 as "the longest-running misinformation campaign in U.S. business history"; the Cooler Heads Coalition, which sought "to dispel the myths of global warming"; the Competitive Enterprise Institute, a research and advocacy group that advocated against safety and environmental regulation; and the Environmental Education Working Group, which sought to undermine environmental education programs in schools. Today, some corporations belong to dozens of such coalitions. Enron, for example, belonged to quite a lengthy list of them: the African Growth and Opportunity Act Coalition, Alliance for Capital Access, Alliance for Lower Electric Rates Today (ALERT), American Council for Capital Formation, American Institute for International Steel, American Legislative Exchange Council, Americans for Affordable Electricity, Americans for Fair Taxation, Business Council for Sustainable Energy, Citizens for a Sound Economy, Coalition for Competitive Energy Markets, Coalition for Gas-Based Environmental Solutions, Competitive Power Coalition, Direct Access Alliance, DOD Competition Coalition, Electric Power Supply Association, Emissions Marketing Association, Energy Group, International Climate Change Partnership, Mid-Atlantic Power Supply Association, National Wetlands

Coalition, New York Energy Providers Association, Pew Center on Global Climate Change, Power Trading Council, and Texas Renewable Power Coalition.

Over time, the new political infrastructure honed a variety of techniques. Alongside traditional tactics such as lobbying and junkets, innovative new methods emerged such as "astroturfing." As defined by *Campaigns & Elections* magazine, an astroturf campaign is a "grassroots program that involves the instant manufacturing of public support for a point of view in which either uninformed activists are recruited or means of deception are used to recruit them." Like short-order democracy cooks, the Washington-based consulting firms that specialized in astroturfing could serve up a fully orchestrated "grassroots" citizen campaign—just name the issue.

On the fringe of the new corporate politics was a grab bag of techniques used to smear or silence corporate opponents. To place environmentalists in a bad light, public relations firm Hill & Knowlton distributed a memorandum on the letterhead of the group Earth First that called for activists to commit violence "to fuck up the mega-machine." More common was the use of lawsuits to intimidate corporate critics. According to law professors George Pring and Penelope Canan, thousands of such suits were filed from the mid-1970s to the mid-1990s. Pring and Canan coined the term "strategic lawsuit against public participation," or SLAPP. Their research showed that the targets of such suits rarely lost in court but nevertheless were "frequently devastated and depoliticized" and that the suits discouraged others from speaking out.

With funding from a number of corporate sponsors, the Animal Industry Foundation (AIF) led efforts to enact "agricultural product disparagement laws" in numerous states. Such legislation provided new opportunities for SLAPP suits, the most famous of which was the suit brought by the Cactus Cattle Corporation against Oprah Winfrey and her guest Howard Lyman, following the April 16, 1996 episode of the *Oprah* show, which dealt with the potential dangers resulting from the practice of using processed dead livestock in cattle feed.

A transcript of the show indicates no possible slander of any individual, or even of any company—merely of the practice of feeding dead cows to other cows. Lyman, a former rancher and a staff member of the U.S. Humane Society, warned that the United States was risking an outbreak of mad cow disease by "following exactly the same path that they followed in England." Citing USDA statistics, Lyman noted that one hundred thousand cows die of disease each year, and that "the majority of those cows are rounded up, ground up, turned into feed, and fed back to other cows." He warned that since mad cow disease is transmitted by eating animals infected with the disease, "If only one of them has mad cow disease, it has the potential to affect thousands."

Oprah reacted viscerally, "It has just stopped me cold from eating another burger."

As is typical in SLAPP cases, Winfrey and Lyman won the suit, but it was six years before the final appeal by the litigants had run its course. The fact that Winfrey was forced to spend millions in legal fees and expenses sent a chilling message to consumer advocates. Authors of books on the topic found it more difficult to find a publisher, producers of documentaries found it more difficult to secure funding and airtime. Free speech on food safety issues had been effectively squelched.

Another thrust of the corporate political agenda was to foster a sympathetic climate for corporate antiregulatory ideology among the federal judiciary. To this end, several procorporate foundations developed "judicial education" seminars, which involved free trips for federal judges to attend training sessions at resorts such as Marco Island, Florida. Here corporate perspectives on environmental regulations, antitrust law, and other topics were presented along with golf, fishing, and other recreations. The organization that pioneered the judge junkets, the Law and Economics Center, was founded in 1974 and funded by a number of corporations including Ford Motor Company, Abbott Laboratories, and Proctor and Gamble, as well as right-wing foundations such as the Carthage Foundation and the Olin Foundation. LEC's program included such seminars as "Misconceptions About Environmental Pollution and Cancer." Later, additional conservative groups joined the judicial education movement, including the Foundation for Research on Economics and the Environment (FREE) and the Liberty Fund. Topics at a typical seminar sponsored by FREE at the Elkhorn Ranch in Big Sky, Montana, included "The Environment—a CEO's Perspective," taught by retired Texaco CEO Alfred DeCrane, "Progressive Myths and the Lords of Yesteryear," and "Why We Should Run Public Lands Like Businesses."

According to LEC's newsletter, many judges reported that the seminars had "totally altered their frame of reference for cases involving economic issues." One such judge was Spencer Williams, who attended a Law and Economics seminar at the Key Biscayne Hotel in Miami while presiding over a predatory pricing case being heard in U.S. district court. Returning from the seminar, the judge wrote to the LEC, "As a result of my better understanding of the concept of marginal costs, I have recently set aside a $15 million antitrust verdict."

FOUNDATIONS, THINK TANKS, coalitions, litigation centers, PR agencies, publications, judicial education—all these contributed to the corporate political comeback. But there was one final old-fashioned ingredient to add to the mix: *money*. Obviously, in politics, money isn't everything. Although some politicians will sell their votes in exchange for some crisp bills passed in a cloakroom, that's not how the pros play the game. Smart lobbyists direct contributions strategically rather than tactically, contributing year in and year out to the members of crucial committees, to *both* political parties, and sometimes even to a politician's pet causes rather than to the actual individual candidate. But although money has to be used in the right way, it is the element that makes all the other elements work properly.

Only one problem stood in the way of corporations putting together a system for deploying political money at the federal level: a Progressive Era law known as the Tillman Act. The Tillman Act originated in an 1898 scandal in the Republican Party involving Ohio mining magnate Marcus Hanna, a major player in the party and a fund-raiser for William McKinley. It was Hanna who made the memorable observation, "There are two things that are important in politics. The first is money, and I don't remember what the second one is."

Under Hanna's direction, the Republican Party systematically extracted contributions from banks and corporations, each according to its "stake in the general prosperity." The scandal led to calls for campaign finance reform, which went unheeded until 1904, when Alton B. Parker, the Democratic presidential nominee, charged that corporations were providing gifts to President Theodore Roosevelt in return for access and influence. Roosevelt denied the charges, and in his annual messages in 1905 and 1906 he called for campaign finance reform. Under the sponsorship of Senator Benjamin "Pitchfork" Tillman, Congress began considering such legislation, which finally passed and became law in 1907.

The Tillman Act banned contributions by corporations to federal campaigns. In 1947, the Taft-Hartley Act included labor unions in the ban as well.

On the surface, the 1970s did not look like an auspicious time to undo the ban on the use of corporate political donations. In fact, corporate donations had a particularly bad image at the time after revelations during the Watergate scandal that numerous businesses had doled out money to President Nixon from secret political slush funds. In one well-known incident, the chairman of Archer Daniels Midland had walked into the White House and handed the president's personal secretary an envelope stuffed with a thousand $100 bills. Eventually, twelve corporations were shown to have donated $750,000 in cash to Nixon. Given public outrage over such activities, it was unlikely that the Tillman Act ban on corporate contributions to candidates would be revoked. A more sophisticated avenue needed to be developed.

The solution came from an improbable source: the labor movement. After the Taft-Hartley Act of 1947, which banned labor unions from contributing to federal candidates, labor unions had invented the *political action committee*. PACs had provided a way for union members to pool their individual donations together, creating greater leverage. But even after corporate PACs were legalized by the Federal Election Campaign Act in 1971 and 1974, corporations found them of little use because the law allowed them to solicit stockholders for PAC contributions, but not employees.

The legal status of corporate PACs was dramatically changed by the Federal Election Commission in a little-known 1975 decision known as the SUN-PAC ruling. SUN-PAC not only gave the green light to corporate PACs but also gave corporations permission to solicit contributions from their employees and to use their own treasury funds to manage their PACs.

Prior to the SUN-PAC ruling, the use of PACs had depended on the rare stockholder who happened to have a high degree of interest in the company's political agenda. After the ruling, corporations were freed to "work" their own employees for contributions.

In the mid-1980s, researchers at the University of Massachusetts and the University of Maryland began a series of anonymous interviews inside corporations about how PAC money is raised. The results were revealing. At some companies, the researchers found no attempt to

pressure employees to contribute to the company PAC. At other companies, the official stance was "no pressure," but such pressure did indeed
exist. A typical pattern was for the head of government relations, one of
the firm's lobbyists, and the supervisor of a work unit to jointly lead a
meeting of that unit's employees: "We talk about the PAC and what it
means to the company and what it means to them as individuals, and we
solicit their membership; if they are members we solicit an increase in
their gift." Then the employees' boss was asked "to get up and say why
they are members and why they think it's important for an employee to
be a member."

The Massachusetts and Maryland university researchers concluded
that, given the nature of employer-employee relations, the pressure to
contribute to PACs is real, if somewhat veiled: "If your boss comes to you
and asks for a contribution saying he or she hopes that all team players
will be generous, it's not easy for you, an ambitious young manager, to say
no."

Not surprisingly, the researchers found that positions taken by corporate PACs on legislative issues were not derived by a democratic
process among the employees making the contributions. In every company surveyed, all such decisions were made by senior management. In
effect, the PAC served as a means for a corporation to make direct political contributions—the exact opposite of the intent of the Tillman Act.

After the SUN-PAC ruling, the use of PACs by corporations exploded.
In 1974, labor PACs outnumbered corporate PACs by 201 to 89. Ten years
later, the numbers were reversed, with corporate PACs far outnumbering
labor PACs, 1,682 to 394.

For lobbyists, PACs became a resource to be systematically managed,
with overhead expenses paid for out of company coffers. Making this
resource even more effective was the arrival of organizations devoted
specifically to coordinating PAC activity among corporations. These included the Business-Industry Political Action Committee (BIPAC), the
National Association of Business Political Action Committees, and the
National Chamber Alliance for Politics. Such coordination allowed PAC
money to be deployed with maximum effectiveness.

PAC MONEY WAS ONLY PART of the picture. Another important source
of corporate money in federal politics was "soft money," a category of

contribution approved by the Federal Election Commission in 1978 that allowed corporations, unions, and wealthy individuals to contribute money to the parties for "party-building" purposes unrelated to influencing federal elections. This money had to be kept in separate party accounts known as "nonfederal accounts." In practice, this money flowed from national parties to state parties, where it was spent in ways that supported candidates. Although some of the largest donors of soft money were labor unions, corporations overall outpaced labor unions in soft money contributions by a margin of ten to one. In 1999, labor unions contributed $33 million in soft money; business interests contributed $368 million.

In 2002, spurred by public rage over the Enron scandal, the U.S. Senate passed the McCain-Feingold bill banning soft money contributions, and the House passed the similar Shays-Meehan bill. The two bills were then reconciled as the Bipartisan Campaign Reform Act (BCRA). The new law offered the hope that the flow of soft money would be cut off, thereby reducing corporate influence over federal legislation. Unfortunately, the likelihood is that corporate political money will merely be rerouted through political action committees. PACs are certainly a less convenient way of raising money, since they require a large amount of logistical attention in order to assemble contributions in $1,000 blocks. Nevertheless, as has been shown by the nature of the corporate political mobilization since 1971, that sort of logistical expertise is where corporations, with their in-house organizational resources, have their biggest advantage in the political process.

So what about a simple, direct approach? Why not simply ban corporations from the political arena—period? Far from being a pie-in-the-sky proposition, such laws once existed in some states. Consider Wisconsin, for example. Until 1970, that state had the following statute on the books:

> No corporation doing business in this state shall pay or contribute, or offer consent or agree to pay or contribute, directly or indirectly, any money, property, free service of its officers or employees or thing of value to any political party, organization, committee or individual for any political purpose whatsoever, or for the purpose of influencing legislation of any kind, or to promote or defeat the candidacy of

any person for nomination, appointment or election to any political office. [Wis. Laws, Section 4479a (Sec. I, ch 492, 1905)]

Clearly, the enactment of such a statute at the federal level would accomplish far more than merely removing corporate campaign contributions from the political process. If written broadly, it could also stop corporate political lobbying, corporate media blitzes on referendums, and corporate influence machines like the American Legislative Exchange Council. With such legislation in place, corporations could still send their representatives to testify before legislative committees— on invitation only. The sixty thousand corporate lobbyists who work the hallways of the Capitol—a hundred for every congressman and senator—would have to go home, and the democratic institutions of American society, including courts, legislatures, and regulatory bodies, would all hang out a prominent sign: for human beings only.

Of course, the enactment of a "corporations out of politics" statute at the federal level seems quite improbable. For that reason, activists have viewed states—especially states that allow citizen ballot initiatives—as the most promising place from which a redemocratization process can emerge. Indeed, when citizens organize rebellions against corporate rule, states and local jurisdictions have offered some of the most creative and promising approaches. Unfortunately, the possibility of new reforms taking root at the state level has been seriously limited by decisions of the United States Supreme Court since 1976 that narrow the options of states to reform campaign financing. Those decisions are the subject of the next chapter.

CHAPTER THIRTEEN

Speech = Money

Using the First Amendment to block campaign finance reform

Money doesn't talk, it swears.
—Bob Dylan

AT SIX FEET THREE INCHES and three hundred pounds, lobbyist Arthur H. Samish cut an imposing figure, and he had an ego to match. "To hell with the governor of California," Samish once told a grand jury, "I'm the governor of the legislature." In 1949, Samish posed for *Collier's* magazine cradling a ventriloquist's dummy in his arms and saying, "This is my legislature. How are you Mr. Legislature?"

California legislators were not amused. As one commentator wrote, "Many legislators in the 1930s and 1940s didn't mind being manipulated by a powerful lobbyist; they just didn't like being laughed at for it." Enraged, the legislature voted to ban Samish from lobbying in Sacramento.

By then, Samish had amassed a $10 million fortune representing liquor, oil, transportation, racing, and other interests. He pretended to retire, saying, "Thank heavens, it has been proved I do not control the legislature."

Of course, Samish didn't actually close his lobbying business. From a suite at the Senator Hotel, he continued to direct his "Gestapo" of seventeen operatives. The liquor industry was a particularly lucrative client, and Samish's successors continued to block any increases in alcohol taxes. Among Samish's legacies in California was one of the lowest alcohol taxes in the country. As late as 1989, the tax on wine remained a constant one cent per gallon.

But California was changing. The California Highway Patrol pushed the state to see alcohol as a public safety issue. Mothers Against Drunk Driving (MADD) turned personal grief into political mobilization. In the late 1980s, a broad coalition of groups organized to pressure the state legislature to impose a nickel-a-drink tax on bars and restaurants, with revenues earmarked for trauma centers, law enforcement, alcoholism prevention and treatment, child abuse prevention, and services for addicted newborns. But despite polls showing that 73 percent of Californians supported such a tax, the measure went nowhere in the legislature.

Stymied in the legislature and encouraged by passage of a voter initiative raising the tobacco tax, the coalition that had backed the nickel-a-drink bill decided to take the matter directly to the citizens of California by means of an initiative on the 1990 state ballot. Soon, thousands of volunteers across the state were setting up tables on sidewalks and in malls to collect the signatures needed to qualify the initiative, Proposition 134.

Responding immediately, liquor industry leaders held emergency meetings to plot a counter-strategy. The president of the California Wine Institute called Proposition 134 "the most serious threat to this country since Prohibition," and an industry newsletter reported that the industry would spend "whatever is necessary" to defeat the tax. Led by donations from Seagram & Sons and Guinness Corporation, the industry committed an unprecedented $38 million to oppose the nickel-a-drink tax initiative. National industry groups joined the effort, motivated by concerns that if the California initiative succeeded, voters in other states would pass similar measures. A spokesman for the Washington, D.C.–based Beer Institute, which donated $1.8 million, said, "Things that happen in California have a way of creeping eastward." Attack ads were drafted, a one-penny-a-drink counterinitiative was launched in order to muddy the waters, and an industry front group, Taxpayers for Common Sense, was created in the offices of liquor executives.

The combination of negative advertising, counterinitiatives, front groups, and an overwhelming financial advantage proved effective. In the crucial area of broadcast advertising, the balance of resources was not even close. While the liquor industry spent $18 million on ads that slammed the nickel-a-drink initiative, proponents had only $40,000 with which to counter them. With plenty of funds left over, the industry iced the cake with a $5.5 million direct mail campaign. On election day, confused voters rejected both the citizen initiative and the industry alternative. Andy Legg of the California Highway Patrolman's Association, a supporter of the tax, said, "We couldn't make the public understand how important the tax was; we were just outshouted."

Across the country, the industry techniques used to kill Proposition 134 have since been honed to perfection. In cases where corporate opponents of citizen initiatives spend at least twice as much as proponents of such initiatives, the rate of success by the corporations is approximately 90 percent. As a result, citizen groups have taken the logical next step of attempting to restrict corporations from pouring massive funds into distorting the initiative process.

Consider the state of Montana, which for nearly a century was run as a virtual colony by the aptly named Anaconda Copper Company. Anaconda was born in 1895 out of a set of mergers that followed an intense power struggle for industry dominance known as the War of the Copper Kings—some of it literally fought as physical combat in the tunnels of the mines at Butte in the 1890s. The company had a tradition of corruption and hardball political tactics. At one point, displeased with the decision of a state judge in favor of one of its rivals, Anaconda shut down all its mines and smelters in the state for three weeks, cutting off thousands of workers from their paychecks, until the governor called a special session of the legislature to pass a new bill that resolved the dispute in favor of the company. Over the next sixty years, Anaconda maintained its grip on the state, owning all but one major state newspaper and continuing to dominate the Montana legislature. While Anaconda's mines and smelters devastated large tracts of the state, the company's political allies quashed attempts to enact legislation to protect the health of the state's citizens. Other mining companies took advantage of the anything-goes regulatory environment created by Anaconda, with tragic results.

In the town of Libby, Montana, two companies—first the Zonolite Corporation and then the W.R. Grace Company—operated a vermiculite mine from 1924 to 1995 that spewed five thousand pounds of highly toxic asbestos dust into the air every day, according to W.R. Grace's own tests. The connection between asbestos and fatal lung disease had been known since the 1920s, but efforts by the companies to protect their employees from exposure were minimal at best. Internal reports documenting the problem were concealed, and workers were told that the type of asbestos contained in the mine's dust was a nonhazardous variety. By 1964, when Grace assumed ownership of the mine, the evidence had become impossible to ignore: numerous workers in Libby were dying slow, excruciating deaths caused by debilitating lung ailments including fatal asbestosis (a thickening and hardening of the lung tissue), mesothelioma (cancer of the lung's lining), and lung cancer (cancer of the lung itself). An X-ray survey in 1969 showed that almost half of the people who had worked at the mine for eleven to twenty years had lung disease; among workers with twenty-one to twenty-five years tenure, the rate was 92 percent. In 1999, a survey by the *Seattle Post-Intelligencer* confirmed 192 deaths, with an additional 375 people diagnosed with fatal lung disease.

At the root of the appalling conditions in Libby and elsewhere was the political power of the mining industry. A former Bureau of Mines inspector told the *Post-Intelligencer:* "You would have to have bodies stacked like cordwood and the public screaming for someone's head before we could get the government's lawyers to do anything."

In the 1970s, a window opened briefly as Anaconda turned its attention to more lucrative mining opportunities in Chile and other countries. With the grip of the company loosened, a coalition of ranchers, environmentalists, labor unions, and others succeeded in enacting a new state constitution as well as a series of stronger environmental laws. In 1996, the coalition, assisted by campaign-finance reformers from other states, undertook the ambitious project of excluding corporate money from citizen ballot initiatives.

Campaigning from the backs of pickup trucks, at barbeques, town meetings, and county fairs around the state, activists gathered signatures proposing a ballot initiative that would prohibit corporations from spending general funds in connection with any future ballot initiatives. Despite heavy corporate opposition, Initiative 125 passed with 52 percent of the vote.

Initiative 125 changed the fundamental terms of Montana politics, allowing activists to consider putting measures on the ballot that otherwise would have been unthinkable because of the financial resources of the mining industry. Proposals could now be debated in the civic arena— via editorials, talk shows, public debates, door-to-door leafleting. A corporation could not rely on an expensive television and radio advertising blitz to present its case.

Two years after the passage of the campaign finance initiative, an initiative was placed on the ballot that banned the use of cyanide in gold mining. After a vigorous debate, the law was passed. At this point, Montana's corporations played their trump card, arguing in federal court that Initiative 125 violated the First Amendment. The federal judges agreed, citing the 1978 *First National Bank v. Bellotti* decision in which the U.S.

Supreme Court overturned a similar Massachusetts statute. Ruling in favor of the Montana Chamber of Commerce in the case of *Montana Chamber of Commerce v. Argenbright,* the U.S. Ninth Circuit Court of Appeals declared Montana's I-125 to be unconstitutional.

How did the first amendment become a tool for striking down grassroots campaign finance reform? The answer lies in a series of U.S. Supreme Court decisions between 1976 and 1986. Because several of these decisions were written by Justice Lewis Powell, it is helpful to recall a portion of his "Attack on American Free Enterprise System" memorandum entitled "Neglected Opportunity in the Courts":

> American business and the enterprise system have been affected as much by courts as by the executive and legislative branches of government. Under our constitutional system, especially with an activist-minded Supreme Court, the judiciary may be the most important instrument for social, economic and political change.

In his Senate confirmation hearings, two months after writing the memorandum, Powell presented himself as a moderate. And indeed, after joining the Supreme Court, Powell tended to be a bridge-builder between conservatives and liberals on social issues such as abortion. But in his advocacy on behalf of large corporations, he was anything but moderate. Powell took the lead in a significant new expansion of the legal foundations of corporate power.

During Powell's tenure, the two most significant Supreme Court decisions on campaign finance reform were *Buckley v. Valeo* and *First National Bank of Boston v. Bellotti.* These decisions placed two serious obstacles in the path of campaign finance reform. First, the Court interpreted very *broadly* the connection between corporate political spending and free speech, thus setting a high constitutional bar in front of any efforts to restrict political spending. Second, the Court interpreted very *narrowly* the issue of corruption, excluding systemic corruption—as opposed to direct favor trading, or quid pro quo corruption—as an acceptable justification for restricting corporate political contributions. Because of these two obstacles, the ability of state

and federal legislatures to deal with the overwhelming influence of corporate money in the political process is extremely limited.

Buckley v. Valeo (1976) did not deal specifically with corporations;
rather, it was a broad ruling on whether the post-Watergate reforms
contained in the Federal Election Campaign Act (FECA) amendments
of 1974 were constitutional. But *Buckley* established two important
principles that would later be applied to cases involving corporations.
One can be characterized as "speech = money." In essence, the Court
ruled that since spending money is often necessary to communicate a
message to a large audience, restrictions on political spending or donations must satisfy the same difficult standard that restrictions on
speech must satisfy in order to be considered constitutional. Such restrictions are justified only if there is no other way to protect a vital
public interest, such as upholding the public's confidence in the integrity of the electoral system.

Buckley reflected the view that the biggest danger posed by unre-
stricted money in politics is quid pro quo corruption—that is, the use of
political contributions to gain favors from a politician. To avoid such corruption, the *Buckley* decision upheld FECA's restrictions on *donations* to
candidates. But *Buckley* overruled FECA's restrictions on a candidate's
own ability to *spend* money on his or her own campaign, based on the
logic that a candidate cannot corrupt himself or herself.

If the justices had looked at how financial power actually translates
into political power, they would have seen that quid pro quo corruption
is just a small part of the problem. For example, by refusing to allow
statutory limits on spending by rich candidates on their own campaigns,
the Court made it difficult for ordinary citizens to compete in the political arena unless they curry favor with other sources of money—such as
corporations. Thus, by bending over backward to protect the rights of
rich candidates, the Supreme Court created a system where money over-
whelms any other factor.

In contrast to *Buckley,* which overturned limits on the political spending of individuals, *First National Bank of Boston v. Bellotti* (1978) protected political spending by corporations on state legislative initiatives.
The specific circumstances of the decision grew out of a Massachusetts
law that banned corporations from buying advocacy advertisements on
citizen initiatives. A consortium of major corporations, led by First

National Bank of Boston, joined in a lawsuit against the law, and the U.S. Supreme Court sided with the consortium.

In overturning the Massachusetts law, the majority in *Bellotti* attempted to sidestep the tricky issue of whether a corporation should be entitled to the free speech protection of the First Amendment. Instead, the Court chose to interpret the issue as one of the *public's* right to hear the information provided by the corporate ads. According to the decision of the Court, the public's right to a "free discussion of governmental affairs" was at stake as well as the need to stop government "from limiting the stock of information from which members of the public may draw." Then the opinion stated, "The concept that government may restrict the speech of some elements of our society in order to enhance the relative voice of others is wholly foreign to the First Amendment."

The reasoning of the majority in *Bellotti* had a winning sort of simplicity. Who, after all, would support restricting the amount of information available to the public? But the dissenters in *Bellotti* raised straightforward objections. The argument opposing the idea of corporate First Amendment rights was written by Justice White, who began by noting that thirty-one states restrict corporate political activity. He argued that corporations are clearly not capable of the principle purpose of the First Amendment, that of "self-expression, self-realization, and self-fulfillment," nor of "mental exploration and the affirmation of self." Of course, conceded White, not all communication is necessarily so noble. The First Amendment also protects communications "which have no purpose other than that of enriching the communicator." But White noted that the Massachusetts law did not actually block corporations, their executives, their shareholders, or their employees from communicating their ideas in any way. Rather, the law merely blocked certain kinds of corporate political *spending*. Thus, it merely limited the ability of corporate leaders to use the company as a megaphone for political positions. Because it did nothing to inhibit corporate executives from speaking out, forming political associations, or buying advertisements with their own personal funds, the Massachusetts law did not violate the First Amendment.

Justice Rehnquist, one of the most conservative members of the Supreme Court, joined White in opposing the notion that corporations were being entitled to First Amendment protection on par with citizens. Rehnquist noted that properties such as "perpetual life and limited liability" may "pose special dangers in the political sphere," since they allow corporations an inherent advantage over other players in the political process. Because of these advantages, legislatures are fully justified in limiting corporate political activities. Otherwise, the voices of ordinary citizens may simply be drowned out in the media. As for the idea that limiting corporate "speech" might limit the amount of information available to society, Rehnquist argued that the opposite might well be true. If a single corporate voice is amplified with a deafening repetition of advertisements, the opportunity for alternative viewpoints to be heard is arguable diminished.

The two sides in the *Bellotti* case reflected two distinct views about the essential nature of the corporation. One side saw corporations as "elements of our society" on a par with human beings; the other side saw corporations as something quite different from human beings—as entities that enjoy special properties and that therefore pose "special dangers."

THE COURT'S DECISION in the *Bellotti* case represented a significant expansion in corporate power, but it did not come about in isolation. It is useful to look at the case in the context of the extensive series of corporate rights decisions that began with *Santa Clara* in 1886, as well as in the context of internal tensions within the Constitution itself between the rights of property and the rights of individuals. As early as the Boston Massacre and other riots that preceded the revolution, in which freed slaves and impoverished sailors took the lead in skirmishes against the British, there had been tension between what John Adams termed the "motley rabble of saucy boys, negroes and molattoes, Irish teagues, and outlandish Jack Tarrs" and wealthy gentlemen such as Washington, Jefferson, and Madison. Though obscured by the rhetoric of the revolution, the class divisions in America are deeply rooted.

Democracy, in the view of the privileged group to which the framers of the Constitution belonged, was a fine thing as long as it didn't get out of hand. Benjamin Rush, an influential doctor, coined a term for a new mental illness: "anarchia," which he defined as "an excessive love of liberty."

The original framing of the United States Constitution, written by a group of predominantly wealthy gentlemen meeting in secret, took pains to protect the interests of the wealthy few against the rest of the population. Even the Bill of Rights can be looked on as two separate sets of guarantees, embodying two contradictory political objectives. On the one hand, First Amendment rights such as freedom of speech and freedom of assembly represent the ordinary citizen's defense against potential abuse by powerful instruments of the state. On the other hand, the Fifth Amendment forbade the uncompensated taking of property—a guarantee that majority rule would not be used to appropriate the wealth of the elites.

In light of this tension within the Constitution, it makes sense that the set of rights developed by the Supreme Court to shield corporations from state and federal legislation have been mainly extensions of the provisions of the Constitution that were designed to protect the property rights of individuals. What is suprising about the "speech = money" decisions of the 1970s, 1980s, and 1990s, is that the First Amendment was now being turned into a shield for wealth, property, and corporate power. Such an outcome could only occur by means of a careful compartmentalization of rationales. Thus, Supreme Court decisions that pretended to walk a careful line—protecting corporate free speech rights on the one hand while permitting certain legislation aimed at preventing corruption on the other—actually relied on highly artificial ways of conceiving both the nature of "free speech" and the nature of "corruption." By "speech," the Court had come to accept the idea that expenditures of money by immense business entities in political campaigns deserved the same degree of protection as utterances by human beings. By corruption, the Court had limited itself to the notion of quid pro quo corruption, where particular movements of money could be connected directly to particular actions in politics.

Such twisting and contorting of rationales is not new, as the history of the *Santa Clara* decision amply demonstrates. Indeed, as described in the next chapter, the entire body of Supreme Court jurisprudence underlying corporate rights is a hodgepodge of inconsistent rationales, illustrating that as a general rule, corporate rights have not migrated to earth from disinterested Olympian heights. Rather, power has dictated certain results, and reason has found ways to accommodate it. But that accommodation has never been easy, given the fact that the framers of the Constitution declined to place explicit corporate rights in that document.

CHAPTER FOURTEEN

Judicial Yoga

The tangled logic of corporate rights

W HAT LEGAL RATIONALES has the Supreme Court relied on to establish corporate rights? How well do those rationales stand up to an audit of their logical coherence?

At first glance, the Supreme Court's development of corporate rights has the appearance of an orderly and careful progression. It begins with the foundation decision in the 1886 *Santa Clara* case declaring corporations to be entitled to the same "equal protection" as persons under the Fourteenth Amendment. Then, over the course of the following century, the Court examines first one case and then another, gradually expanding the set of corporate rights. (The entire corporate bill of rights is shown in Table 1.1.)

That image of coherence and care is deceptive. The judicial reasoning that underlies the creation of corporate rights has cracks—deep internal inconsistencies. Unfortunately, the process by which the Supreme Court builds a body of jurisprudence out of multiple decisions does not serve to expose these sorts of cracks, but rather to hide them. With the passage of time, the defective old bricks acquire a sheen of legitimacy, weathering into handsome, venerable foundations.

ALL LEGAL RATIONALES about corporate rights, whether supporting or opposing, must start with a basic question: *What is a corporation?* From a legal standpoint, the answer is simple. A corporation is a type of organization in which a separate legal identity is created from that of the owner or owners. Legally, that separate identity comes into being when the government issues a charter of incorporation.

A business can exist without the blessing of the government. A corporation, by definition, cannot. This fundamental distinction lies at the basis for the oldest theory of the corporation, which was used to deny corporations all but a few functional rights from 1789 until 1886, and which has continued to serve as the primary argument in recent dissenting opinions in corporate rights cases.

In the 1819 *Dartmouth College* decision, Chief Justice John Marshall wrote that a corporation is an "artificial being, invisible, intangible and existing only in contemplation of law." Thus, a corporation can't assert rights against its creator, the legislature that issued its charter. The legislature is free to pass laws and regulations as it sees fit—or even to revoke a corporation's charter and end its existence. In the *Dartmouth* case, the Supreme Court actually blocked New Hampshire's bid to radically alter the charter of Dartmouth College, agreeing with Dartmouth's contention that its charter should be considered a preexisting contract with King George and therefore protected by the Constitution's contracts clause. However, in the same decision, the Court made it clear that as long as a state legislature included a clause in future charters reserving its right to alter or revoke them, the legislature could do so with impunity. Although the case did begin the process of creating a distinct legal status for corporations, it also established clearly that legislative power trumps corporate authority.

This *artificial entity theory* does not deny that corporations can have some rights, but it limits those rights to the functional ones necessary for the corporate entity to participate in the legal arena: the right to own property, the right to enter into contracts, and the right to defend its property and enforce its contracts in court.

Implicit in the artificial entity theory is the philosophy that legitimate power can only emanate from democratic institutions. The theory reflects the wariness toward corporations inherited from the colonial period, a belief that corporations will inevitably seek power over their legislative masters. Such fears have even older roots in traditional English law. For example, *mortmain* ("dead hand") clauses in church charters limited the amount of land that the congregation could own in order to prevent the accumulation of real property in immobile corporate hands.

Concerns about runaway corporate power induced legislatures to use the corporate charter as a restrictive tool, confining each corporation in a tight legal box. Together, the artificial entity definition and the charter system provided the justification along with the means for strict state control of corporations.

T HE FIRST SERIOUS EFFORT to create a theory of the corporation that would justify giving corporations constitutional rights was articulated by Justice Stephen Field in his ninth circuit court opinions in the *San Mateo* and *Santa Clara* cases.

Field argued that to deny corporations "equal protection" under the Fourteenth Amendment would have the effect of denying corporate shareholders their "equal protection" rights. This approach called for looking past the corporate veil and seeing the rights of the shareholders. On its surface, this approach has a simple appeal, especially as articulated by Field's friend Professor Pomeroy, who wrote that "for purposes of protecting rights, the property of the corporation IS the property of the corporators."

But does Pomeroy's equation really make sense? The entire point of the corporate form of organization was to create a category of property that could be *different* from individual or partnership property, both in terms of the privileges it affords and the accountability it demands. For example, the meaning of limited liability is that investors in a corporation are safely beyond the reach of those who sue the corporation.

With ordinary property, the accountability of the owner is straight-forward. If a horse knocks over your fence, you can sue the owner for damages, even if the horse is no longer alive. But if sparks from a corporation's train burn your barn, you can't demand compensation from the bank accounts of the stockholders, only from the bank account of the corporation. In other words, the very aspects of the corporate institutional form that create flexibility also create gaps in accountability. So it seems reasonable for society to address those gaps with regulatory measures.

G IVEN SUCH PROBLEMS WITH Field's and Pomeroy's justification for corporate rights, a new rationale was eventually developed. Legal schol-ars call this second approach the *natural entity theory* of corporate rights.

The natural entity theory involved looking not at the shareholders but at the corporation itself as an upstanding, respectable participant in society. Given its central role in society, the corporation deserves the same rights as humans beings, even if the Constitution doesn't actually say it does.

Unlike Field's shareholder-oriented theory, the natural entity theory never had an articulate advocate on the Supreme Court. Indeed, as legal historian Morton Horwitz has argued, the natural entity theory did not even exist in America at the time of the *Santa Clara* decision. And in later decisions, it was never presented in a straightforward way as a rationale. Rather, the theory seeped into the Court's decisions more indirectly, as a presumption rather than as an explicit argument.

What gave the natural entity theory a sheen of respectability was a wave of European scholarship that arrived on the American intellectual and legal scene during the 1890s. In Germany, an academic movement known as *organicism* had been exploring the social meaning of groups and associations for a long time, and about a decade after the *Santa Clara* decision some of the key works produced by that movement were published in English for the first time. The movement's central figure was German medieval law scholar Otto Gierke (1841–1921), whose writings were translated into English by Frederic William Maitland in 1900 as *Political Theories of the Middle Ages*. According to Gierke, under Pope Innocent IV in the thirteenth century, the church initiated a long and undesirable process of attempting to monopolize the organization of society, making every other institution subordinate to itself. When the state replaced the church as the primary institution in society, it too sought to make its authority universal.

To Gierke, the democratic revolutions spawned by the Enlightenment were only partial successes. Although they elevated the status of individual humans, they failed to elevate the status of the intermediate institutions that are also organic elements of society. Democracies had worked out the relation between the individual and the state. But the rich and lively web of organizations that constitute society—schools, churches, clubs, businesses, unions, and other entities—also required legitimacy and protection against the state, and that need remained unmet by political systems that only granted rights to individuals. According to Gierke's historical research, the "collective personality" of organizations was well established during early medieval times, when communities of various sorts asserted "organic" rights—that is, rights that reflected the needs of the community as a whole. He proposed that such rights be resurrected.

Gierke's arguments appealed to a diverse audience. Some supporters were traditionalists concerned about the social fragmentation induced by the Industrial Revolution. Others were socialists and anarchists who saw communal values buttressing their challenges to the bourgeois power structure. As the literature of the movement permeated the British and American intellectual worlds, legal scholars, historians, social theorists, and philosophers on both sides of the Atlantic pondered the question of "group personality." Initially they focused on premodern social and economic institutions, seeking to understand how industrialization had corroded those forms during the transformation of Western society from its medieval roots into its modern form. Eventually they included modern organizations, including corporations, in the discussion.

Although Gierke's ideas may sound appealing, they run into a simple problem when applied to the American context: the United States Constitution. The natural entity theory holds that shielding associations from the state should be a fundamental principle of law—a right. But the Constitution disagrees. Organizations of various stripes, including corporations, did in fact exist at the time the Constitution and the Bill of Rights were enacted. If the founding fathers had wanted to create special rights for groups such as corporations, they had every opportunity to do so in framing the Constitution. In fact, the Constitution did confer special protection on two groups—the press and religious institutions—but not on any others. The history of the East India Company, the Boston Tea Party, and the Constitutional Convention all reveal absolutely no desire on behalf of the framers of the American system to afford any rights whatsoever to corporations. Indeed, they indicate the opposite: a bias toward *restraining* corporations. (See again chapter 5 for a detailed discussion of this subject.) Thus, it is fair to say that those who supported using Gierke's theories of group personality as a rationale for corporate empowerment were essentially undertaking to transplant a European notion into a constitutional framework distinctly unsympathetic to it.

YET QUITE BY COINCIDENCE, the terminology of the organicist movement seemed tailor-made for the American debate over corporate rights. Organicist scholars used the term *corporate personality*, which is confusingly similar to the legal notion of *corporate personhood*. The relation between the terms is merely semantic, not substantive, yet it led to confusion. Prior to the 1880s, it had always been clear that the legal personhood status enjoyed by corporations under English and American law was merely a functional category that referred to the fact that corporations can access the courts on matters of property and contracts.

The term "legal person" had never implied that corporations were entitled to a broader set of human rights. Indeed, in England, as described in chapter 7, incorporation had never been a protectable property right.

As legal historian Morton Horwitz has pointed out, the ideas of the European organicists were never raised in the Supreme Court arguments in the *Santa Clara* case. Only in the decade following *Santa Clara*, the 1890s, did these ideas become a justification for corporate rights. From the 1890s until the 1920s, legal scholars, philosophers and others became caught up in a seemingly endless series of debates over the meaning of corporate personality and the connection between corporate personality and legal personhood.

These rarified and generally pointless debates finally drew to a halt after philosopher John Dewey argued convincingly in a 1926 essay that the whole discourse about corporate personality was too abstract to have any practical value. After Dewey, proponents of corporate rights abandoned any further efforts to produce a coherent justification for granting corporations an ever-increasing body of rights. In general, Supreme Court decisions have granted new corporate rights with virtually no supporting argument, or alternatively have used a strange medley of rationales.

For FORTY YEARS—from 1922 to 1962—the trend by the Court toward creating a corporate bill of rights came to a halt, and no new rights were granted to corporations. During this period two justices, Hugo Black and William O. Douglas, sensed an opening, and they wrote stinging dissents advocating the reversal of the *Santa Clara* decision. In a dissent to the 1938 *Connecticut General Life Insurance Company v. Johnson* decision, Justice Black wrote:

> Both Congress and the people were familiar with the meaning of the word "corporation" at the time the Fourteenth Amendment was submitted and adopted. The judicial inclusion of the word "corporation" in the Fourteenth Amendment has had a revolutionary effect on our form of government. The states did not adopt the amendment with knowledge of its sweeping meaning under its present construction. No section of the amendment gave notice to the people that, if adopted, it would subject every state law and municipal ordinance, affecting

corporations, and all (administrative actions under them) to censorship of the United States courts. No word in all this amendment gave any hint that its adoption would deprive the states of their long-recognized power to regulate corporations.

Similarly, in a 1949 dissent to *Wheeling Steel v. Glander,* Justice Douglas wrote:

> It may be most desirable to give corporations this protection from the operation of the legislative process. But that question is not for us. It is for the people. If they want corporations to be treated as humans are treated, if they want to grant corporations this large degree of emancipation from state regulation, they should say so. The Constitution provides a method by which they may do so. We should not do it for them through the guise of interpretation.

But *Santa Clara* was not reversed. By now, the concept of corporate rights had become deeply embedded in American law and had gained a momentum of its own. And beginning in 1962, the Court resumed expansion of corporate rights, giving corporations:

❖ The Fifth Amendment right against being tried twice for the same offense (*Fong Foo,* 1962)

❖ The Seventh Amendment right to a jury trial in a civil case (*Ross v. Bernhard,* 1970)

❖ The First Amendment right of "commercial free speech" (*Virginia Board of Pharmacy v. Virginia Citizens Consumer Council,* 1976, and *Central Hudson Gas,* 1980)

❖ The Fourth Amendment right against unwarranted regulatory searches (*Marshall v. Barlow's,* 1978)

❖ The First Amendment right to spend money to influence a state referendum (*Bellotti,* 1978)

❖ The First Amendment right of "negative free speech" (*Pacific Gas & Electric Co. v. Public Utilities Commission,* 1986)

In all these cases, the Supreme Court seemed to carefully avoid citing any of the defective rationales that had earlier been used. Instead, it began using two new methods of justification: one based on history, the other based on the intended purpose of a particular constitutional right.

The Supreme Court used the historical argument in *Marshall v. Barlow* (1978). The Court ruled that government safety inspectors could not enter corporate property without a search warrant, under the Fourth Amendment's protection of "the right of the people to be secure in their persons, houses, papers, and effects." Though corporate property would seem to fall under none of those categories, the majority decision in the case relied on the assertion that at the time of the American Revolution a prime cause of colonial anger was British searches of colonists' shops. The dissenting justices in the case objected that equating major corporations with colonial shops made little sense. (They might have added that a true reading of history would reveal that colonial attitudes were quite distinctly *anticorporate* and would hardly have lent corporations any such constitutional protection.)

The Supreme Court made the argument based on the intended purpose of a right in extending First Amendment "free speech" rights to corporations. The Court faced a dilemma. Such rights are intrinsically associated with human qualities such as "will" and "conscience." Only in a metaphorical sense can such qualities be ascribed to business organizations. But in the *Bellotti* decision, the Court found a way to get around this objection by adopting an approach that didn't depend at all on the nature of the corporation. Rather than claiming that a corporation has any intrinsic human qualities that would entitle it to human rights, it came up with the roundabout rationale that the protections of the First Amendment were protections of *speech,* not of the *speaker.* In the *Bellotti* decision, Justice Powell wrote, "The inherent worth of the speech in terms of its capacity for informing the public does not depend upon the identity of its source, whether corporation, association, union, or individual."

Similarly, in striking down a state law that sought to limit corporate advertisements promoting electrical consumption during a period of energy shortages (*Central Hudson Gas,* 1980), the majority decision stated that its purpose was not to protect the rights of the corporation, but rather to protect the right of the public to receive the maximum amount of information possible on a given issue.

But if the goal is to maximize speech rather than to protect a particular speaker, what happens when the rights of two different speakers come into conflict? The answer, of course, is: "Management decides." This became clear in the case of *Pacific Gas & Electric v. Public Utilities Commission.*

In *Pacific Gas & Electric* (1986), the Court established a novel new corporate right, that of "negative free speech." In this case, the management of an electrical utility company had a newsletter expressing one set of political views on energy policy, but the state regulatory body, wishing to increase the diversity of opinions, passed a rule requiring the utility company to enclose the newsletter of a consumer group four times each year in its billing envelopes. The utility company objected to the newsletter, and the U.S. Supreme Court ruled in favor of the company.

Under the principle of protecting "speech" rather than the rights of the corporate "speaker," one would have expected the Supreme Court to support the Public Utilities Commission's rule. After all, the effect of the rule was to *increase the amount of information available to the public* by forcing the company to disseminate a newsletter with views different from those of the management. But the Court ruled in favor of management, contradicting its own rationale in the *Central Hudson* decision. In the majority opinion, written by Justice Powell, the Court concluded that forcing an electric utility to enclose a message from a ratepayer group in its billing envelope violated the utility's First Amendment free speech right *not* to be associated with statements it disagreed with. According to the Court's decision, being required to enclose such a message would violate the corporation's rights, because it would implicitly force Pacific Gas & Electric "to respond to views that others may hold."

How can the *Pacific Gas & Electric* decision be explained? Since it clearly contradicts the Supreme Court's own previous rationale for extending First Amendment rights to corporations—the notion of increasing the amount of information available to the public—some other rationale must be sought. Evidently, the Supreme Court concluded that corporate managers deserved a higher level of constitutional protection than other corporate stakeholders, such as ratepayers or employees. To give First Amendment protection to an official newsletter while denying it to a rate-payer newsletter, an employee newsletter, or a stockholder newsletter is in effect to grant constitutional protection to management over and above other groups involved with the corporation.

A few members of the Supreme Court recognized the fundamental flaw in the *Pacific Gas & Electric* decision. Justice William Rehnquist dissented forcefully from the decision:

> Extension of the individual's freedom of conscience decisions to business corporations strains the rationale of those cases beyond the breaking point. To ascribe to such artificial entities an "intellect" or "mind" for freedom of conscience purposes is to confuse metaphor with reality.

What appears to have happened is that the Court came to a gradual acceptance of the privileged status that corporations had gained in American society. And that rise in status was created, at least in part, through Court decisions that had created the "corporate bill of rights." Ironically, the justices who might have been expected to be the philosophical heirs to the dissenting tradition of Black and Douglas, liberals like Justice Brennan and Justice Marshall, had now emerged as leading advocates, alongside avid pro-corporate advocates such as Lewis Powell, of granting First Amendment rights to corporations.

Like a myopic Dr. Frankenstein, the Court had worked piecemeal and haphazardly, grafting a finger here, an eyebrow there, until the result was a full-fledged legal superperson. Only sporadically, in dissents interspersed across the decades, was there an explicit recognition that the cumulative impact of the growing body of corporate rights was to tie the hands of legislative bodies seeking to control corporate power. In general, the justices displayed no awareness that the Supreme Court's creation of a corporate bill of rights amounted to an immense transfer of power from democratic institutions to private ones. The process was not driven by any overarching theory—to this day, the Court has yet to sustain any consistent rationale to support its creation of the corporate bill of rights. On the contrary, the process has been a perfect illustration of the Orwellian ability of large, unaccountable institutions to bend even ordinary language into a tool to serve their own needs—the gravitational force exerted by power. Far from laying orderly tracks, that force of power seemed to operate between the cracks of reason, leaving in its wake only muddled, blurry traces.

ONE OF THE MOST disappointing aspects of the dramatic expansion of corporate rights since 1970 has been the acquiescence and even support for that process by the leading advocate for an expansive interpretation of constitutional rights: the American Civil Liberties Union. Generally, the role of the ACLU in the judicial process is to seek the protection and expansion of human freedoms. But on the issue of corporate rights, its position has actually served to diminish human rights by expanding corporate ones.

Take the example of *Pacific Gas & Electric v. Public Utilities Commission.* The ACLU has cited this Supreme Court decision approvingly as an example of the Court blocking "compelled speech." According to the ACLU, compelled speech is speech in which "the government has compelled someone to support a particular message through word or action." Such compulsion, according to the ACLU, "violates the principle of individual conscience that is central to the First Amendment." To the ACLU, a utility company that objected to being required to insert a consumer group newsletter in its billing statement has the right to block such a newsletter—just as a student has a right to refuse to say the pledge of allegiance.

But isn't a corporation different from a student? After all, a student really does have a conscience. But where is the conscience of a corporation?

As Adolph Berle and Gardiner Means pointed out in their landmark work *The Modern Corporation and Private Property,* the essence of a corporation is the fragmentation of accountability among various internal groups. Those who occupy the key leadership position (the professional managers) aren't necessarily its owners; those who are owners (the stockholders) are generally neither in charge nor legally liable; and those who are supposed to be exercising strategic direction on behalf of the owners (the board of directors) are rarely sufficiently informed nor sufficiently empowered to actually fulfill their theoretical function.

With such intrinsic fragmentation, a core feature of the corporation is the absence of any discernable mind or conscience. That void makes the theories of corporate rights that rely on the qualities of individuals meaningless. If the Berle and Means analysis of the corporation makes sense, then *none* of the views of the corporation out of which constitutional rights precedents have developed stand up to scrutiny, because all of them turn on the assumption that a corporation is capable of behaving within the same moral and legal framework as a person or a community of people. All of them assume that some group inside the corporation—generally either the owners or the managers—is ultimately in charge and can be used as a morally accountable proxy for the corporation as a whole. Without a *someone,* or at least a coherent group of someones, in charge of the corporation, it becomes a phenomenon without any moral agency—like a hurricane or a beehive. Thus, to dignify a profoundly nonhuman entity by awarding it rights was to confuse basic categories—like trying to control the behavior of animals by handing them pamphlets, or trying to make a machine operate more reliably by promising it a ticket to the movies.

In practice, the ACLU's protection of corporate free speech rights actually boils down to protection of *management* speech. But it is questionable whether even management speech is the expression of a human conscience. After all, fiduciary responsibility requires managers to pursue a course of advocacy on behalf of the corporation that maximizes the corporation's profits—and it is not infrequently the case that such advocacy violates a manager's own conscience.

Such realities are all ignored by the "can't see the forest for the trees" nature of the ACLU's approach to corporate rights. The forest is the reality that the structure of American society limits the opportunity to communicate in the public arena to those with sufficient resources. Day in and day out, corporations use their financial resources to drown out other points of view. Thus the institutions of democratic government may attempt at times to carve out zones in which noncorporate voices can be heard. For example, in the case of *Pacific Gas & Electric,* the fact that a single corporation monopolizes all electrical and gas supplies to a large region containing millions of people, as well as monopolizes all communications with electrical customers within that region, was believed by the Public Utilities Commission to create an unhealthy bias in the information available to customers. The Public Utilities Commission took the reasonable step of requiring the company to occasionally enclose a consumer newsletter in its monthly billing statement.

Instead of focusing on the "trees," the ACLU would serve the goals of the Constitution better if it considered the constitutionality of actions by the government that have ceded vast tracts of the public's media to corporate interests. Perhaps the most crucial example of that sort of concession to corporations has been in the area of telecommunications policy. In his seminal book *Rich Media, Poor Democracy,* University of Illinois professor Robert McChesney recounts the respective histories of the United States and Canada during the 1920s and 1930s in allocating control of the radio spectrum. In the United States, federal regulatory agencies quickly marginalized public broadcasting channels, resulting in an overwhelming domination of the airwaves by corporate interests. In Canada, the government carefully reserved a portion of the spectrum for noncommercial broadcasting.

Were the ACLU to consider broadly the goals of the First Amendment, it might apply its resources to challenging the overall structure of telecommunications policy, toward the goal of providing access to as broad an array of voices as possible.

The ACLU's position on First Amendment issues has led it to oppose a number of attempts to institute campaign finance reform. Here, the issues of "forest and trees" are similar to those in the *Pacific Gas & Electric* decision. In its decision in *Buckley v. Valeo,* the Supreme Court appeared to open one eye—to see at least one part of the forest of contemporary reality. Thus, the Buckley decision recognized that the expenditure of money is intrinsically intertwined in modern society with the ability to disseminate a political message through the commercial media. But the Supreme Court avoided the obvious corollary to its own "speech = money" insight: if the expenditure of money is intrinsic to disseminating a political message, then doesn't that leave those without financial resources essentially *speechless?* Doesn't this imply the need to make the First Amendment meaningful by increasing noncommercial channels for those whose financial resources don't rise to the level of the threshold needed to "play ball" in the commercial system?

IN EFFECT, THE SUPREME COURT, with the blessing of the ACLU, has accepted the ground rules of a system where corporations can dominate the airing of issues—the control of media by a limited number of large corporations, as established by federal telecommunications policies. Once it has accepted the underlying setup, where most of society is rendered speechless and invisible, the ACLU falls into the trap of seeing only the actors who remain in the game. Thus it is the rights of these actors—corporations and the relatively few wealthy individuals who can match the resources of corporations—that the ACLU ends up defending.

Not surprisingly, corporate America was delighted with the ACLU position on free speech. According to one document released by the U.S. House of Representatives' Commerce Committee, "Strategy to Combat Advertising Content Restrictions and Counter-Advertising Requirements," the tobacco industry considered the ACLU to be the "most prominent and valuable of our constitutional ad ban allies."

Why did the ACLU capitulate so easily to the corporate framing of First Amendment issues? It seems that the ACLU is motivated by a "slippery slope" notion, believing that restricting the First Amendment rights for one segment of society will inevitably undermine the protection for other segments. Speech should be protected, no matter what the source. After all, if the speech of pariahs such as pornographers or Nazis deserves protection, then why should not the speech of a mainstream element such as the corporation?

The problem with the ACLU position is that it bases its rationale on the wrong metaphor. Protecting corporations is not a way of avoiding the slippery slope, analogous to protecting the speech of an unpopular speaker. After all, a corporation is not a speaker at all—*speaker* is entirely the wrong metaphor. More aptly, the corporation might be compared to a megaphone. Suppose you go to a PTA meeting, and you notice that one of the other parents has brought along a megaphone that allows him to drown out everyone else. By asking that person to put the megaphone down, you're not depriving him of the opportunity to speak. You're merely protecting the ability of other speakers to be heard.

Similarly, campaign finance laws that restrict corporate political expenditures have the effect of protecting First Amendment rights. How? They prevent the corporate megaphone from drowning out other points of view. When such regulations are not in place, a large corporation is often capable of using its superior financial resources to overwhelm other opinions. With regulations in place, corporate managers remain free to express their own opinions, either personally or on behalf of the company. But other points of view are protected too, including those of employees, stockholders, dissenting managers, and the public at large.

THE FALLACY OF SEEING THE CORPORATION as a speaker is illustrated by a recent case involving Nike, Inc. In 1996, Nike began to face serious charges of sweatshop conditions in the Asian factories operated by its subcontractors. Three hundred thousand to five hundred thousand people, mostly young women, work in those factories, located primarily in Vietnam, China, Indonesia, and Thailand. Reports in the news program *48 Hours* and in the *New York Times, Financial Times, San Francisco Chronicle, Kansas City Star, Oregonian, Buffalo News,* and *Sporting News* contained a wide range of allegations. The *Times* reported "grim conditions" and widespread human rights abuses in factories where Nike shoes were made. A spot audit of one Vietnamese factory found 77 percent of workers suffering respiratory problems. An investigator for Vietnam Labor Watch found a pervasive "sense of desperation" based on interviews with the young women making Nike shoes there. In China, the Hong Kong Christian Industrial Committee found workers subjected to eleven- to twelve-hour days, compulsory overtime, and violation of minimum wage laws. Other reports described physical, verbal, and sexual abuse, and exposure of young workers to toxic chemicals, noise, heat, and dust without adequate safety equipment.

In response to the allegations, Nike mounted a publicity blitz in which it denied the charges and asserted that its workers were paid double the minimum wage, on average; its workers received free meals and health care; its workers were not subjected to corporal punishment or sexual abuse; and its products were made in accordance with health and safety regulations.

Marc Kasky, a San Francisco resident, became convinced that much of the information being used by Nike in its publicity campaign was false. Kasky decided to take action, and coming to the conclusion that Nike's statements did not even agree with the company's own internal audits, he filed a false advertising lawsuit in state court under California's Business and Professions Code.

In response to Kasky's lawsuit, Nike's lawyers used an interesting legal strategy. Rather than argue that the company's advertisements were factual, the lawyers asserted that factuality was irrelevant in the case because Nike was protected by the First Amendment. Thus, the company could publicize any sort of information it wanted—even "facts" that it knew to be completely false.

As the case worked its way to the Supreme Court (which ultimately refused to hear the case, leading the parties to settle out of court), the legal arguments became complex. Kasky's attorneys argued that Nike's statements constituted "commercial speech," which is subject to a lower

level of First Amendment protection because of the need to ensure public safety from misrepresentations about product safety and ingredients.
Nike's lawyers, on the other hand, argued that the sweatshop issue was a
political debate, and that the entire purpose of the First Amendment was
to ensure that no one in such a debate could be subjected to governmental restriction.

Once the debate was set in these terms, Nike enjoyed a tremendous
advantage. The ACLU rushed to defend the company's freedom of
speech, as did a number of corporations, editorials in major newspapers,
and even the AFL-CIO. Typical of the arguments was that of the ACLU's
amicus brief, which cited "the fundamental First Amendment principles
that protect the rights of those on both sides of a debate to speak their
minds freely."

Here is the crux of the issue: the corporate mind. When a corporation
issues a press release or runs an advertising blitz, who is actually speaking its mind? Obviously, a corporation itself does not have a mind. It is
merely a collection of papers—the name on a financial statement. There
are, of course, managers, directors, employees, lawyers, and public relations firms involved in such campaigns. But do the statements issued by
a corporation actually reflect the personal opinions of any of those people? Perhaps, perhaps not. But what is certain is that holding a company
accountable for the accuracy of its advertisements and official statements
about safety conditions, worker pay, incidents of verbal or sexual abuse
by factory supervisors, or other such information hardly seems a restriction on anyone's freedom of speech. Kasky's suit was not directed at after-
hours statements made by human beings who happened to work for
Nike—rather, the suit aimed at official statements of the company.

The situation might be compared to the responsibilities of a corporation in the financial arena. In official representations about its financial status, a corporation is accountable for the truthfulness of all
representations. On the other hand, if an executive wants to go to a cock-
tail party or a family reunion and brag about how successful her company
is, she should have every right to do so.

Ultimately, society must be able to make a distinction between the
rights and prerogatives of a $10 billion corporation such as Nike and an
ordinary human being like you or me. No one would ever propose that a
machine that emits words is entitled to free speech. It is human speakers

that the First Amendment protects, not machines. Contrary to the fears of the ACLU that requiring corporate statements to be truthful puts society on a slippery slope toward restricting human speech, the actual slippery slope is different. The real slippery slope is the ever-increasing tendency to treat corporations as though they were human beings.

But what about the other rationale for extending First Amendment rights to corporations—the notion that protecting corporate speech is not so much about protecting the corporation as a speaker as about protecting society as a listener? According to this listener-oriented rationale, society depends on the lively, unimpeded flow of information, the "free market of ideas." Truth and falsehood, it is thought, can best be sorted out if all providers of information, no matter who or what they might happen to be, are afforded the maximum leeway to say whatever they want, whether truthful or not.

The problem with applying this rationale to corporate speech is that in many cases only the corporation is in a position to know the facts about its own operations. For that reason, few people would argue against requirements that corporate representations about finances and product ingredients be truthful. But why should the truthfulness of corporate statements about the treatment of workers in Third World factories be any less important?

It must be remembered that in China and other countries where many companies, including Nike, manufacture their products, it remains difficult and even dangerous to independently ascertain what goes on inside the workplace. Thus, the "free market of ideas" can't be relied upon to reveal the truth. The only way society will know how the workers who make Nike shoes are paid and treated is if Nike, Inc. is required to report such matters truthfully.

As the following chapter shows, the pressures on corporations to paint a false picture to the outside world are significant and pervasive. For that reason, the idea that giving corporations "the right to lie" under the First Amendment is a way of maintaining the "free market of ideas" is wrongly conceived. Indeed, just as laws against fraud and monopoly are needed to maintain the integrity of markets for goods and services, so likewise laws against deliberate corporate deception are actually quite vital to protect the "free market of ideas."

CHAPTER FIFTEEN

Crime Wave

The roots of the scandals of 2002

Some will rob you with a six-gun, and some with a fountain pen.
—Woody Guthrie

IT STARTED QUIETLY ENOUGH. On October 4, 2001, two executives of Enron Corporation worked the phones from the company's Houston headquarters, breaking the news to analysts for the nation's major credit-rating agencies that the company was expecting to report significant losses for its third quarter. Later that week, the company's board of directors met and were also informed of the losses, which were described as significant—$600 million. For most companies, a loss of that magnitude would be a highly serious matter. But to Enron, it looked like little more than a speed bump. Company executives explained the losses as a onetime setback with no significant effect on the company's future. The directors later said that they left the meeting feeling that the company was doing fine.

Enron, after all, was the epitome of success. For five years running, the company had been named "most innovative" by *Business Week*. Enron didn't just dominate markets—it invented them. Around the world, the United States pushed governments like Argentina, Mozambique, the Philippines, and India to privatize key state enterprises and sell those enterprises to Enron. When financing was needed, the U.S. government provided the loans. No company in American history has ever been more closely connected at the highest levels of government. At least twenty-eight former U.S. officials worked for the company as employees, officers, directors, consultants, or lobbyists. The Bush administration counted five former Enron executives in its inner circles. Over the course of his career, Bush himself had received more money from Enron than from any other contributor: $572,000, according to the Center for

Public Integrity. In preparing the administration's energy policy, Vice President Dick Cheney's staff met six times with Enron representatives. And on the recommendation of Enron CEO Kenneth Lay, President Bush chose Pat Wood as head of the Federal Energy Regulatory Commission, the main watchdog agency to keep tabs on Enron's gas and electricity businesses. Of course, Enron knew better than to work with just one side of the political aisle. Its ties to Democrats, though weaker than to Republicans, were nevertheless significant. Three-quarters of the Senate had received contributions from the company's PACs.

In hindsight, the announcement of Enron's $600 million loss was merely a prelude—a clearing of the throat. Not long after reporting the loss, the whispering began in Washington, Houston, and Wall Street. Rumors swirled that the credit rating agencies had found Enron's accounting to be perplexing. Soon, the story emerged that executives inside the company had created secret partnerships into which they had channeled hundreds of millions of dollars. It was also rumored that Enron had created over twenty-eight hundred phony subsidiaries in off-shore locations. Both rumors turned out to be true. Much larger losses were in the offing—perhaps even civil and criminal charges. Investors hurried to unload their shares, the stock price tumbled, and within weeks, $60 billion of investor equity had disappeared into the ether.

For employees of the company, what stung most were revelations that twenty-nine company executives, while knowing the company was in danger of collapse, had sold large amounts of their own stock—some $1.1 billion, according to a shareholder lawsuit. Yet during the period when the value of the company's stock was sliding most rapidly, Enron had blocked employees from selling shares in their own retirement portfolios. At angry meetings attended by laid-off employees, the sense of betrayal was intense.

And then, like a grass fire leaping a highway on a windy day, the Enron scandal seemed to ignite scandals at other companies. By July 2002, the scandal sheet included over a dozen corporations, including Adelphia, AOL Time Warner, Arthur Anderson, Bristol-Meyers Squibb, Global Crossing, Halliburton, Johnson & Johnson, Qwest Communications, Tyco, WorldCom, and Xerox.

The nature of the scandals varied, but some features appeared repeatedly. In most cases, executives had used illicit accounting schemes to artificially enhance the company's financial appearance, thereby enhancing the stock price. One motive was clear. High stock prices maximized the value of the stock options that had become a major part of executive compensation packages. The use of options—rather than a straight salary—had been intended to motivate corporate leaders and to align their interests with those of the company's shareholders. Instead, the effect had been the reverse.

The rise in popularity of stock options in the 1980s and 1990s was part of a remarkable increase in executive compensation during that period, especially for CEOs. In 1980, the average CEO of a large corporation earned 42 times the average hourly worker's pay; by 2001, the ratio had soared to 411 times. The increase reflected a major change in the image and status of business leaders. In the 1950s and 1960s, the CEO was viewed in the context of a managerial team. Stability was valued; the ethos was bureaucratic rather than entrepreneurial. By current standards, salaries were astonishingly low. For example, in 1950, the pretax income of the best-paid CEO in the United States, Charles E. Wilson of General Motors, was $626,300 (or $4.8 million in 2003 dollars), a modest salary by today's standards. Moreover, tax rates were steep for high-income earners. Had Wilson paid federal income taxes on his entire compensation, his after-tax disposable income would have been only $164,300 ($1.3 million in 2003 dollars).

Why was CEO compensation so much lower only decades ago? According to economist Paul Krugman, in previous generations salaries were linked to the size of the company, not to its growth rate, and salaries were kept in relative check by the lingering effect of a New Deal social ethos that "imposed norms of relative equality in pay." Krugman quotes John Kenneth Galbraith's popular 1967 book *The New Industrial State*: "Management does not go out ruthlessly to reward itself—a sound management is expected to exercise restraint. . . . Group decision-making insures, moreover, that everyone's actions and even thoughts are known to others. This acts to enforce the code and, more than incidentally, a high standard of personal honesty as well."

In the 1980s, the image of the CEO as restrained team player was abandoned in favor of a new one: swashbuckler. High-profile CEOs like Lee Iacocca added to the traditional role of manager the additional roles of supersalesman, public advocate, even best-selling author. Clearly, a CEO such as Iacocca was worth a mammoth paycheck. Another version of the star CEO emerged in the improbable persona of the hard-driving, twenty-something nerd-entrepreneur epitomized by Bill Gates. Even though few CEOs could claim the selling abilities of an Iacocca or the genius of a Gates, such celebrity business leaders did much to exorcise the image of CEOs as the bureaucrats and social pariahs depicted in the Powell memorandum. Indeed, they were becoming the new generation's equivalent of rock stars.

Reinforcing the phenomenon of the CEO celebrity was a new school of thought on compensation pioneered by Chicago-school economists Michael Jensen and William Meckling, who published dense journal articles in the mathematical argot of neoclassical economics challenging the old methods for compensating CEOs. According to Jensen, Meckling, and others, companies would produce better results overall if executive compensation were linked to stock market performance rather than to company size. Thus was born the stock option as an integral part of executive compensation packages.

The logic of stock options was clear enough—in theory, they created incentives for outstanding performance, while holding CEOs accountable to clear goals set by the board of directors. The problem was that in many large corporations, the independence of boards is an illusion. In reality, many CEOs had the power to create lucrative compensation targets, then revise the rules of the game if results fell short of the target. If the stock price met the original goal, the CEO hit the jackpot. If the stock price underperformed, the option was repriced, giving the CEO another chance. Few CEOs could resist such a game. In 1980, fewer than a third of CEOs received stock options; by 1997, options packages had become the norm among the top two hundred corporations, and the average value was $32 million. By 2001, the average had climbed to $50 million.

So extensive was the awarding of options to CEOs that control of many corporations literally changed hands. According to corporate governance expert Robert Monks, ownership by top management expanded during the 1990s from 2 percent to 13 percent of all outstanding corporate equity—a share easily sufficient to secure control of many large corporations.

In addition to drastically polarizing the distribution of wealth in America, options produced a number of unforeseen perverse effects, especially an increasing tendency for corporations to manipulate their financial results. The stratagems included shifting revenues or expenses either forward or backward, hiding liabilities, reporting bogus revenue, treating onetime gains as normal revenue, and treating normal expenses as capital expenditures. As noted by accounting experts such as Howard Schilit of American University, such irregularities began to appear with mounting frequency throughout the 1990s, though they stayed below the public radar until the huge financial meltdowns of Enron, WorldCom, and other companies in 2001 and 2002.

THE PERVERSE EFFECTS of options provided something people craved: an explanation for why things had gone so terribly wrong at so many companies. But this explanation did not really address the root of the problem. After all, the American business system is world-famous for the strengths of its checks and balances, its multiple layers of oversight. *Layer one* is the accounting standards maintained by the Financial Accounting Standards Board, which are intended to ensure that the financial information received by investors and bankers allows an accurate assessment of corporate performance. *Layer two* is the periodic audit, conducted by large professional accounting firms. *Layer three* is the threat of investor lawsuits: if companies or accounting firms lie to investors, both can be sued in civil court. *Layer four* is the Securities and Exchange Commission, empowered to ensure the integrity of individual companies and the soundness of the system as a whole. *Layer five* is Congress, especially the oversight committees that scrutinize the performance of the SEC and other regulators. *Layer six* is the media, afforded special protections by the U.S. Constitution to shine the spotlight of public attention on whomever and whatever it chooses.

With so many layers of oversight, how could things have gone so far off track? Maybe the answer was actually a simple, straightforward one— old-fashioned greed and perfidy, unleashed in the heady environment of a colossal boom. Such an interpretation had a basic appeal, since indicting the morals and character of a few isolated rogues suggests readier solutions than blaming—and thereby being forced to address—the system itself. And so, as the scandals of 2001 and 2002 refused to leave the headlines, President George W. Bush spoke out in support of basic ethical standards. Declaring that "too many corporations seem disconnected from the values of our country," Bush denounced "destructive greed" and proposed increasing the maximum prison sentence for executives found guilty of fraud from five years to ten.

The Bush response is notable for its chutzpah. After all, the spotlight of scrutiny provoked by Enron and other scandals had widened to include both Bush himself and Dick Cheney. Bush found himself answering questions about why he had earned hundreds of thousands of dollars selling stock in his company, Harken Energy, shortly before the company announced a raft of bad news that sent the stock plunging. The investigation of the affair, conducted by the SEC during the first Bush administration, appeared to have been extremely mild. Now, questions were being asked not only about the new President Bush's business record but about Vice President Cheney's as well, and the SEC opened an investigation into charges that Halliburton, the company Cheney had run prior to becoming vice president, had engaged in dubious billing and accounting practices under his watch.

With the Bush administration absorbed in its own damage control, it was the Business Roundtable that stepped in with what appeared to be a deeper explanation of the corporate crime wave, along with a proposal for curing the patient. According to the Business Roundtable, the problem in the industry was essentially one of business not doing enough to keep pace with the times. As the Enron scandal peaked in March 2002, the Roundtable released a statement declaring that the problems with Enron were a "troubling exception" in a system with an "overall record of success." Nevertheless, Roundtable president Franklin Raines announced that the organization was in the process of an expedited review of its 1997 corporate governance standards. Two months later, the group released the results of the review, a series of "best practices" recommendations for the organization of corporate boards and committees, the approval of stock options, and the disclosure of pertinent information.

As for the use of stock options for executive compensation, the Roundtable recommended no essential changes. Instead, it affirmed the appropriateness of a "management compensation structure that directly links the interests of management to the long-term interests of shareholders, including short-term and long-term incentives."

If ever there were an area where Congress might want to heed the advice of groups *other* than big business, it would be a spate of scandals involving big business itself. Yet the legislation adopted in response to the scandals, the Sarbanes-Oxley Act, represented a mild set of measures that barely exceeded the "best practices" recommendations of the Roundtable: requiring CEOs to certify their company's financial reports, tightening the regulations for corporate auditing committees, banning inside loans to executives and board members, prohibiting accounting firms from serving as consultants to their clients during audits (but not prohibiting accounting firms from advising their clients at other times), requiring disclosure of off-balance-sheet items, and increasing fines for fraud and other violations.

Not surprisingly, the Roundtable applauded Sarbanes-Oxley, the legislative enactment of its assertion that big business merely needed an accounting tune-up, and that voluntary measures taken by the corporate sector would be sufficient to get the house of corporate America back in order. Congress readily agreed; neither Republicans nor Democrats fought for stronger measures. That response by the Republicans was understandable, given the party's traditional identification with the interests of big corporations. But what had happened to the Democrats?

The answer can be found by following the money. In the ten years preceding the scandal, corporations had doled out over $1.08 billion in campaign contributions: $636 million to Republicans and $449 million to Democrats. No one, it seemed, had any incentive to rock the boat. In the decade prior to the Enron scandal, there had been three major fights in Congress having to do with accounting industry practices and accountability. In all three cases, big business lobbying overwhelmed potential reforms:

❖ *Stock options:* In 1993, the Financial Accounting Standards Board (FASB) attempted to close the loophole that allowed companies to reward stock options to employees and executives without reporting those options as expenses. Big business mounted a huge lobbying effort, and Congress, led by Senator Joseph Lieberman, a Democrat, pressured the FASB not to treat stock options as a corporate expense.

❖ *Tort reform:* Part of the Contract with America that fueled the Gingrich revolution of 1994, in which Republicans gained a majority in the House of Representatives, was tort reform. Proponents of tort reform denounced the prevalence of frivolous lawsuits and passed legislation making it much more difficult for investors and others to sue corporations and their accounting firms. In 1995, Congress passed (over President Clinton's veto) the Private Securities Legislative Reform Act limiting the

rights of investors to sue management. It also shielded accounting firms from being charged with aiding and abetting fraudulent activities. The result was a slack environment where there
was little fear of lawsuits.

❖ *Conflicts of interest within auditors:* In April 2000, SEC chairman
Arthur Levitt proposed that auditing firms not be allowed to
consult with the same companies that they were auditing, since
wearing both hats puts auditing firms in a position where they
have an interest in not rocking the boat. Levitt was not speculat-
ing about problems that might happen as a result of such conflicts. Already, he had ample evidence that the practice of issuing
"managed earnings" had "absolutely exploded." And Arthur Anderson had already been fined $7 million for its role in advising
Waste Management Inc., which paid $457 million in penalties
for overstating its earnings between 1993 and 1997. To defeat the
proposal, Anderson was joined by two other major accounting
firms, KPMG and Deloitte & Touche, in an all-out lobbying
campaign that included nearly $23 million in campaign contri-
butions to both parties. Seven lobbying firms worked on Capitol
Hill to kill the proposal. After the committee that oversees the
SEC threatened the agency's funding, Levitt reluctantly caved in
to the pressure and withdrew the proposal.

So what was the lesson of the crime wave of 2002? First, it should be
clear what the lesson *wasn't.* Personal corruption, conflicts of interest at
accounting firms, the weakening of investor lawsuit remedies, the accounting standards applying to stock options, the definition of Generally
Accepted Accounting Principles, or whether the Financial Standards Accounting Board should be independent or federally controlled—all these
were merely symptoms. The deeper problem was overwhelming corporate influence in democratic government, which had become so pervasive
that the lines separating corporate power and governmental power had
become blurred.

Consider the decision to go to war against Iraq. In its public statements justifying the attack, the Bush administration cited the heightened
national security concerns since September 11, 2001. Yet ideas such as

"regime change" and "preemptive war" had actually been developed by corporate-supported policy development groups even before the 2000 election. The founders of one such think tank, the Project for a New American Century (PNAC), included a number of men who later became top members of the Bush administration: Donald Rumsfeld, Dick Cheney, Paul Wolfowitz. Indeed, former executives, consultants, and shareholders of top defense contractors fairly peppered the policymaking ranks. Eight came from Lockheed Martin, the largest defense contractor; seven came from Northrop Grumman, the third largest defense contractor. One investigator of the relationship between the Bush administration and the defense industry described it as a "seamless web." Yet aside from a few allegations of conflict of interest, that web did not appear to depend on any actual illegalities. In that regard, the defense industry followed a pattern that can be seen in any number of other areas where corporate influence has an overriding effect on public policy: energy, finance, pharmaceuticals, telecommunications, media, agriculture, tobacco, high tech, criminal justice, and many more.

In contrast to the more subtle methods used by corporate interest groups—the think tanks, the white papers, the political action committees—some of the crimes of 2002 seem almost quaint, the villains old-fashioned. CEOs like Tyco's Dennis Kozlowski and WorldCom's Bernie Ebbers treated company funds like personal piggy banks, fleeced shareholders with false accounting, and looted employee pension plans without shame. Yet compared to the sophisticated networks of influence that constitute business as usual, these greedy corporate shysters look rather clumsy, like small-time crooks.

Scandals break out periodically in American business, and when they do, a window is opened briefly that allows public debates over the role of corporations in politics and society that normally do not take place. Yet even at the height of these recent scandals, the terms of the debate were extremely narrow. No one seriously proposed limiting corporate power in any radical way, much less excluding it altogether from the political process. In 2002, the window opened wider than usual but not nearly wide enough.

CHAPTER SIXTEEN

Global Rule

*How international trade agreements
are creating new corporate rights*

T HE DAY THAT CORPORATIONS gained the right to vote—July 1, 1997—
Hong Kong was unpleasantly hot and sticky, at least for the human
beings who marked the occasion. Of course, the corporations themselves
didn't mind. As the Union Jack went down and the flag of the People's Republic of China flew for the first time over the Hong Kong Special Administrative Region, a new "mini-constitution" went into effect, designed
by shipping tycoon Tung Chee Hwa and supported by the Beijing government and the Communist Party. It divided the sixty seats in Hong
Kong's new legislature as follows: twenty elected by voters, ten elected by
a selection committee controlled by Beijing, and thirty elected by "functional constituencies," which included professionals such as lawyers and
architects but also corporations based in Hong Kong.

Advocates of democracy such as Christine Loh of the Citizens Party
cried foul, pointing out that businesses in Hong Kong already enjoyed
sufficient influence in the governmental process and didn't need the actual right of voting in order to have their interests represented. By its
very nature, she asserted, the system devalued the rights of Hong Kong's
2.7 million human voters. Professor Byron Weng of the Chinese University of Hong Kong gave precise measure to the injustice. According to
Weng's calculations, one corporation, the Sino Group, now enjoyed a
quantity of direct electoral power equivalent to 6,100 human voters—
this due to Sino Group's control of various subsidiaries, each enjoying
a separate vote.

Corporations voting? To our American mentality, the notion sounds
absurd. But it does raise a question: What is the ultimate limit on corporate empowerment? As the Hong Kong example makes clear, corporations aren't the ones that are going to suggest limits. They'll take what

they can get, advancing their agenda of empowerment both in the political arena of each individual nation and on the international stage by means of bilateral and multilateral agreements.

GLOBALIZATION IS NOTHING NEW. In the sixteenth and seventeenth centuries, trading and settlement corporations such as the British East India Company, the Virginia Company, and the Royal African Company were the cutting edge of British imperial expansion around the world. The typical pattern was for corporations to lead the way, then eventually be supplanted by Crown colonies. In America, the conversion of corporate settlements into Crown colonies took place in the 1600s; in India, company rule lasted until 1858. As late as the 1890s, the British South Africa Company fought wars of conquest against the Matabele and Shona kingdoms of present-day Zimbabwe, and it was not until 1924 that the company became a British Crown colony. Other countries followed similar patterns. After conquering Indonesia in the 1600s, the Dutch East India Company ruled the archipelago until 1798, when it was dissolved and replaced by a Dutch civil administration. In northeastern China, Mantetsu, the South Manchurian Railway Company, ruled an area the size of France and Germany combined from 1905 until it was replaced by a Japanese colonial administration in the 1930s.

More typical than direct corporate rule was the domination of weak Third World governments by corporate interests, backed up by occasional military interventions. The template for such "banana republics," of course, was Central America, where nineteenth-century railroad entrepreneur Minor Cooper Keith led the building of an extensive railroad system, then moved into fruit as a sideline enterprise. The 1899 merger of Keith's Tropical Trading and Transport Company with the Boston Fruit Company, its chief competitor, created the United Fruit Company, which built towns, hospitals, and schools, sponsored archeological excavations, and played political puppeteer to generations of Central American dictators. Keith himself was known in the 1920s as the "uncrowned king of Central America."

In 1954, United Fruit played a leading role in a CIA-sponsored coup that overthrew the elected president of Guatemala, Jacobo Arbenz. Before the coup, the company flew dozens of American journalists to Guatemala on lavish, stage-managed trips, and presented them with evidence that communism was threatening the country. Back home, the journalists quickly spread the story of a communist menace. United Fruit used its contacts in Washington, including Secretary of State John Foster Dulles, formerly an attorney for United Fruit, and his brother Allen Dulles, the head of the CIA, to make its case for intervention in Guatemala. In the run-up to the coup, United Fruit shipped weapons on its company boats and housed coup leaders on company property.

Such collaborations between corporate interests and spy-agency coup-planners were repeated elsewhere during the Cold War. In 1960, the Belgian mining company Union Minière, which had run the Congo province of Katanga as a virtual colony since 1908, worked with the CIA and the Belgian government in destabilizing and overthrowing the government of popular leader Patrice Lumumba, who was assassinated and replaced by the dictator Joseph Mobutu. Similarly, in 1972, following the election of a socialist, Salvador Allende, as president of Chile, International Telephone and Telegraph Corporation (ITT), worked with the CIA on a plan to create "economic collapse" that would destabilize Allende's government. Like Lumumba, Allende was killed and replaced by a military dictator.

WITH THE END of the Cold War, such naked tactics became less tenable, and the ways in which multinational corporations sought to influence national governments became more sophisticated. Increasingly, the global economy was shaped by a framework of international accords known as the *Bretton Woods system*. These agreements had arisen during talks between Winston Churchill and Franklin Roosevelt in the summer of 1944. As Allied troops fought their way from the Normandy beaches into France, delegates from forty-four countries met at the New Hampshire ski resort town of Bretton Woods to establish a set of international financial institutions, including the World Bank, which provided reconstruction loans for Europe after the war, and the International Monetary Fund (IMF), which took on the role of providing short-term loans for national governments. Four years later, the General Agreement on Tariffs and Trades (GATT) was initiated as an ongoing series of negotiations to smooth out barriers to international trade and investment. In 1994, the World Trade Organization was created as the third main Bretton Woods institution.

All three institutions—the World Bank, the IMF, and the WTO— have become integral to the expansion of transnational corporations, especially in the Third World. The international debt crisis of the early 1980s was a watershed in the development of that role. During the previous decade, low interest rates had encouraged a wave of borrowing from American and European banks. Long-term external debt owed by low-income countries increased from $21 billion to $110 billion between 1970 and 1980. In 1980, interest rates began to climb, and numerous countries found themselves unable to meet their repayment schedules. The outcome of the crisis was the creation of the "structural adjustment" loan by the IMF and the World Bank, first applied to the Philippines in 1980 and then to Mexico in 1982. Such loan packages provided emergency funds for refinancing a country's debt burdens, but not before securing the government's agreement on a number of conditions aimed at improving its balance of payments. Among the austerity measures insisted upon by the IMF were cuts in social services and privatization of state-owned enterprises.

The requirement by structural adjustment programs that governments sell state-owned businesses created a host of new opportunities for transnational companies in public utilities, toll roads, bus systems, oil pipelines, and power plants. One such company was Enron, which generated $23 billion in foreign revenues in 2001. Aided by World Bank privatization pressure on Third World governments, Enron struck deals around the world with numerous countries, including India, the Dominican Republic, Panama, Columbia, and Guatemala. In many cases, Enron also received financing for these deals from the World Bank and from national governments, including over $3 billion from the U.S. government.

Although structural adjustment provided one mechanism for transnational corporations to expand their reach, other factors also played a role, such as the special industrial zones that were created in scores of countries, most notably China. In 1980, after decades of economic isolation, China began opening five special economic areas, setting off an episode of economic expansion that one economic expert, Nicholas Lardy of the Brookings Institute, described as "unparalleled in modern economic history." In the 1990s, the Chinese special economic areas attracted $300 billion in investments. Corporations such as Wal-Mart, Kmart, and J.C. Penney entered into deals with subcontractors that offered unlimited access to China's nonunion factory workforce.

Worldwide, companies operating outside their home country more than tripled in number between the late 1960s and the 1990s. By the 1990s, transnationals accounted for about a third of all private-sector capital. American companies were the most aggressive in buying overseas manufacturing assets and moving domestic manufacturing offshore. By the late 1990s, American corporations were producing twice as much abroad as European and Japanese multinationals combined. But the internationalization of ownership also affected the United States domestically, as the foreign-owned share of U.S. manufacturing assets grew from 3 percent in 1970 to 19 percent in 1990.

As they straddled countries, corporations found themselves facing multiple regulatory systems. What to do? In the United States itself, a similar problem had been solved a century earlier by creative interpretation of the commerce clause and by development of new doctrines of corporate rights. Why not try the same thing on a global scale—develop a new trump card for nixing unwanted regulation?

Guided by that general objective, two channels were developed. One was the GATT process, the ongoing series of multilateral negotiations involving over one hundred countries. But GATT's sheer size made the process slow and unwieldy. A quicker channel proved to be regional treaties, starting with a U.S.–Canada Free Trade Agreement (FTA) in 1987. In 1994, Mexico joined the regional agreement and the FTA was subsumed into the North American Free Trade Agreement (NAFTA). A third treaty, the Free Trade Area of the Americas (FTAA), is currently being negotiated.

The regional agreements provide powerful new global rights for corporations—legal mechanisms that allow a corporation based in one country to overturn the laws or judicial decisions of a different country. In 1987, two international corporate rights (*national treatment* and *minimum standard of treatment*) came into being with the ratification of the FTA. When that agreement was subsumed into NAFTA, it added a third corporate right (*compensation for regulatory takings*).

The right of national treatment, defined by NAFTA's Article 1102, requires that governments treat foreign corporations as favorably as domestic ones. The right of minimum standard of treatment, defined by Article 1105, means that all corporations must be treated according to the requirements of international law. The right of compensation for tak-ings, defined by Article 1110, requires that if new regulations reduce the value of a corporation's property or expected future profits, the firm is allowed to sue the host government for damages in a special court of arbitration.

NAFTA's corporate rights are stronger than those available to corpo-rations through the rules of the 144-member World Trade Organization (WTO). Although the WTO allows a *government* to challenge the do-mestic laws of another government, NAFTA allows a *corporation* to sue a foreign government directly in response to a law, a regulation, or even a court decision in that government's sovereign domain. Such challenges are considered by secret arbitration boards that do not allow any public participation.

Among NAFTA's three corporate rights, the most potentially explosive is the right of compensation for regulatory takings. In the negotiations that led up to that right, and in the lobbying to persuade the U.S. Con-gress to approve the agreement, the takings right was presented as a pro-tection against the sort of expropriation that took place in 1938 when Mexico nationalized its oil industry. Indeed, the language of NAFTA refers to any action that is "tantamount to" an "indirect expropriation."

But NAFTA's protections for corporations are actually much broader than would be necessary if the objective were merely to prevent a gov-ernment from seizing corporate property. Rather, the indirect expro-priation right contained in NAFTA appears identical to a right that property rights advocates in the United States have unsuccessfully sought to establish through a new interpretation of the Constitution's "takings" provisions. The campaign to expand the takings provision was pioneered in the 1970s by conservative American law professors such as Richard Epstein of the University of Chicago, and it has been backed by a powerful array of conservative funders including Richard Mellon Scaiffe and William Simon. The organizational face of the movement, known as the Takings Project, seeks to persuade legislators and judges to adopt the doctrine, and it regularly hosts federal judges at judicial edu-cation sessions held in posh retreats.

Takings advocates base their notions on the Fifth Amendment of the United States Constitution: "Nor shall private property be taken for public use without just compensation." Obviously, the key word here is *taken.* For example, when the government uses the power of eminent domain to seize a corridor of land to build a highway, the owners of that land are entitled to payment for the land. But what happens when a general tightening of environmental standards causes the owner of certain types of land to find his or her options for developing that land to be more circumscribed? Is the owner entitled to compensation for the diminishment of value?

The managements of many corporations, especially those in highly polluting industries, would, of course, like the answer to be yes. So far, however, the courts have declined to interpret most reductions in potential use of property as takings, for the practical reason that doing so would paralyze a vast array of regulations, especially those protecting the environment. The defining case is *Penn Central Transportation Co. v. City of New York* (1978), in which the Supreme Court established a balancing test that considered the economic impact of a regulation, the effect of the regulation on "distinct investment-backed expectations," and the nature of the government action. Under the test, most regulations do not fall into the category of takings unless they completely destroy the value of a piece of property.

In April 2002, the Supreme Court reaffirmed the basic principles of *Penn Central,* ruling in *Tahoe-Sierra Preservation Council, Inc. v. Tahoe Regional Planning Agency* that landowners were not entitled to any compensation due to a thirty-two-month moratorium on property development imposed to allow the preparation of a land use plan. Described by environmentalists as "the best news from the Court on takings in twenty years," the decision made it clear that the Supreme Court acknowledged the role of regulation and had no intention of creating a new property right that would make land use regulations and other sorts of environmental protections untenable.

But even as the *Penn Central* and *Tahoe-Sierra* decisions indicated that the Supreme Court was not willing to create a new right to compensation from regulatory takings for United States corporations and other property owners against their own government, NAFTA was making it possible for U.S. companies to assert exactly that right in Mexico, and for Mexican and Canadian companies to do the same in the United States. In 2001, pending claims in such suits totaled an estimated $13 billion.

THE POTENTIAL FOR corporations to use their new global rights to attack environmental regulations is illustrated by a case involving Metal-Clad Corporation, a waste disposal company based in the United States, that bought an abandoned toxic waste dump in the Mexican state of San Luis Potosi near the town of Guadalcazar. Although MetalClad had received a permit from the Mexican federal government, it began building a new facility on the site before receiving a permit from the local authorities. Following objections by local residents, the governor of the state ordered a geological study, which found that the facility was located on an alluvial stream and might contaminate the local water supply. Local police posted a stop work order on the site, and when MetalClad attempted to hold a grand opening for the dump, the community staged a protest. In response, MetalClad sought $90 million in compensation under the provisions of NAFTA, alleging that its national treatment rights had been violated and that the action of the Mexican government constituted a regulatory taking. In August 2000, a NAFTA tribunal awarded Metalclad $16.7 million, which was paid by the Mexican government.

In a similar case, which remains unresolved, Methanex Corporation, a Canadian producer of methanol used to manufacture the gasoline additive MTBE, sued the United States government under NAFTA for $970 million after California governor Gray Davis, with the backing of the California legislature, ordered the phasing out of the additive. Davis's action followed the discovery that MTBE, which smells like turpentine and creates a foul taste in drinking water, had turned up in Shasta Lake, in drinking wells in the Lake Tahoe basin, in thirty public water systems, and in thirty-five hundred groundwater sites. In addition, a study by the University of California had revealed MTBE to be carcinogenic in rats and mice. On its Web site Methanex stoutly defended its case against the United States, asserting that far from any adverse health effects "pure MTBE has been successfully and extensively used as a medicine to treat gallstones in humans."

Often the mere threat of a NAFTA lawsuit is sufficient to produce the desired effect. For example, in 2001 Canada issued new regulations prohibiting the use of descriptors such as "light" and "mild" on tobacco products. According to Canada's health minister, Allan Rock, such regulations were believed to mislead smokers into thinking that these products were less harmful. In its comments on the ban, Philip Morris objected to the position of Canada's health department, arguing that "light" and "mild" were appropriate terms to use on packaging. But Philip Morris didn't stop there. The company threatened that unless Canada backed down and removed the new regulations, it would sue Canada in a NAFTA arbitration proceeding. When issued by a well-heeled company such as Philip Morris, such threats, even if not carried out, can easily cause a nervous government agency to back down. How Canada will respond remains to be seen.

A CHEMICAL CALLED MBTE, a type of binding arbitration known as a NAFTA tribunal, and a treaty provision known as Article 1110—all these dauntingly obscure, esoteric, and technical particulars would seem to be an unlikely foundation on which to base an international mass movement. Nevertheless, by the mid-1990s, activists around the world had become aware of the corporate rights provisions of NAFTA and were determined to prevent such rights from being implemented on a global scale. Thus, when news of a proposed new agreement known as the Multilateral Agreement on Investments (MAI), which had been negotiated in secret for two years, was leaked to the public in 1997, citizen groups mobilized quickly to oppose the agreement.

The provisions of the proposed MAI were breathtaking in scope. Its protections for corporate investments were similar to those of NAFTA, only now they would apply on a global scale. Foreign corporations would be able to sue national governments directly in closed arbitration courts, demanding compensation for environmental or other laws that had the "effect of taking" corporate assets.

The secrecy of the MAI negotiations and the dramatic nature of its terms evoked protests around the world from hundreds of labor, environmental, human rights, consumer, development, and other groups. Over 565 organizations in over seventy countries sponsored a statement urging the suspension of the MAI negotiations. In a major victory for this far-flung opposition, the European Parliament voted 437 to 8 on March 9, 1998 in favor of a resolution opposing the agreement. A month later, the MAI was removed from the agenda of the Organization for Economic Cooperation and Development.

It was a stunning victory for the ad hoc coalition that had mobilized to stop the agreement, and an indication of the depth of opposition to the extension of corporate rights in the global arena. The international uprising against the MAI stands as the first example of the aggregate organizing power of worldwide civil society in the age of the Internet. Moreover, it marked the crossing of a threshold. Where past movements had focused on particular problems associated with multinational corporations, the new one focused on corporate power itself—specifically, the international institutions and trade agreements that leveraged corporate power while undermining democracy.

CHAPTER SEVENTEEN

Fighting Back

A movement emerges to challenge corporate hegemony

Each of us is laboring under the psychic weight
of powerful absurdities, children.
—Reverend Billy

NOBODY KNEW QUITE WHAT TO MAKE of the tall, smooth-faced man sporting a white dinner jacket and a hundred-watt smile. Clearly, the Reverend Billy Talen was an evangelist of some sort. He preached on sidewalks and street corners—anywhere he could gather a small crowd. But his message didn't quite match that of the other soapbox preachers on the streets. His denomination was neither Baptist nor Methodist, but rather the Church of Stop Shopping, whose physical location was wherever the Reverend Billy happened to be holding forth. His sermons had the twinkle of the inspired parodist, but his mission was not to mock Christianity. His heresy, instead, was to mock the true religion of the modern world—capitalism—and to desecrate its places of worship: the retail outlets of Disney and Starbucks. With passion and self-deprecating humor, Reverend Billy sermonized against sinful practices such as child labor, sweatshops, environmental pollution, and disregard for the dignity of workers. He admonished his followers to renounce their credit cards, their shopping carts, and all other such evil accoutrements. Yet, sipping a double low-fat latte with a hazelnut shot, he also admitted his frailty and weakness in the face of uncontrollable temptation. "We're all sinners! We're all shoppers!" he announced. "Hallelujah!"

According to a Starbucks internal memorandum dated April 24, 2000, "Reverend Billy sits quietly at a table with devotees and then begins to chat up the customers. He works the crowd with an affirming theme but gradually turns on Starbucks. Toward the end, he's shouting." The memo added: "According to a store manager, he may stand on your tables."

Raised in Michigan by conservative Dutch Calvinists, Talen discovered his calling as an anticorporate Jeremiah after moving to New York in the 1990s and watching Mayor Giuliani's heavy-handed "cleanup" of the city.

"Times Square used to be a place full of these great individual stories," he told one reporter. "But slowly, I noticed all those people—the shoe shiners, the hookers, the dealers, the street preachers—everyone who gave that place its own special life was being pushed out and replaced by these corporate identities."

In making his own personal rebellion against the corporate steamroller, Talen decided to join the ranks of the marginalized street preachers. Many of those walking past Reverend Billy may have interrupted their own reveries to wonder briefly whether the man was clinically crazy or just garden-variety perverse. After all, New York, along with the rest of the United States, was in the midst of the most astonishing new outburst of prosperity since World War II. Why didn't the man get a real job—take those verbal talents and that boundless energy to the nearest brokerage house, get himself a telephone headset and a Bloomberg screen, and start selling bonds?

THE REVEREND BILLY's style of activism may have been idiosyncratic, but the impulse was becoming widespread. Remarkably, despite the glow of the business triumphalism that dominated the 1990s, a quite different upsurge was also taking place. All over the United States, people were talking about corporate power in ways that did not necessarily fit conventional categories.

To some, it may have seemed an exceedingly inappropriate time to be critiquing the corporation, that rock of the capitalist system. After all, hadn't communism—the Russian version, that is—just announced its own demise? Wasn't this to be the occasion for celebrating the watershed that Frances Fukuyama called "the end of history," a time when the world settled on a single political-economic system featuring corporate capitalism and constitutional democracy? Wasn't it now just a matter of working out the details?

Despite the sheen of apparent prosperity and the dismissals of the pundits, a new movement was definitely on the rise, and its concerns were real. The grip of large corporations on American society had never been stronger, and it was manifested in various ways. Despite strong public support for environmental standards, the United States had rejected the Kyoto treaty regulating greenhouse gases, a result of corporate pressure on senators. Unlike every other industrialized country, the United States still lacked comprehensive health care for all its citizens, again because of corporate opposition. Statistics showed that 17 percent of the population lacked medical insurance, and life expectancy in the United States was equivalent to that of Cuba and lower than Costa Rica. Unions, traditionally the strongest counterbalance to runaway corporate power, had been systematically undermined. By 2000, union membership was down to 14 percent of the work- force, compared with 26 percent in 1953. The results of corporate political ascendance could be seen in the dramatic decline in the share of the federal tax burden paid by corporations, down from 33 percent in the 1940s to 15 percent at the end of the twentieth century. Statistics also showed that the gap between rich and poor in the United States was rapidly widening. Between 1979 and 1994, 97 percent of the gain in national income had been concentrated in the 20 percent at the top of the income pyramid. By 1998, the top 1 percent of the American population owned more of the country's wealth than the bottom 90 percent. If the wealth of the country were divided equally, every American household would have had $270,000 in net assets in 1998. Instead, because of the skewed distribution, median household assets were only $61,000.

Throughout the 1990s, it was clear that there weren't just a lot of Reverend Billys running amok in America—they were also starting to conspire together, openly, vigorously, with creativity and even humor. In August 1995, former *Texas Observer* editor Ronnie Dugger penned a blunt assessment of the state of American society in *The Nation* magazine. His article opened: "We are ruled by Big Business and Big Government as its paid hireling, and we know it." The article went on to recount the history of the populist movement of the 1880s and 1890s, drew parallels to the 1990s, and called for the revival of a political movement focused on reclaiming democracy from the corporate embrace.

Dugger's article touched a nerve. In its wake, seventeen hundred letters arrived at *The Nation's* offices, with most writers wanting to know how they could get actively involved in Dugger's idea of a populist revival. The result was a new organization—the Alliance for Democracy—just one of a myriad of seemingly independent sparks that ignited during the

1990s. These sparks touched on a broad spectrum of themes, not just political, all aimed at forcing the issue of corporate power onto the mainstream agenda.

No event showed the blossoming of the issue more dramatically than the demonstrations that rocked Seattle in November 1999. Outside the Seattle Convention Center, where representatives from scores of nations met to negotiate during meetings of the World Trade Organization, unionists marched alongside environmentalists, farmers from Saskatchewan joined with indigenous leaders from Venezuela, and giant puppets helped inspire the throng. People linked arms and resolutely blocked the entrances to the convention center as police crammed plastic-handcuffed arrestees into waiting buses. Predictably, the corporate media focused on the smashing of plate-glass windows by a small number of protesters, while deliberate police brutality against scrupulously nonviolent demonstrators went unreported. On the boardwalk fronting the pierside Seattle Public Market, patrons emerged from their dinners of oysters and beer to encounter the sound of concussion grenades and the acrid odor of tear gas, a smell that would soon be noticed in other cities as well: Quebec City, Washington, Los Angeles, Prague, Gottenburg, Genoa.

Yet Seattle was neither a beginning nor an end—it was more like a midterm report. For years, an activist upsurge had been gathering force, not just in the United States but around the world. Indeed, the notion that the worldwide movement against corporate power had begun in the United States was itself a case of American narcissism. Prior to Seattle, similar demonstrations had already taken place in numerous cities, including Jakarta, Vancouver, and Brasilia. The largest, in Hyderabad, India, a year before the Seattle demonstrations, had attracted hundreds of thousands of protesters.

In the United States itself, the movement had been gathering force throughout the 1990s, propelled particularly by the sweatshop issue. In her best-selling book *No Logo*, Canadian journalist Naomi Klein described how in 1995 and 1996, dubbed the Year of the Sweatshop by activists, "a kind of collective 'click' on the part of both the media and the public occurred on both sides of the Atlantic." Students were picketing Gap stores and boycotting Nike shoes in an effort to raise awareness about sweatshop manufacturing conditions. Again and again, labor groups and student groups stung large corporations such as Disney and

Nike with sweatshop revelations. Most infamous was the discovery that Kathy Lee Gifford's brand of clothing was being made in New York sweatshops and by children in Honduras.

Besides the sweatshop issue there were related concerns: the social impact on Third World societies of the structural adjustment programs mandated by the World Bank and the International Monetary Fund; the dangers of genetic engineering; the predatory trade practices of the new agricultural and pharmaceutical conglomerates; the impact of corporate media on children.

Corporations hired private detectives to spy on activists and law firms to drag them through the courts. Such efforts sometimes backfired. In Alaska, the Wackenhut Corporation, a private security firm, was hired by the Alyeska Pipeline Service Company to investigate oil broker Charles Hamel, a critic of the handling of the 1989 Exxon Valdez oil spill. Wackenhut set up a phony environmental organization, the Ecolit Group, hoping to gather information on oil company critics. It bugged hotel rooms, secretly videotaped meetings, and spied on activists. Eventually, the operation came to the attention of the U.S. House of Representatives' Committee on Interior and Insular Affairs, which found that Wackenhut had "engaged in a pattern of deceitful, grossly offensive and potentially, if not blatantly, illegal conduct to accomplish their objectives . . . [in] Alyeska's disastrous campaign to silence its critics."

In London, McDonald's Corporation hired two different spy agencies—without telling either about the other—to infiltrate a tiny group of environmental activists. (Not surprisingly, the spies spent much of their time writing reports on each other.) McDonald's then sued the group, but remarkably, two of its members succeeded in holding a squad of corporate lawyers at bay in the longest libel trial in English history. In the course of the trial, the plaintiffs called up expert after expert, defending the charges they had made about McDonald's environmental and labor practices. The British press followed the story closely, and the two activists, Helen Steel and Dave Morris, became international folk heroes.

The movement was notable for its subversive creativity. Artists "liberated" billboards, tweaking words and graphics to perform acts of media jujitsu, or more often, as noted by author Naomi Klein, to "x-ray" the ad, "uncovering not an opposite meaning but the deeper truth hidden beneath the layers of advertising euphemisms." Groups like Art and Revolution specialized in creating giant papier-mâché puppets that gave demonstrations a festive atmosphere. Magazines like *Adbusters* and groups like Project Censored, PR Watch, and Fairness and Accuracy in Reporting all sought to question the assumptions of mainstream media and advertising.

Economist PAUL KRUGMAN defined "Seattle Man" as a person "who is passionately committed to a simpler view, without any ambiguities. Seattle Man believes that globalization is purely and simply a way for capitalists to exploit the world's workers." Krugman had it right about the passion, but not about the "simpler view." In fact, one of the most productive aspects of the movement was the depth of its attention span, its capacity to engage with complex issues of systemic power that had not previously been able to gain entry into the public dialogue. For a movement even to raise such issues in a sustained manner was a significant accomplishment, as well as the foundation for a new type of democratic activism.

Some who had witnessed the trajectory of earlier movements pointed out that unless this impulse to address power on a deeper level was sustained and developed, efforts to solve such problems as sweatshops would eventually run out of steam. For example, by 1997, much of the movement against sweatshops was already becoming ensnarled in the question of how to respond to industry offers to create voluntary standards known as *codes of conduct*. Generally, such codes are accompanied by third-party auditing plans and others measures that seem to hold out the hope of enforceability. Yet experience has made activists skeptical of such measures, because they typically enable corporations to parlay a weak, unenforceable promise of better worker conditions into a "no sweat" label or certification. For that reason, corporate attorneys themselves have described codes as a way to "muzzle the offshore watchdog" groups.

The most high-profile code of conduct negotiations revolved around the Clinton administration's Apparel Industry Partnership, an initiative that included a number of corporations, unions, human rights groups, and religious groups. After months of negotiations, most of the labor and human rights groups balked at the terms of the code, and dropped out of the negotiations. In the end, both the worker standards of the agreement and the enforcement provisions proved disappointing. Worker standards included wages below the living wage and a sixty-hour work week. Meanwhile, the enforcement provisions required only 10 percent of a company's factories to be monitored each year, and allowed companies to choose their own monitors. Most disappointingly, workers were offered no guarantee of freedom to form unions and bargain collectively. Thus, the end product served to ratify the very conditions that had led to sweatshops in the first place—the powerlessness of nonunionized workers under the thumb of repressive governments like China, Indonesia, and Vietnam.

Debacles such as the Apparel Industry Partnership led many activists to advocate even harder for strategies that addressed the roots of corporate power. One was longtime environmental and labor activist Richard Grossman, who set out to engage others in an extended exploration of the simple question so often asked by progressives: Why do even the most vital citizen movements often fizzle out, while the power of corporations keeps increasing?

Grossman had been involved in the highly successful antinuclear movement of the 1970s. He had seen the movement grow and find its voice—from timidly arguing in the late 1960s for safer nuclear plants to assertively demanding "no nukes" ten years later. "But we blew it," he said, noting that decades after the peak of the antinuclear movement there had been very little progress in the development of solar and other alternative energy sources. The reason, Grossman believed, was that the movement had missed what should have been its main target: the way giant electric utility corporations are controlled.

Reflecting further on the failure to fundamentally change the electric utility companies, Grossman said, "The whole notion of what a public utility was created to be—to serve the people—is so far from our historical and cultural memory that the utility corporations like Pacific Gas & Electric are walking away not only with vast bundles of ratepayer cash, but with even more special privilege to govern over us."

GROSSMAN HAD BEEN DIGGING into American history. In 1993, he and Frank T. Adams revived the tradition of the political pamphlet with a recounting of the pre–Civil War history of the corporation in America. *Taking Care of Business: Citizenship and the Charter of Incorporation* revived the history of how states used the charter system to control corporations. Grossman, Adams, and others organized a research and education group known as the Program on Corporations, Law, and Democracy (POCLAD) that conducted further research and educational seminars on the early history of the corporation in the American republic.

POCLAD's message was as straightforward as it was radical. In America, the most basic principle of government is that the people are in charge. Dealing with the problem of corporate power is essentially a matter of getting people to wake up and assert their sovereignty. Grossman wrote:

> In 1628, King Charles I granted a charter to the Massachusetts Bay Company. In 1664, the King sent his commissioners to see whether this company had been complying with the terms of the charter. The governors of the company objected, declaring that this investigation infringed upon their rights. On behalf of the King, his commissioners responded:
>
> "The King did not grant away his sovereignty over you when he made you a corporation. When His Majesty gave you power to make wholesome laws, and to administer justice by them, he parted not with his right of judging whether justice was administered accordingly or not. When His Majesty gave you authority over such subjects as live within your jurisdiction, he made them not subjects, nor you their supreme authority."
>
> From childhood, this King had been led to act as a sovereign should. What about us?

The message was simple. The trick, of course, was making it real, given the myriad ways in which corporations had developed and buttressed their power through a century of court decisions, legislative measures, and political organizing. After researching various state constitutions, Grossman concluded that one fulcrum for challenging a corporation was its state-issued charter. And so the organization began seeking to revive an avenue of recourse, charter revocation, that had often been used in the nineteenth century to discipline errant corporations.

In 1998, POCLAD launched its first experiment at making a corporation's charter into a target of action. Together with dozens of environmental and human rights organizations, POCLAD's lawyers filed a book-length complaint with California's attorney general, Dan Lungren, documenting the case against the oil giant Unocal Corporation,

a company with a history of collaborating with some of the most oppressive governments in existence, and with a long track record as a
corporate scofflaw.

In the United States, Unocal had repeatedly been convicted of violating environmental and worker safety standards, yet it continued to break
the rules. The company had pled guilty to deceiving both the courts and
its shareholders. In Burma, the company had taken advantage of the oppressive conditions created by a ruthless military dictatorship and used
forced labor to build its pipeline there. In Afghanistan, the company had
entered into a partnership with the Taliban regime, despite that government's oppressive treatment of women and homosexuals. The POCLAD
complaint asked the state of California to formally address Unocal's pattern of unlawful behavior by revoking its charter of incorporation.

As described in chapter 5, charter revocation was not uncommon in
nineteenth-century America. It remains a legal option in every state,
and it is quite common for smaller corporations to be suspended by
state authorities for failure to comply with basic regulatory requirements. For example, in fiscal year 2001–02, the state of California suspended the charters of fifty-eight thousand corporations for failure to
pay taxes or file proper statements. Once suspended, a California corporation may no longer do business or have access to the courts. It is effectively terminated.

In the late 1990s Florida revoked the charters of a number of corporations involved in stock fraud schemes that cost investors $81 million. In
1998, New York's attorney general, Dennis Vacco, announced action to
revoke the charter of the Council for Tobacco Research. According to
Vacco, CTR violated its official mission of providing "truthful information about the effects of smoking" and instead "fed the public a pack of
lies in an underhanded effort to promote smoking and to addict America's kids." In response to Vacco's petition, a state court appointed a re-
ceiver for CTR, and the organization agreed to donate its assets to two
cancer research institutes.

Despite such examples, to Attorney General Lungren the demand
that Unocal's charter be revoked must have seemed like a message from
outer space. The idea of terminating the charter of a large corporation
with billions in annual revenues, thereby forcing it to dissolve as a legal
entity, with its assets sold to new owners, was simply unthinkable. And
so Lungren dismissed the petition out of hand. Nevertheless, as a law

enforcement official, Lungren should have recognized that statutes can only be enforced when sanctions provide a credible deterrent. And in the case of corporate offenders such as Unocal, ordinary sanctions no longer appear sufficient. Particularly in the areas of labor law, pollution control, and government contracting, some corporations regard complying with the law to be more expensive than breaking it. Moreover, in contrast to human ex-convicts, who in some states are barred from voting, even a pattern of repeated legal violations does not disqualify corporations from actively lobbying Congress to repeal the very same statutes. Consider the case of the False Claims Act, which punishes corporations that defraud the government. In 1994 the group lobbying to weaken the law included twenty corporate violators, among which a total of ninety-three settled fraud cases were documented.

Despite its failure to spur Lungren to action against Unocal, POCLAD judged the experiment a success. Slowly but surely, the unthinkable was beginning to become thinkable—the first step toward becoming real. The complaint against Unocal had helped reawaken the notion that a corporate charter is not a natural right. It is granted by the citizenry of a state, and by the same token, the citizenry may revoke it.

IF POCLAD'S PROJECT of reviving the dormant practice of charter revocation seems quixotic, consider the attempt to invoke the Alien Tort Claims Act (ATCA) in human rights cases. ATCA was one of the first statutes to be enacted after the ratification of the Constitution in 1789. This dusty law, which had lain in hibernation for *two centuries*, had been written originally for suing pirates and protecting diplomats. Nevertheless, in 1979, lawyers for a Paraguayan couple successfully invoked ATCA as the basis for a suit against a Paraguayan police officer accused of murdering the couple's son.

ATCA applies to violations "against the law of nations"—that is, laws committed outside the context of the United States legal system. With its revival, a mechanism now exists for addressing horrific crimes whose victims would otherwise have never found justice. ATCA has led to a number of suits against corporations. In 1996, the International Labor Rights Fund assisted Burmese villagers in filing a suit against Unocal, charging that the company had used forced labor in building a pipeline there. Other suits have targeted Shell (for alleged human rights abuses in

Nigeria), Texaco (for allegedly dumping toxic waste in Ecuador), Coca-Cola (for allegedly using paramilitary forces to suppress union activity in Colombia), Del Monte (for allegedly hiring thugs to torture union leaders in Guatemala), DynCorp (for allegedly spraying Ecuadorian villagers with toxic chemicals), and the Drummond Company (for allegedly hiring gunmen to assassinate union leaders in Colombia).

HUMAN RIGHTS ABUSES are not just an overseas phenomenon. It must be kept in mind that slavery lasted from 1621 to 1865 in the United States, and when it was over African Americans were left with no personal, family, or institutional assets with which to build new lives. On January 16, 1865, General William Tecumsah Sherman issued Special Field Order No. 15, granting land south of Charleston for settlement by freed slaves, who were to receive forty acres and a mule. In March of the same year, Congress passed a law allowing "every male citizen, refugee or freedman . . . not more than forty acres of land." But by April of that year, with President Lincoln dead, President Andrew Johnson had vetoed the bill.

But the promise was not forgotten. Tired of waiting for the day when Congress might pass some sort of legislation providing reparations, one activist turned to corporate America. On March 26, 2002, New York researcher Deadria Farmer-Paellmann filed a class-action lawsuit on behalf of herself and other descendents of slaves against corporations that had built their assets by means of slave labor. Farmer-Paellman was inspired by the success of similar suits against Volkswagen, Siemens, Deutsche Bank, and DaimlerChrysler for Nazi-era slave labor. Those cases had compensated victims directly, but in the case of the Farmer-Paellmann lawsuit, any settlement would be directed to a humanitarian trust fund.

Initially, Farmer-Paellmann's suit cited FleetBoston Financial Corporation (for financing slaving ships), Aetna Inc. (for insuring slaves), and CSX (for using slave labor to build railroads). Later, she added more companies as further documentation of slavery-related activities emerged, including JP MorganChase, Lehman Brothers Holdings, Brown Brothers Harriman, American International Group, Lloyd's of London, Loews Corporation, Union Pacific, Norfolk Southern, WestPoint Stevens, R. J. Reynolds Tobacco Holdings, Brown and Williamson Tobacco, and Liggett Group.

Aetna Corporation offered an apology. "We express our deep regret over any participation at all in this deplorable practice," spokesman Fred Laberge told Reuters, adding, "We are actively engaged in determining what actions might be taken." Later, the company issued a brief statement: "We have concluded that, beyond our apology, no further actions are required."

Farmer-Paellmann responded, "The profits Aetna gained from the crime against humanity that was chattel slavery helped it to become a multibillion-dollar corporation today. That's unjust enrichment."

THE FARMER-PAELLMANN LAWSUIT is a reminder of the Supreme Court's own misguided decisions in the nineteenth century: declaring people to be property, giving property the rights of people. Over a century later, the harms from both mistakes continue to reverberate. In an article in the *Hastings Law Journal,* legal scholar Carl J. Mayer proposed a succinct constitutional amendment stating clearly that the rights contained in the Constitution are reserved for human beings, not corporate entities. Mayer suggested the following language:

> This Amendment enshrines the sanctity of the individual and establishes the presumption that individuals are entitled to a greater measure of constitutional protection than corporations.
>
> For purposes of the foregoing amendments, corporations are not considered "persons," nor are they entitled to the same Bill of Rights protections as individuals. Such protections may only be conferred by state legislatures or in popular referenda.

The prospects for such an amendment remain distant. Nevertheless, various groups have given the idea their support, including the Green Party; the Alliance for Democracy; the Community Environmental Legal Defense Fund; Public Citizen; the Program on Corporations, Law, and Democracy; and the Women's International League for Peace and Freedom. Author and activist Thom Hartmann has taken the proposal even further, suggesting that "corporations aren't persons" amendments should be passed at all three levels of government: local, state, and federal.

Hartmann writes, "I'm not so naïve as to think this is something that will happen quickly.... It may be in my children's or their children's lifetime that humans finally take back their governments and their planet from corporations, and it may even be generations beyond that." On the other hand, Hartmann refuses to rule out that the amendment could serve as a near-term catalyst: "Sometimes the Constitution is amended quickly in response to an overall public uprising, as happened with the amendment to end Prohibition and the amendment to lower the voting age to eighteen."

Like Hartmann, other "personhood" campaigners have not been dissuaded by the seemingly remote prospects of a constitutional amendment. They reason that even if the amendment is not adopted, the activity of promoting it is sufficiently valuable in its own right as a means of educating the public on a topic that for a century has languished in obscurity.

It should be noted that the reversal of the rights acquired by corporations as a result of Supreme Court decisions does not depend on the enactment of a constitutional amendment; it is fully in the power of the Court. On many occasions, the Supreme Court has reversed its own well-established doctrines and precedents. For example, *Plessy v. Ferguson* (1896), which legitimized the Jim Crow system of segregation, was demolished by the Court's 1954 decision in *Brown v. Board of Education.* Similarly, *Butler v. Thompson* (1951) and *Breedlove v. Suttles* (1937), which upheld poll taxes, were overridden by *Harper v. Virginia Board of Elections* (1966). And the social Darwinist doctrine established in *Chicago, Milwaukee* (1890) and epitomized by the *Lochner* decision of 1905 was effectively overturned by the decision in *West Coast Hotel Company v. Parrish* (1937). Even very old decisions have been reversed: *Erie Railroad Co. v. Tompkins* overruled *Swift v. Tyson,* a decision ninety-five years old; *Graves v. New York* overruled *Collector v. Day,* a decision sixty-eight years old; and *United States v. South Eastern Underwriter's Association* overruled in part *Paul v. Virginia,* a decision seventy-five years old.

In all these cases, no constitutional amendment was necessary. Instead, the heat that softened the wax of established Court doctrine, allowing it to be reshaped, was an underlying shift in public opinion, amplified by a mobilized grassroots movement. This experience suggests that activists should simply look for ways to contest corporate rights wherever the opportunity presents itself, especially at the grassroots level.

Along such lines, promising steps have already been taken by some local governments. In one case, the tiny city of Port Arena, California, became the first municipality in the United States to pass a resolution advocating the rejection of corporate personhood rights. In another, Porter Township, Pennsylvania, passed a "Corporate Personhood Elimination and Democracy Protection Ordinance," declaring that corporations operating in the township may not exercise constitutional rights to override township decisions.

The Porter Township ordinance came about as a result of a fight between nearby Rush Township and Synagro Corporation, a large sludge-hauling company. In the 1990s, a teenage boy had died from a massive infection after riding his all-terrain vehicle in a field that had been spread with sludge by Synagro. In response, township supervisors in Rush Township, where the death had occurred, adopted Pennsylvania's first sewage-sludge testing ordinance. Synagro then sued Rush Township for violating its constitutional rights. In addition, Synagro attempted to intimidate the Rush Township supervisors by suing each personally for $1 million.

In forming its own response to the sewage sludge issue, Porter Township considered the option of working through Pennsylvania's Environmental Hearing Board (EHB), but the officials of the township concluded that the EHB was too beholden to corporate interests. Rather than providing an effective means to protect citizens from environmental hazards, the EHB procedures served to bog activists down in endless hearings and comment periods. Moreover, the final outcome of the process generally favored the polluters rather than the communities seeking protection. As a step toward regaining control over local environmental decisions, the attorney advising Porter Township, Thomas Linzey of the Community Environmental Legal Defense Fund, proposed the "personhood elimination" ordinance in conjunction with a set of township ordinances for testing sludge.

Speaking to a local meeting of about one hundred people in the Limestone Fire Hall, Linzey noted that formally denying corporate rights moved the focus to basic concepts of power: "If corporations can veto local decisions, we can't get to democracy.... That's what this is about— who is in charge." After Porter Township enacted its ordinance, Linzey reported that his phone was "ringing off the hook" with calls from other local governments around the United States.

Wʜᴀᴛ ᴍᴏsᴛ ᴅɪsᴛɪɴɢᴜɪsʜᴇs the tactics of the new populists is an aversion to conventional solutions that regulate corporations without addressing the underlying structures of power. Richard Grossman writes, "Too many organizing campaigns accept the corporation's rules, and wrangle on corporate turf. We lobby Congress for limited laws. We have no faith in regulatory agencies, but turn to them for relief. We plead with corporations to be socially responsible, then show them how to increase profits by being a bit less harmful. How much more strength, time, and hope will we invest in such dead ends?"

The skepticism of Grossman and others was well founded. Far too often, agencies created to limit corporate harms have morphed over time into enablers of the same harms. And far too often, "corporate responsibility" ends up as "greenwashing"—measures whose main purpose is to provide a public relations cover for continued abuses.

Some activists averred, agreeing that while most conventional approaches to regulating corporations generally do nothing to address the underlying problem of power, it was nevertheless possible to discern strategies that do exactly that. Sociologists Dan Clawson and Alan Neustadtl spent over fifteen years studying the means by which corporations influence political decisions, especially through political action committees. For the most part, Clawson and Neustadtl agreed with skeptics of regulatory approaches, concluding that because "money can be used in a million different ways" most types of campaign finance regulation can't achieve their goal of limiting corporate influence: "Campaign finance could be thought of as similar to a balloon. . . . Regulators . . . can push the balloon down in one place—but that makes it pop out farther somewhere else. . . . The regulatory model of campaign finance reform is doomed to failure."

But if placing limits on particular channels of corporate money won't work, what will? Clawson and Neustadtl want to reframe the question. Rather than "How can we stop corporate money?" they propose asking instead "How can we fund elections without corporate money?" The two advocate a system of public campaign finance known as "clean money reform," which has been passed by citizen initiatives in Maine, Vermont, and Arizona. Under such a system, private financing of elections is not banned, but candidates who wish to eschew private fund-raising can receive public monies as a replacement.

The public finance approach uses conventional channels of government, and it can hardly be seen as a direct challenge to corporate power.

Nevertheless, such measures do undermine that power because they provide candidates a way to oppose corporate interests without committing political suicide. Thus, public financing provides a noncorporate safe haven within the corporate-dominated political process, and that haven in turn can provide the starting point for further action. Clawson and Neustadtl describe the approach as a "nonreformist reform," a phrase coined by social theorist André Gorz to describe reform measures that strengthen rather than co-opt the democratic energies of citizens movements, and that create leverage for further change.

The beauty of such a strategy is its pragmatism. Ideally, citizens would simply invoke their sovereignty over the political process, excluding corporations from politics by democratic fiat, as was once done in various states. But if corporations block the enactment of such direct measures, or if courts overturn them, then pursuing subtler initiatives like "clean money reform" offers a guerrilla strategy, a set of tactics that allow a weaker force to defeat a stronger one. Note that in this case the "weaker force" just happens to be the sentiment of an overwhelming majority of the population who, according to the *Business Week* poll cited in chapter 1, think that corporations have "too much power."

WHAT ABOUT OTHER guerrilla strategies, where corporate power can be incrementally tamed by means of smart, well-focused initiatives? One recent proposal involves exploiting the power of information. In 2003, a coalition consisting of labor and citizen groups such as Amnesty International, the AFL-CIO, Global Exchange, Oxfam America, and the Sierra Club proposed a new set of International Right to Know standards. Under these standards, corporations would be required to release information on the environmental impacts of their actions, on safety standards including worker exposure to chemicals, on labor practices such as child employment, on agreements with local security forces, and on human rights practices such as forcible relocations carried out to accommodate U.S. business interests.

The International Right to Know standards aim to build on the success of the Emergency Planning and Community Right to Know Act, a 1986 statute that requires companies to disclose information on toxic chemicals, enabling a public database known as the Toxic Release Inventory, which has drawn praise from environmental groups. According to

EPA data, industries reduced toxic releases by almost 50 percent in the first decade of the inventory.

The International Right to Know effort also builds on the successful experience of the Foreign Corrupt Practices Act (FCPA). Passed in 1977, that act has led to only sixteen prosecutions for bribery in the first eighteen years of its existence. Nevertheless, it is credited with drastically reducing the use of foreign bribes by American corporations. What appears to have made the FCPA work is the reporting provisions, which require companies to keep better records of expenses.

On the surface, the principle of transparency would hardly seem a threat to corporate power. But the right to know is a basic enabling right, a first step toward mobilization of communities to deal with toxic releases and other corporate impacts. Al Capone, it should be recalled, was brought down not on a murder rap but on charges that he failed to accurately report his federal income.

WHICH APPROACH IS BETTER: to highlight the issue of corporate sovereignty by direct provocation or to develop stealthier tactics that seek to undermine corporate power without deliberately confronting it? In an era of corporate political ascendancy, common sense would point to pursuing a greenhouse strategy—plant many seeds and see what sprouts. Common sense would also suggest looking for lessons in past struggles.

One of the most promising aspects of the movement has been its efforts to encourage a wider understanding of America's own heritage of anticorporate struggle. Such approaches to American history turn the conventional story upside down—rather than focusing on the great men who wrote the rules, they describe the rise, again and again across the sweep of American history, of popular movements that dared to make "impossible" demands—from abolition of slavery to gay liberation.

As those exploring a populist agenda have delved into history, they have begun to ask what happened to earlier movements such as the agrarian populists, the pre–World War I socialists, and radical unions like the Industrial Workers of the World (IWW), the "Wobblies."

The Populist Party, the political arm of the National Farmers Alliance, was founded in Texas in 1878. At its height, the party reached into forty-three states and territories, had four million members, and controlled five state legislatures. On its heels came the Socialist Party, which gained the support of millions of Americans in the first two decades of the twentieth century. In 1912, there were over twelve hundred socialist officeholders at the local, state, and federal level. American socialism was rooted both in urban and rural areas, with a diverse character that blended European notions with homegrown American ones.

The Populists envisioned a pluralistic economy, including local cooperatives, and governmental ownership of some large businesses, including railroads. The Socialists advocated state ownership of most capital-intensive business. In contrast to the Socialists and the Populists, the Progressive movement, whose most prominent leader was Theodore Roosevelt, advocated leaving corporations untouched but cushioning their impact on society through such means as antitrust statutes and social legislation.

By 1920, both populism and socialism had been eliminated as mainstream options in American politics, and with the demise of those movements the scope of mainstream political discussion on the corporation narrowed dramatically.

Why did these popular movements collapse? The question was particularly relevant to the activists of the 1990s as they grappled with the fact that neither major party in the United States showed the slightest appetite for challenging corporate political dominance. Significantly, America lacked the socialist parties and labor parties that provided a political base for opposing corporate positions in Europe. Why had politics in the United States evolved so differently?

Some historians ascribe the difference to an "American exceptionalism" rooted in this country's celebration of individualism. Yet even if such an element in the national character might explain a cultural aversion to statist socialism, it would explain the demise of the Populists and the anarchist Wobblies. Other historians emphasize the ethnic and racial diversity of the American workforce, which supposedly makes unifying the labor movement a daunting project. Still others cite the absence of a class system based in feudalism, which has allowed Americans to place their bets on upward mobility rather than on class warfare.

Progressive historians seeking to explain the decline of political movements that might have provided a more sustained challenge to corporate power have also found evidence for a more straightforward explanation: simple repression. Repeatedly, but especially during the crucial period from the 1870s to the 1930s when the modern corporate-oriented system defined itself, such movements were shattered through combinations of illegal violence and the aggressive application of hostile legal doctrines.

For the most part, antiunion measures were carried out by company security forces and the local police. Federal labor injunctions also played a big role. And from time to time, during periodic "scares" such as the anarchist scare of 1901–03, the wartime repression of 1917-18, and the great Red scare of 1919–20, federal law enforcement agencies added their muscle to the dirty work. On a single night in January 1920, federal agents under the direction of Attorney General A. Mitchell Palmer rounded up some five thousand to ten thousand people in radical hangouts such as poolrooms and meeting halls. Although targeted at aliens, the dragnet caught thousands of American citizens. In addition to the arrests, thousands of people were beaten and over five hundred deported during the nationwide hysteria.

The Palmer raids are a well-known chapter in American history, as are other events prior to the Great Depression such as the Ludlow Massacre (twenty-one people killed), the Homestead Strike (thirteen killed), the Lattimer Massacre (nineteen killed), the Great Steel Strike (twenty killed), and the 1877 Railroad Strike (ninety killed). The conventional telling of American history depicts those events as battles in an honorable war, in which Labor gamely battled Capital until Capital grudgingly agreed to give Labor a seat at the negotiating table.

But a more complete reading of labor history tells a different story, one of divergent fates. One wing of the labor movement, represented by Samuel Gompers and the American Federation of Labor, defines itself more narrowly and conservatively, and consequently risks far less repression. It survives. The other wing of the movement, represented by such organizations as the Knights of Labor and the IWW, seeks to fundamentally confront the basic tenets of corporate power. This branch is suppressed, not in epic battles but through a countless series of small, ugly incidents: organizers harassed, imprisoned on specious charges; police joining cause with company goon squads; Wobblies forced to run the gauntlet between vigilantes armed with clubs, forced to stand all night in jail cells up to their knees in freezing water; agricultural workers beaten and shot; organizers excluded by injunction from entire mining districts.

Until the 1930s, it was considered subversive merely to be involved in the radical wing of the labor movement, as reflected in the sentencing statement of one judge: "I find you, Joyce, to the president of the union, and you, Malony, to be secretary, and therefore I sentence you to one year's imprisonment." According to labor historians Philip Taft and Philip Ross, a "grossly underestimated" count of casualties in labor unrest from 1873 to 1937 is seven hundred killed and thousands seriously injured, mostly in little-known incidents. Surveying that period, historian Robert Goldstein concluded that "American labor suffered governmental repression that was probably as severe or more severe than that suffered by any labor movement in any other Western industrialized democracy."

LIKE THE HISTORY of the labor movement, the history of how the media evolved in the United States shows how the "mainstream" was defined in narrow terms favorable to corporate interests. One example is the formation of federal radio policy in the 1920s and 1930s. At a time when Canada and the countries of Western Europe were moving to organize strong public media institutions such as the CBC and the BBC, comparable efforts in the United States were defeated.

Corporate ownership of the media has become considerably more concentrated in the past two decades. The first edition of Ben Bagdikian's *The Media Monopoly,* published in 1983, described how fifty media conglomerates dominated the mass media in the United States. By the sixth edition of the book, published in 2000, mergers had shrunk the set of dominant conglomerates to a mere six. A study of sector-by-sector concentration showed the following: in film production, six firms accounted for over 90 percent of revenues in 1997; in theater ownership, twelve companies controlled 61 percent of screens in 1998; in the newspaper industry, 25 percent of revenues were now created in metropolitan "clusters" where a major urban daily controlled a constellation of suburban and regional papers; in book publishing, seven firms dominated; in cable television, three firms owned all or part of 56 percent of channels; in music, five corporate groups accounted for over 87 percent of the U.S. market; in cable television, seven firms controlled over 75 percent of channels and programming; and in book retailing, 80 percent of books were sold by national chains. In radio, a single corporation, Clear Channel Communications, owned more than twelve hundred local radio stations in 2002. Its nearest competitors, CBS and ABC, owned only one-fifth as many stations.

Led by organizations such as Fairness & Accuracy in Reporting and the Institute for Public Accuracy, media activists have organized grassroots efforts focused on blocking new Federal Communications Commission moves toward further relaxing rules that prevent media consolidation, such as a single company owning both newspapers and television stations in the same community. Activists exposed the "inside-the-Beltway" tactics of the media conglomerates, revealing, for example, that FCC employees, members of Congress, and senior staffers had been taken on over seventeen hundred all-expenses-paid trips between 1995 and 2000.

In addition to focusing on national FCC policy issues, local media activists have battled corporate advertising in schools and cafeterias, and have worked to support noncorporate alternatives such as the Pacifica radio network. Hundreds of community groups have sought to establish low-power FM radio stations, designed literally to "fly through the cracks" in the radio spectrum.

The increased concentration of media ownership is an issue with direct connections to the issue of corporate power. With a half-dozen immense corporations dominating media, and with "noncommercial" media such as National Public Radio increasingly dependent on corporate funding, opportunities for discussion about systemic issues of power have become increasingly rare. In this context, delving into such topics basically becomes a reason "not to get invited back on the show"—as though a sort of Emily Post of political manners had said, "It's not polite to talk about corporate power in a public forum, just as we don't argue about religion at a family reunion."

At times such taboos have been breached, a famous example being the statement Dwight D. Eisenhower issued on his last day in office, January 17, 1961. In his "Farewell Radio and Television Address to the American People," Eisenhower warned that "acquisition of unwarranted influence, whether sought or unsought, by the military-industrial complex" posed "the potential for the disastrous rise of misplaced power." He concluded: "We must never let the weight of this combination endanger our liberties or democratic processes. We should take nothing for granted."

But even Eisenhower's dramatic statement seemed to confirm the existence of the taboo rather than refute it. If not, why did Eisenhower wait to talk about the problem of a military-industrial complex until just three days before he left office? Why no mention of it during seven previous State of the Union addresses? Why no specific names of companies exerting inappropriate influence? And why no specific proposals for dealing with the problem? Both the timing and the vagueness of the warning speak volumes about the unspoken "house rules" of American politics. Eisenhower had strayed close to an off-limits area, and he knew it.

PREACHING A SERMON on top of a table at Starbucks, picketing a Gap store, participating in a charter-revocation campaign, suing a multinational for human rights violations, joining the campaigns of media reform activists—the diversity of actions gives the new populist movement a haphazard look. But the movement should not be underestimated. The emergence of a sustained attempt to openly address corporate dominance in American society is a significant achievement. Its politics reflect our country's founding values. Its greatest asset is our culture's deeply ingrained antiauthoritarian streak, which is as much a part of the American heritage as the fragments of broken tea chests scattered at the bottom of Boston Harbor.

CHAPTER EIGHTEEN

Intelligent, Amoral, Evolving

The hazards of persistent dynamic entities

Freed, as such bodies are, from the sure bounds to the schemes of individuals—the grave—they are able to add field to field, and power to power, until they become entirely too strong for that society which is made up of those whose plans are limited by a single life. —Supreme Court of Georgia, Railroad Co. v. Collins, 1929

E ARLY MORNING AT THE Dallas/Fort Worth Airport. As I step out to the taxi curb, I feel a coolness in the air that I suspect will not stick around once that big Texas sun reports for duty. I have arrived on a red-eye flight, and as I take a taxi into the city I imagine the inhabitants waking up and drinking their breakfast coffee. I've never been to Dallas before (*"The place where Kennedy got shot"* keeps sneaking into my thoughts), but the driver of my cab, a man full of stories and warm southern exuberance, quickly puts me at ease. Turning off his meter, he takes me the long way to my hotel, pointing out the local sights.

Far less welcoming is the darkened hall of grandiose proportions where I eventually find myself, in the midst of a hushed, submissive audience. In front is a podium raised to an unnatural height, where Lee Raymond, chairman and CEO of ExxonMobil Corporation, announces the company's recent triumphs and outlines its strategy going forward. Above the stage is the glowing logo of the corporation, and next to the logo, in a touch of exquisite irony, a glistening blue image of Planet Earth hangs in midair as though floating through space.

It is a piece of choreography disguised as a democratic proceeding: the annual meeting of a Fortune 500 corporation. To the right of Raymond sits a group of seven men and three women. Their role appears to be the opposite of that of the chorus in a Greek play: to be seen, but not to make a sound. They are the nominees for the board of directors, each hand-picked by management. Everything is preordained, except that there seems to be a small fly in the ointment. A party pooper.

In the aisle to my left a well-dressed woman approaches a freestanding microphone. This is the portion of the meeting during which stockholders are allowed to present statements for or against resolutions that have been proposed for a vote. The woman's voice is soft but firm, "Mr. Chairman, on behalf of the members of the Sisters of St. Dominic and the Capuchin Order of the Roman Catholic Church, I wish to argue in support of Resolution 8 tying the compensation of management to certain indices of environmental and social performance by the company—"

For a heartbeat, the lock-step march of the meeting seems in jeopardy.

"Whatever you have to say," cuts in the chairman, "the matter has already been decided in the negative by proxies received prior to this meeting. You have one minute forty seconds."

"Mr. Chairman, you have the power to restrict this debate, but your authority is not legitimate. I represent twenty thousand nuns and clergy who have an ownership stake in this company. Their pensions depend on its financial results, but at the same time they wish to see financial performance balanced against other factors including the urgent need to protect the environment and to safeguard human rights."

"You have fifty-five seconds remaining."

Speaker after speaker approaches the microphones to make statements on behalf of a variety of resolutions to reform the company. One asks for a policy forbidding discrimination against gays and lesbians. Another proposes that ExxonMobil alter its stance on global warming. Yet another opposes drilling in the Arctic National Wildlife Refuge.

The most startling of the proposals requests that ExxonMobil end its involvement in the Indonesian province of Aceh, where the company maintains a close relationship with military forces that have been ruthlessly suppressing a local separatist movement. According to a lawsuit filed in federal court by the International Labor Rights Fund, ExxonMobil provided buildings used by the Indonesian military to torture local activists, and its bulldozers dug the mass graves used to bury the victims. There will be no real debate on any of these matters. The atmosphere is oppressive, even intimidating. Security guards stand ready to forcibly eject from the hall any speaker who deliberately exceeds the meager time limits.

Of course, if this were a small family business, no one would expect nuns, environmentalists, and human rights activists to have any say over its dealings, nor would the public be interested. But according to the glossy materials in my hand, ExxonMobil represents the reunification of two of the thirty-four strands of John D. Rockefeller's Standard Oil empire: Standard Oil of New York (renamed Mobil in 1966) and Standard Oil of New Jersey (renamed Exxon in 1972). Its total revenues now exceed $200 billion annually. This is not a business, it is a world power. Its operations affect not only its tens of thousands of employees and millions of customers, but large areas of the planet. On a strictly dollar-for-dollar basis, the revenues of ExxonMobil exceed the governmental budgets of all but seven of the world's nations.

The man at the podium commands a private domain. That he conducts himself like a dictator is no accident. In fact, his power actually exceeds that of most dictators. Around the world, they are more likely to hurry to answer his phone calls than he would be to answer theirs.

As I watch this larger-than-life executive assert his power, I reflect on the notion that the corporation is a nobody—an entity divorced from human values or designs. That notion would seem to be belied by the very real somebody who is running this meeting, this human being named Lee Raymond, whose political views clearly drive this corporation and its policies. Thanks to Mr. Raymond, ExxonMobil has set itself apart. For example, on global warming, most of the other oil giants have taken a different stance. They have announced that they agree with the science that has forecast global warming and that they endorse the Kyoto Protocols on global warming. Competitors like British Petroleum (the largest maker of photovoltaic cells) and Royal Dutch/Shell (one of the biggest developers of wind farms) are racing to anticipate and ride the trend toward renewable sources of energy. Similarly, not every company opposes gay rights, as ExxonMobil does. Numerous corporations, seeking to retain talented staff, provide health benefits to domestic partners.

These policy differences among oil companies would seem to belie the notion of corporations as mindless, impersonal entities. Clearly, policy is in the hands of human beings, each free to adopt a wide scope in their tactics and strategies. Still, I would argue that this freedom is constrained. Let's imagine, for a moment, that the night before the meeting Lee Raymond had been visited by a series of Dickensian ghosts, who had rattled their chains and urged him for the sake of his grandchildren's lives and his own eternal soul to sacrifice a hefty share of ExxonMobil's profits in order to take the company on a radically divergent path toward social justice and environmental protection. At the annual meeting, Raymond—a young grandchild in each arm—had announced his intention of moving the company in the new direction, making a passionate speech about human rights and the fate of the planet.

What would have happened next? It is predictable enough. Either (a) Raymond's board of directors would have fired him posthaste, or (b) both Raymond and the board would soon have been staring down the barrel of a class-action shareholder lawsuit charging them with violating their legally mandated fiduciary responsibility toward the owners of the company.

In fact, that's exactly what happened to none other than Henry Ford, who wanted to plough his company's retained earnings into building more factories, in order to "employ still more men, to spread the benefits of this industrial system to the greatest possible number, to help them build up their lives and their homes." Unfortunately for Ford, his shareholders took him to court, demanding that the company's retained earnings be distributed as dividends. Even though Henry Ford had pioneered the assembly line, the Michigan Supreme Court ruled bluntly in 1919 in *Dodge v. Ford Motor Co.* that he could not devote the company he had created to his personal goal of creating as many factory jobs as possible, if doing so would reduce the profits of the company. Profits, said the court, were the only goal that Ford was allowed to pursue:

> A business corporation is organized and carried on primarily for the profit of the stockholders. The powers of the directors are to be employed for that end. The discretion of directors is to be exercised in the choice of means to attain that end, and does not extend to a change in the end itself, to reduction of profits, or to the nondistribution of profits among stockholders in order to devote them to other purposes.

Since Ford defended his plan of reinvestment in terms of social goals rather than in terms of maximizing shareholder returns, he lost the case.

Americans have always been fascinated by the personalities of business tycoons. But if we really want to understand what it would take to put corporations on a more socially healthy course, we have to look past the personalities and opinions of the human beings who manage these institutions. In truth, the power yielded by Lee Raymond has little to do with the man himself. CEOs will come and go, while ExxonMobil, this immense, morphing, shapeless entity, lives on. It is the company's power, not Raymond's intellect or force of will, that causes presidents and dictators to pick up the phone.

The purpose of this book has been to reveal the roots of that power. Corporate power may seem impregnable, a vast, looming shape. But when we pan in closer with our historical lens, tracing how the institution known as the corporation was constructed piece by piece, the looming shape comes into focus as a specific legal contraption, a thing made of nuts, bolts, wheels, belts, and wiring. The better we can diagram this device, the more easily we can change it.

At one time, the institution known as the state seemed similarly impregnable. Prior to the late eighteenth century, virtually all cultures were organized as monolithic top-down power structures enforced by monopolies of overt violence and by ideologies such as "divine right of kings" that taught subservience and compliance. One way of thinking about the American Revolution is to see it as a reengineering of the state. Like a computer programmer debugging a piece of software, the framers of the American system rolled up their sleeves, tweaked this and that, and came up with a new design.

One can see this practical bent in *The Federalist Papers,* where Alexander Hamilton writes about society like a mechanic considering different bolts and screws:

> The science of politics, like most other sciences, has received great improvement. The efficacy of various principles is now well understood, which were either not known at all, or imperfectly known to the ancients. The regular distribution of power into distinct departments; the introduction of legislative balances and checks; the institution of courts composed of judges, holding their offices during good behavior; the representation of the people in the legislature, by deputies of their own election; these are either wholly new discoveries, or have made their principal progress towards perfection in modern times. They are means, and powerful means, by which the excellencies of republican government may be retained, and its imperfections lessened or avoided.

Social change, according to this vision of things, isn't just a matter of asserting values. It's also a matter of innovating and implementing specific ways for realizing those values, mechanisms like democratic selection of leaders, separation of powers, human rights, and judicial review.

For example, the concept of human rights can be seen as a safety feature—an organizational airbag that helps prevent large, powerful institutions from crushing vulnerable human beings. To make any such design feature work, it must be accompanied by legal systems to interpret it and police power to enforce it.

As new design ideas for the state were implemented in America and elsewhere, it became apparent that some worked better than others. For example, compare the American experience with that of the French in crafting a working system of human rights. Although France's Declaration of the Rights of Man and the Citizen is more extensive than America's Bill of Rights, the two countries diverged in mechanisms for enforcement. In France, enforcement was placed in the hands of the National Assembly and its representatives on the Committee for Public Safety. In America, Chief Justice Marshall's assertion of Supreme Court authority in *Marbury v. Madison* (1803) established judicial review in a separate branch of government. In France, the human rights system quickly broke down; in the United States it worked, however imperfectly. International human rights expert Geoffrey Robertson attributes the difference to the fact that *Marbury v. Madison* "provided human rights in the U.S. with a set of teeth, by endorsing courts rather than legislatures as their enforcement mechanism."

Just as it was necessary to innovate and implement specific new features in order to democratize and constrain state power, the same applies to corporate power. A short list of changes might include the following: (1) revoking the doctrine of corporate constitutional rights; (2) curbing corporate quasi-rights as appropriate—for example, requiring corporations to renew their charters every five years; (3) banning corporations from political activity; (4) shoring up the boundaries of "noncorporate" spaces in society—for example, prohibiting advertising aimed at children; (5) expanding the scope of worker and customer rights vis-à-vis corporations; (6) strengthening countervailing institutions, especially unions; and (7) promoting noncorporate institutions like public schools and economic forms like municipal utilities, family farms, consumer cooperatives, and employee-run enterprises.

OF COURSE, THE NOTION that we might simply decide on some design changes and then implement them, as though corporate power were a malfunctioning carburetor that needed some new seals and valves, is disingenuous. Unlike car parts, corporations are not passive objects. They're run by smart, resourceful people, who can be expected to defend their power. When you fix the carburetor on your car, the carburetor does not start thinking about how to undo the fix. This makes the problem of corporate power different from more routine problems. As the history of the late nineteenth century shows, corporations are veritable Houdinis in their capacity to slip out of legally imposed strictures. Corporate power is like a germ that develops a resistance to the newest antibiotic, like the mouse that learns to steal the cheese from the trap, like the recidivist who gets out of prison and then commits another crime. Corporations have a well-earned reputation for capturing regulatory agencies, undoing legal restrictions, and otherwise meddling in their own future.

It is the iterative, self-amplifying quality of corporate power that makes static metaphors inadequate. The corporation's ability to influence the shaping of its own legal framework—like a computer program capable of rewriting its own code—calls for a richer conception, one that captures the corporation's restless, dynamic qualities. The best strategy, perhaps, is to assume the role of naturalist and pretend we are looking at a new form of life, a previously unknown organism. We need to study it with fresh eyes. We might take as our model the discoverer of the microbe, Dutch dry-goods merchant, janitor, and amateur lens grinder Antoni van Leeuwenhoek. In 1672 van Leeuwenhoek sent a memo to the Royal Society of England, the main scientific body of the time, titled "A Specimen of some Observations made by a Microscope contrived by Mr. Leeuwenhoek, concerning Mould upon the Skin, Flesh, etc.; the Sting of a Bee, etc." In that document, van Leeuwenhoek reported his conclusion that many of the common substances we assume to be simple, uniform fluids or materials are actually vast, cavorting, tumbling herds of tiny "animalcules."

Outright derision and dismissal greeted the receipt of van Leeuwenhoek's letters by the Royal Society. If van Leeuwenhoek's outrageous notion was correct, then vast portions of the world previously labeled "scum" or "film" or "rot" would have to be reassigned into an entirely different ontological district—moved by a Dutchman's optical contraption from the static realms of the "dead" to the heavens of the "quick." It took years for the Royal Society to accept these findings. But the discovery of life at a very small scale proved to be a breakthrough of incalculable value, enabling phenomena that had previously been mysterious to become comprehensible, and opening the door to such advances as inoculation and antibiotics.

If we look at the corporation like a naturalist studying a new life form, we see that it has an evolutionary history, a characteristic structure, a set of behaviors. The genius of the corporation is the simplicity, flexibility, and modularity of its design. It scales to any size, serves virtually any function, adapts to any culture, and is robust—capable, at least in principle, of functioning indefinitely. It is programmed to survive, to maintain its structure and functional integrity, to grow, to avoid danger and recover from damage, to adapt, and to respond to the outside world.

There is nothing malicious or even conscious about the tendency of the corporation to seek power. The process is slow and incremental; the world is bent in tiny steps. But over time, such small acts result in the wholesale transformation of society.

Does that sound far-fetched? If so, consider the changes that propelled the conversion of the corporation from its legally restrained status prior to the Civil War to a liberated and empowered one at the end of the nineteenth century. Next, trace the trend of empowerment through the twentieth century, to nation-sized, politically aggressive corporations such as ExxonMobil. Finally, extrapolate the trend another century or two, as corporations continue to tinker with and alter the constraining web of laws that define their power, as they seek to overcome problems, eliminate threats, or achieve goals.

The notion of creating a technology so dynamic and lifelike that it becomes dangerous to ourselves has been a theme in the modern mind since 1818, when Mary Shelly's novel *Frankenstein* transposed the medieval legend of the golem—the creature composed of clay and animated by kabalistic incantations and procedures—to the industrial age. In general, such tales paint visions of horror and tragedy. The horror has to do with powerful life forces escaping the normalizing checks of nature. The tragedy has to do with the notion that in humans the talent for creating such trouble exceeds the capacity to prevent or manage it.

Because it is so adaptable, the corporation seems on an inexorable course toward permeating every aspect of life, not just the traditional economic spheres but increasingly such public spheres as schools and prisons, and such personal spheres as preparing meals and entertaining children. In many ways the corporation is coming to know us better than we know it. It involves itself with us intimately. It participates in our birthing, our education, even our sexuality; it tracks our personal habits, entertains us, imprisons us; it helps us fight off dread diseases, manufactures the food products that we eat, barters and trades with us in a common economic system, jostles us in the political arena, talks to us in a human voice, sues us if we threaten it.

In recent years, scientists have speculated about the potential of various existing or future technologies to veer out of human control. Nuclear power, genetic engineering, artificial intelligence, and the microscale engineering known as nanotechnology have all been the subject of such concerns, however theoretical. Writing in *Wired* magazine, computer scientist Bill Joy warned about the trajectory of research on nanotechnology, describing a nightmare scenario in which an artificially created micro-organism, lacking any natural predators but capable of reproducing itself and metabolizing any sort of living substance, spreads out of control through the biosphere, reducing everything in its path to "grey goo."

It is time for those who worry about runaway technologies to include the corporation among the objects of their concern. In this case, the invention is not a new one or a futuristic one. The experiment is taking place all around us. The laboratory is the world. The scientists are Tom Scott, Stephen Field, Lewis Powell, and many other legislators, businessmen, and jurists of yesterday and today. The chromosome of the creature is the legal system, the Constitution, the framework of global agreements. Innovations like the holding company, the SUN-PAC decision, and NAFTA are brilliant gene splicings.

So WHERE IS THE GREY GOO? I just looked out my window, and I saw the sky, some trees, a rooftop. If our world is being chewed up by a swarm of organizational locusts, the process must be rather slow and quiet. Of course, that's exactly the point that the environmental movement has been making now for decades, and their concerns about global warming, species extinction, and general environmental degradation are based on fact, not speculation. The sky may not literally be falling, but it's filling up with greenhouse gases, and the rest of the biosphere is under continual assault. Again and again, when people organize to find political solutions to such problems, the chief obstacle blocking their way is the opposing political muscle of corporations like ExxonMobil.

There are two benefits to seeing the corporation as a technology, and a dynamic one at that. First, this recognition quickly reorganizes the question of whether corporations deserve rights. Rather than what *rights* corporations deserve, the question is reversed: What sort of *restraints* will prevent runaway corporate power? The basic approach is suggested by Isaac Asimov's "Three Laws of Robotics":

1. A robot may not injure a human being, or, through inaction, allow a human being to come to harm.

2. A robot must obey the orders given it by human beings except where such orders would conflict with the First Law.

3. A robot must protect its own existence as long as protection does not conflict with the First or Second Laws.

Obviously, a democratic society can't control corporate power by means of three simple rules. Nevertheless, Asimov's point is exactly right: either we control our creations, or they control us. There is no middle ground. Giving corporations constitutional rights does the exact opposite of what is needed. Rather than being prevented on constitutional grounds from implementing laws such as campaign finance reform, legislators need a free hand in creating a legal framework that can hold corporate power in check.

The second benefit to seeing the corporation as a dynamic technology—as a quasi-living thing—is that it allows us to place corporations into a familiar category of problem. Humans have a long and deep experience with the shaping and softening process known as "domestication," in which the useful qualities of a species are fostered while the dangerous ones are pruned away. The work of domesticating the corporation can't be accomplished with a single piece of legislation, and it's not even realistic to think it can happen in a single generation. It will involve a great deal of legislation, including constitutional change. It will involve the evolution of a clearer vision that *rights* are a human privilege, not an institutional one. It will involve the end of the notion that powerful organizations ought to enjoy indefinite terms of existence.

It will require broadening the notion of human rights to incorporate the various forms of interaction between humans and corporations—as consumers, as workers, or in other contexts. It will require clear boundaries and firewalls that maintain politics as a "humans-only" space. It will require similarly clear definitions of other humans-only spaces: the family, education, and so on. Finally, and most importantly, it will require a deep change in attitude, an embedded skepticism. The corporation is a powerful tool, and that makes it a dangerous one. After we domesticate and democratize it—assuming we manage to do so—we'll still have to warn our kids: "Watch out. Keep an eye on this thing. And don't ever forget: it can bite."

CHAPTER NINETEEN

So What's the Alternative?

The vision of economic democracy

*Somehow we have persuaded ourselves that the capitalist economy must
be fueled only by greed. This has become a self-fulfilling prophecy. Only
the profit maximizers get to play in the marketplace and try their luck.
People who are not motivated by profit-making stay away from it [and]
condemn it.* —Muhammad Yunus

U P TO THIS POINT, the method of this book has been forensic: sifting
through evidence, tracing steps. Peering back as far as the thirteenth
century, we've reconstructed the origins and evolution of a powerful entity, the modern corporation. In particular, we've looked at how courts
and legislatures have forged the body of legal privilege that reinforces
corporate power in the United States.

Now I want to squint in the opposite direction, into the future. Is it
inevitable that large, privileged corporations will continue to tighten their
hold over both our economy and our political system? Can we imagine
a different future?

There are several possibilities, the first of which is simply a continuation of the trend toward concentration of corporate power and polar-
ization of wealth. Eventually, such a trend can be expected to run into
serious trouble. Ironically, the more the corporation succeeds in routing
its erstwhile opponents—from unions to environmentalists to antitrust
enforcers—the more it corrodes the civic foundations and resource base
that enable its own success. After all, a functional economy is a rule-based
system, like a basketball game. If the economy winds up under the control of a small number of extremely large corporate players, the ordinary
processes of government become increasingly incapable of refereeing the
action, and the game turns into a melee.

We can see this kind of breakdown in the history of post-Soviet Russia, where raw power and endemic corruption have replaced more orderly processes. Typically, such economies veer toward authoritarianism as a political strongman assumes the role of top bully. But as Germany and Italy in the 1930s, Brazil and Chile in the 1970s, and Argentina in the 2000s all illustrate, concentrating political power does not cure problems; instead, it produces still greater bureaucratic rigidity, social stress, environmental degradation, ideological repression, and economic dysfunction.

Authoritarianism may arrive precipitously; it may also be the result of a more gradual process, where democracy dies a "death of a thousand cuts." After studying a cross section of seven societies during fascist episodes, social scientist Laurence Britt published a list of common symptoms: (1) nationalism, (2) disdain for human rights, (3) use of enemies or scapegoats as a unifying cause, (4) militarism, (5) rampant sexism, (6) controlled mass media, (7) obsession with national security, (8) close ties between ruling elites and predominant religion, (9) protection of corporate power, (10) suppression of organized labor, (11) disdain for intellectuals and the arts, (12) obsession with crime and punishment, (13) cronyism and corruption, (14) fraudulent elections. By such indicators, it is hard to avoid the diagnosis that America is already running at least a low-grade fever.

More hopeful would be a scenario in which the pendulum swings toward a softer variant of corporate capitalism. Under this course, the corporation as we know it does not radically change, but society gets better at pushing back against its influence and excesses. Environmental regulation becomes stricter. Wealth taxes blunt the worst extremes of wealth and poverty. Antitrust regulations break up the largest corporate empires. Restrictions on corporate political activity revitalize democratic institutions. We might also call this second scenario *Euro capitalism,* since it basically extends the model that is currently unfolding under the European Union. For such a scenario to unfold in the United States, an essential requirement would be the ending of corporate constitutional rights that currently stand in the way of legislation such as campaign finance reform.

A third possibility might be called the eclectic economy. In this scenario, the corporation does not disappear but its influence is moderated by the emergence of a range of economic forms, each addressing one or more of the excesses or deficiencies of the modern corporation. Such institutions potentially include worker-owned or locally owned companies, municipal and other public enterprises, consumer cooperatives, networking arrangements among small companies, and "social enterprises" that redefine the bottom line. Like the small, unremarkable mammals of the Jurassic era, many of these institutional players already exist, scampering unnoticed among the legs of the institutional titans. But as new conditions confer unexpected advantages on alternative models, or as today's dominant institution stumbles and society looks for solutions, these diverse forms will provide off-the-shelf models for a more equitable and democratic economic system. The end result is likely to be a medley of institutions, including some typically thought of as classically capitalist or socialist, but also others that belong to a third category sometimes referred to as *economic democracy*. Envisioning this eclectic future requires a less ideological mindset than one normally encounters in such discussions, a new recognition that an economy is a toolbox, not a religion. Its emergence would certainly mark the end of the stale left/right dichotomy that has long constricted American discourse.

As we look at the myriad ways in which corporate capitalism may evolve and diversify, it is interesting to consider that it was little more than a decade ago that various pundits were declaring any discussion of economic alternatives to be irrelevant. As the Soviet Union collapsed and Western European countries like England and Germany privatized many of their state-owned companies, British Prime Minister Margaret Thatcher coined the expression TINA, meaning "there is no alternative" to the model of corporate capitalism. Ironically, as Thatcher and, more recently, Tony Blair, were proclaiming the triumph of a single system, that system itself was diverging into two distinct species. Even after most European nations shed the bulk of their social democratic heritage, they did not morph into clones of American capitalism. Instead, a new model emerged under the aegis of the European Union.

Like the United States, the EU organizes itself around large corporate enterprises, and for that reason many observers see no fundamental difference. Yet the EU appears to have partially sidestepped the problem of corporate dominance in politics and culture that has plagued the United

States. That is not to say that the problem of corporate power is non-existent in Europe. On the contrary, organizations such as Corporate Europe Observatory have amply documented the tremendous influence on EU policy of corporate think tanks and lobbying groups such as the European Roundtable of Industrialists, the Centre for the New Europe, New Defence Agenda, European Seeds Association, and Transatlantic Policy Network.

Yet, despite the growth of corporate influence in Europe, especially in the upper echelons of the EU bureaucracy, there remains something different about European capitalism. After examining indicators of social health such as public health, crime, income equality, environmental protection, mass transit, and amount of time available for family life, observers such as journalists T. R. Reid and Jeremy Rifkin have concluded that Europe is attending better to the *people* side of the economic equation than is the United States. A corporate-based system prevails, but somehow the edges have been significantly softened.

Does the European model of capitalism merely amount to a thicker layer of jam on the same toast? I would argue that more is going on than that, most interestingly in the area of rights. In the United States, fundamental human rights have actually retreated in recent decades while corporate rights have advanced. In Europe, the balance tilts decisively in favor of human rights. The European Social Charter, for example, articulates a number of fundamental rights in the areas of collective bargaining, protection from unjustified dismissal, protection of maternity, right to health care, protection against gender discrimination, and environmental protection.

Unlike the situation in the United States, the regulation of corporate activities in the EU has not been stymied by the judicial doctrine of corporate rights. A telling example is the EU's strict regulation of children's advertising. Under EU law, such advertising is regulated by the Television Without Frontiers Directive, which establishes a set of minimum criteria such as prohibiting advertising aimed at exploiting the inexperience or credulity of children, or showing children in dangerous situations. With that directive as a baseline, eleven out of the fifteen EU countries go even further. Greece bans toy advertisements from 7 A.M. to 10 P.M. The United Kingdom forbids ads that "exhort children to purchase or ask their parents to make enquiries or purchase." Sweden simply prohibits any advertising aimed at children under twelve.

As for campaigning and political advertising, European standards also diverge from those in the United States. For example, most EU countries provide free time on the public airways to political parties, thereby making parties less dependent on corporate money to get their message to the public. All EU countries provide public financing in national legislative elections. In contrast, the United States provides neither free airway time nor public funding in legislative elections. As described in chapter 13, U.S. legislation that aims to reform campaign financing is frequently struck down on First Amendment grounds.

Are there any indications that America might follow Europe's lead in curbing corporate political privilege and creating expressly noncorporate spaces? With polls indicating a strong desire among the public to shore up individuals, families, and communities against corporate interference, the possibility arises for confrontations such as the recent judicial skirmishing over the Do Not Call registry, a legislative initiative enacted in 2003 that allowed persons to block telemarketing companies from calling them at home.

As shown by the vote count—412 to 8 in the House of Representatives and 95 to 0 in the Senate—the Do Not Call registry was a tremendously popular measure. But predictably, after the legislation was signed by President Bush the telemarketing industry used corporate free speech arguments to secure an immediate injunction from a sympathetic federal judge, Edward Nottingham. When the case was heard at the Tenth Circuit Court of Appeals, however, Nottingham's decision was overruled.

The victory of the Do Not Call registry represents at least a half-step toward weakening corporate privileges and softening American capitalism. It suggests an arena favorable to a populist politics: issues in which corporate privilege is framed in direct collision with popular protections, especially those with appeal across the traditional ideological spectrum such as family leave, protection of children, and personal privacy.

PERHAPS THE GREATEST value in the EU example is that it shows how, even without challenging the fundamentals of the corporate model, societies can select a more people-friendly variant from among the available "capitalisms." But why stop there? Why exclude the possibility of experimenting more deeply with the corporate form? The dimensions of such innovation are virtually limitless, and all of them offer the advantage that social entrepreneurs can set about constructing the outlines of an alternative future without waiting for the American political system to abandon its chronic corporate bias.

Take ownership structure, a natural starting point from which flows many possibilities. In the traditional corporation, ownership takes the form of joint stock, either traded on public exchanges (public corporations) or held by a smaller number of investors (private corporations). But there are other ways of setting up ownership.

Green Bay, Wisconsin, is one NFL city where fans need never worry about seeing their championship football team, the Packers, move away. Why? Because the bylaws of the Packers permanently place both the bulk of ownership and full control of the team in the hands of its fans. Community ownership came to the Packers four years after the team's 1919 founding, when a financing crisis forced the team to sell shares to local boosters. Currently, 112,000 shareholders own the Packers, and over half of these owners reside in Wisconsin. Shares cannot be resold, except back to the team, and no single shareholder can own more than 5 percent of outstanding shares.

Although the Packers are the only fan-owned NFL team (league rules now mandate that a single person own at least 50 percent of each team), there are a number of community-owned teams in the minor leagues: Indianapolis, Indiana; Rochester, New York; Columbus, Ohio; Toledo, Ohio; Harrisburg, Pennsylvania; Scranton, Pennsylvania; and Visalia, California.

Meanwhile, the notion of community ownership has extended into the realm of retail enterprises. When a regional chain of department stores called Stage went out of business in the 1990s, local residents in half a dozen Wyoming and Montana towns stepped in to run their own stores, raising capital by selling shares to members of the local community. The stores have succeeded, in some cases despite competition from a nearby Wal-Mart. Residents cite numerous benefits to local ownership, especially in fostering a sense of community.

According to economist Thomas Michael Power, about 60 percent of economic activity is local. Economist Paul Krugman writes: "Although we talk a lot these days about globalization . . . a steadily rising share of the workforce produces services that are sold only within the same metropolitan area." The local ownership model produces a wealth of benefits, including eliminating the *exit power*—that is, the threat of locating elsewhere—that corporations so frequently deploy to win subsidies and concessions on wages, working standards, and environmental protections.

A second institutional innovation is the worker-owned company, a category that has been growing rapidly since new federal legislation established tax benefits for employee stock ownership plans (ESOPs) in 1974. As of 2003, there were eleven thousand ESOPs in the United States, with combined assets of more than $400 billion. Indeed, the number of workers involved in ESOPs (8.8 million) now exceeds the number of workers in private-sector unions (8.4 million).

The existence of an ESOP does not imply that a firm is worker-controlled. One reason is that many ESOP programs issue nonvoting stock. The other is that the worker-owned pool of stock takes time to accumulate. Still, between 1980 and 2000 the portion of ESOPs in which worker-owned shares represented a majority grew from 38 percent to 68 percent.

One of the largest and most innovative ESOPs is W. L. Gore, the $1.4 billion manufacturer of Gore-Tex fabric. At Gore, over six thousand worker-owners in forty-five locations have achieved impressive success (including listing on *Fortune*'s "Best Companies to Work For" list) despite the fact that there are no permanent bosses. Instead, the company uses a decentralized team-based approach, with teams that organize themselves around particular projects. Another success story is Weston Solutions, the nation's second largest environmental services company with over eighteen hundred employees.

A much older cousin to the ESOP, the cooperative enterprise, has existed on the landscape of American business since 1752, when Benjamin Franklin founded the Philadelphia Contributionship for the Insurance of Houses from Loss by Fire. Cooperatives may be owned by workers, customers, or networks of small producers. The Philadelphia Contributionship remains in business, along with tens of thousands of other such businesses serving over a hundred million people. Today there are over eleven thousand credit unions and five thousand food cooperatives in the United States. Hundreds of telephone and electric cooperatives supply power to some thirty million rural customers. Over a million families belong to housing cooperatives, and half a million children attend cooperative nursery school and child care programs. Cooperatives also play a significant role in health care via nonprofit HMOs.

The most notable difference between corporations and cooperatives is that cooperatives operate on the basis of one member, one vote, rather than one share, one vote. In a society where the wealthiest 1 percent of the population owns almost as many corporate shares as the other 99 percent, that difference is hardly inconsequential. Cooperatives, in a nutshell, are run by the same democratic principle as the government itself: representative democracy. And why not? As philosopher David Schweickart notes, "It is a striking anomaly of modern capitalist societies that ordinary people are deemed competent enough to select their political leaders—but not their bosses."

But can democracy really work at the scale of the multi-billion-dollar enterprise? Perhaps the most interesting proof of concept comes from the Mondragon complex of cooperatives located in the Basque region of Spain. In 1943, Don Jose Maria Arizmendiarrieta, a priest in the town of Mondragon, founded a technical school for boys. In 1956, five of his former students along with eighteen other workers established a cooperative factory to manufacture stoves. In 1958, Father Arizmendiarrieta instigated the founding of a machine tools cooperative; in 1959, a cooperative bank. Over the following decades the Mondragon complex grew to encompass more than a hundred enterprises, including Spain's largest manufacturer of refrigerators and Spain's third-largest supermarket chain. In 2004 its total revenues were $6.6 billion, its assets $13 billion, its workforce fifty-three thousand. Each cooperative is run by a board of directors elected by the membership. That board in turn selects delegates to MCC, the cooperative bank that serves as the overall financial hub for the entire Mondragon complex.

If Mondragon shows that alternative businesses can be competitive with the largest corporations, the Grameen family of businesses shows how alternative enterprises can innovate and operate successfully in areas that traditional corporations have previously shunned. Muhammad Yunus, the founder of Grameen, has become renowned as the exemplar of a new breed of businesspeople known as social entrepreneurs—innovators seeking to address unmet social needs by developing new business concepts. While teaching economics at Chittagong University in Bangladesh, Yunus noticed the lack of affordable sources of small-scale finance for poor people, and he began experimenting with lending small sums to women seeking to expand their income-earning potential. Over time, Yunus's ideas have resulted in a multi-million-dollar bank, still serving the original purpose of providing grassroots finance needs to the poor. Grameen Bank is self-sustaining, fueling its own growth through retained earnings. And it has produced a breadth of successful spin-offs: Grameen Cybernet (an Internet service provider), Grameen Fisheries Foundation (an aquaculture enterprise), Grameen Health (a health insurance program), GrameenPhone (a cell phone services provider), Grameen Securities Management Company (providing financial services for other Grameen enterprises), Grameen Shakti (an energy producer), Grameen Shamogree (a finished goods exporter), Grameen Telecom (a bulk telecommunications purchaser), and Grameen Uddog (a fabric dealer). In 1989, Grameen began assisting social entrepreneurs in other countries to establish similar ventures, and by 2003 sixty-five replication projects were running in twenty-seven countries.

Organizationally, Grameen enterprises display a medley of business models, a reflection of Muhammad Yunus's pragmatic style. Grameen Bank is owned 75 percent by its borrowers and 25 percent by the Bangladeshi government. GrameenPhone is a for-profit corporation. Grameen Telecom is a nonprofit corporation.

While nontraditional business models have shown striking adaptability in addressing a variety of economic needs and niches, there remains a place for another alternative: the public enterprise. Although it has long been an article of faith in American culture that public ownership is synonymous with inefficiency, bureaucracy, bad service, and shabby quality, the facts do not necessarily support the stereotype. Take the example of SMUD, the Sacramento Municipal Utility District, a gas and electricity supplier to some 550,000 thousand residential and commercial customers in central California.

SMUD came into being in 1923 after an epic fight between the editorial pens of the *Sacramento Bee* and the giant Pacific Gas & Electric utility. The same year, a similar fight occurred in the city of Fresno. Persuaded of the benefits of public power, the voters in Sacramento approved the formation of a municipal power district while the voters in Fresno voted to stick with PG&E.

Seventy years later, electricity bills in Sacramento were about 45 percent lower than comparable bills in Fresno and other cities served by PG&E—$61 per month for a typical residential customer served by SMUD versus $106 per month for a typical residential customer buying from PG&E. In addition, SMUD had dismantled its nuclear power plant and developed a number of green energy programs, including tree planting to reduce air conditioning loads, low-interest conservation retrofitting, and solar panel financing. As the Enron scandal and other swindles soaked other California ratepayers to the tune of billions in excess charges, SMUD's innovations allowed its customers to duck the crisis.

Why was SMUD able to achieve superior results? Credit goes to SMUD's locally elected board of directors, who have relentlessly pushed the company to stay on the cutting edge of green power while eschewing executive excess. For example, in 2003 the compensation of PG&E's CEO was $34 million; that of SMUD's general manager was $283,000.

As ALTERNATIVES TO investor-owned corporations become more numerous and sophisticated, social entrepreneurs are broadening their thinking to imagine entirely new business models. Muhammad Yunus has proposed the no-loss corporation, a new business structure designed for the needs of social entrepreneurs. Like a nonprofit, the raison d'être of a no-loss company would be to advance one or more social objectives. However, in contrast to a nonprofit, a *no-loss* corporation could seek equity financing from socially minded investors willing to accept a somewhat reduced rate of return. Yunus envisions a new financial infrastructure to assist the needs of such investment avenues: "separate rating agencies, financial institutions, mutual funds, venture capital, and so on."

Slowly, some of the infrastructure that might ultimately serve the vision outlined by Yunus is taking shape. Systematic ratings of social and environmental performance are now being produced by several firms, including Innovest Strategic Value Advisors, CoreRatings, and KLD Research & Analytics. Some financial services firms, including Aviva, ISIS Asset Management, and Henderson Global Investors now have in-house "green teams" that make research into social and environmental records part of the process of qualifying their investments. Various capital funds, including Investors' Circle, Commons Capital, and Community Development Venture Capital Alliance, target their investments toward social and environmental goals. To press their agendas for greater disclosure of relevant data, social investors have formed a variety of coalitions, including the Carbon Disclosure Project, the Extractive Industries Transparency Initiative, and the Investor Network on Climate Risk.

The development of an infrastructure aimed at supporting alternative enterprises illustrates a noteworthy principle: no sort of economic process takes place in the context of the individual firm. Historically, as documented by sociologists like William Roy, the modern corporation evolved in concert with an elaborate support structure of financial markets, legal and accounting services, trade organizations, and so on. Likewise, one of the most interesting aspects of both the Mondragon and the Grameen experiments is the constellation of supportive institutions that has arisen in each case. Mondragon, for example, includes banks, research centers, retail stores, and schools, all servicing its network of businesses. The network provides not only technical support and start-up capital but also mechanisms for assisting individual enterprises during recessions and reorganizations.

Today, in the United States, the movement to create economic alternatives includes networks of entrepreneurs such as BALLE (Business Alliance for Local Living Economies) and the American Independent Business Alliance (AMIBA), regional marketing events known as green festivals, advocacy organizations such as Co-op America, supportive funders such as the Roberts Foundation, and organizations such as Investors' Circle that match investors with entrepreneurs.

DESPITE THE GROWTH of the alternative business movement, it is not easy to see how under normal conditions that movement would come to threaten the dominance of the investor-owned corporation. But normal conditions do not persist indefinitely in capitalist economies. In fact, one of the signature features of such systems is a tendency toward periodic collapses in equities markets and parallel business depressions. Such singular events expand the range of political possibilities, producing new opportunities either for progressive change (the New Deal, for example) or reactionary change (the fascist movements that swept Europe in the 1930s).

In his seminal book *After Capitalism*, philosopher David Schweickart sketches out a hypothetical transition from an economy centered around investor-owned corporations to one where a significant share of large enterprises are worker-owned. Under Schweickart's scenario, a widespread collapse in equity values could prompt the federal government to step into the market in order to buy out ruined investors. But rather than maintain ownership of the companies it had bought out, the government would proceed to transfer them to employee ownership. Meanwhile, federal legislation would establish a network of new financial institutions to support such companies, funded by an economy-wide capital assets tax.

Schweickart's scenario offers two provocative notions: first, that the large investor-owned corporation can be replaced; second, that the exit strategy can be smooth and orderly. No assets are seized, no one is put in front of a firing squad, and the end result is not state ownership of the economy. Rather, what takes place is a drastic broadening of ownership and a parallel expansion of democratic processes into the economic realm.

Of course, the great majority of businesses would be completely unaffected by the transition because they are either family-owned enterprises or investor-owned companies outside the public equities markets. The resulting economy, therefore, would be a mixture of institutional forms.

Even in the absence of a major restructuring of ownership such as that sketched out by Schweickart, the rise of a vigorous alternative business segment in the larger corporate economy has great significance. Assuming that this segment organizes and mobilizes itself politically, it will ensure that the voices representing Big Business can no longer pose as representatives of business as a whole, thereby changing the terms of debate on a range of economic, social, and environmental issues. For comparison's sake, consider the political clout enjoyed by America's family farmers, even though they now represent only 2 percent of the workforce. Thanks to their commitment to their way of life and their tenacity in organizing to protect it, family farm organizations have won dramatic victories, including a complete ban on corporate farming in nine states (Iowa, Kansas, Minnesota, Missouri, Nebraska, North Dakota, Oklahoma, South Dakota, and Wisconsin). Their existence makes it impossible for corporate agriculture to claim a general mandate for policies that fly against the interests of family farmers.

Even more important than the direct political clout of alternative businesses is their ability to serve as a laboratory for a range of principles and innovative approaches. For example, one of thorniest problems arising from the current legal framework of the corporation is the narrow definition of the bottom line. As laid out by Ralph Estes in his book *The Tyranny of the Bottom Line: Why Corporations Make Good People Do Bad Things,* the goal of profit maximization forces corporations to off-load their negative impacts wherever possible—pollution being the most notorious example—onto society at large. In contrast, alternative businesses are less prone to that sort of sociopathological behavior, since their owners (whether that be their workers or the members of the local community) are more likely to be the same people affected by the pollution or other negative side effects generated by the business.

I began this book with a quote that I intended as a comment on the power of the few: "Nothing is illegal if one hundred businessmen decide to do it." But when put in the context of alternative business models, the same quote becomes an optimistic statement. After all, in a business enterprise where ownership is broadened to include the entire workforce or the entire local community, then everyone really is a businessperson, with all the implications of autonomy, initiative, power, and privilege inherent in the word. Alternatively, we can see this as a natural expansion of the meaning of citizenship. In that case, to be a citizen does not merely mean access to the ballot box and the right to speak freely about matters considered politics; it also means enjoying full prerogatives in the sphere that each of us occupies most closely, understands most intimately, and engages most fully: our everyday job.

SUPREME COURT
DECISIONS

TRUSTEES OF DARTMOUTH COLLEGE V. WOODWARD (1819)
New Hampshire had enacted legislation converting Dartmouth College from a private college into a public one. The trustees appealed the action, and the Supreme Court ruled in their favor. According to the decision of the Court, the charter that the trustees of Dartmouth had received from King George in 1769 qualified as a contract entitled to protection under the contracts clause of the Constitution (Article 1, Section 10), which prohibits states from "impairing the obligations of contracts." This decision, Justice Story later wrote, was intended to protect the rights of property owners against "the passions of the popular doctrines of the day." Its effect was to begin the process by which corporations gradually carved out a legal zone of immunity from state legislatures. Subsequently, legislatures found an easy way to get around the problem. They added a new clause to charters stating that the state reserved the right of revocation. But *Dartmouth* is important because it demonstrated that the Court intended to interpret the Constitution (which makes no mention of corporations) liberally enough to give corporations some measure of constitutional protection. At the same time, the ruling made it clear that corporations remain subordinate to state power. Justice Marshall wrote that the corporation is an "artificial being, invisible, intangible and existing only in contemplation of law."

CHARLES RIVER BRIDGE V. WARREN BRIDGE (1837)
John Hancock, other leading citizens of Boston, and Harvard College were stockholders in a corporation chartered in 1785 for the purpose of building a toll bridge over the Charles River. By 1837 their stock had increased tenfold in value. Another company sought to build a second bridge near enough to reduce traffic on the Charles River Bridge, and the Charles River stockholders attempted to block the second bridge. In its decision, the Court refused to uphold the claim that the Charles River Bridge enjoyed exclusive, monopolistic business rights. The effect was to establish the principle that the rights of property are not absolute: they must be balanced against the needs of the community. Chief Justice Taney wrote: "While the rights of property are sacredly guarded, we must not forget that the community also have rights, and that the happiness and well being of every citizen depends on their faithful preservation."

BANK OF AUGUSTA V. EARLE (1839)

This case was the first step in what the Supreme Court in 1898 was to term "the constant tendency of judicial decisions in modern times . . . in the direction of putting corporations upon the same footing as natural persons." The Supreme Court ruled that companies could seek federal enforcement of agreements they made even when operating outside the state where they were chartered. Accustomed as we are today to interstate corporations, this sounds like a natural evolution, but it marked another small shift away from the control of corporations by state legislatures. According to historian Bernard Schwartz, "[Chief Justice] Taney gave legal recognition to the fact that a corporation has the same practical capacity for doing business outside its home state as within its borders." At the same time, the Court limited corporate powers to some extent by refusing to extend the protection of the Privileges and Immunities Clause of the Constitution.

LOUISVILLE, CINCINNATI, AND CHARLESTON R.R. COMPANY V. LETSON (1844)

In this case, the Court assured corporations that they would enjoy the protection of federal judicial review of state statutes.

THE SLAUGHTER-HOUSE CASES (1873)

In this set of decisions the Supreme Court refused to use the Fourteenth Amendment to protect property rights that were infringed by the state of Louisiana. It interpreted the amendment as applying only to freed slaves. The stance of the Court in the decision did not last long: its significance lies in the strong dissent of Justices Field and Bradley, who declared that "Rights to life, liberty, and the pursuit of happiness are equivalent to life, liberty, and property." That minority position gained control of the Court in 1889.

MUNN V. ILLINOIS (1876)

Resentment among farmers toward excessive railroad and grain elevator rates led to the Granger movement, which swept the Midwest in the early 1870s. The Grangers succeeded in getting protective regulations passed in Illinois, Wisconsin, Minnesota, and Iowa. In Illinois, a law setting maximum prices that could be charged by grain elevators led to the dispute resolved in the *Munn* decision. The Court cited a seventeenth-century common law doctrine articulated by Lord Hale, that when private property is "affected with a public interest, it ceases to be *juris privati* only." The *Munn* decision, which empowered the states to regulate corporations, was soon neutralized by the social Darwinist substantive due process doctrine, which prevailed for fifty years. *Munn* remains significant, however, because the "public interest" doctrine contained in the decision provides a strong basis for state regulation of corporations.

SANTA CLARA COUNTY V. SOUTHERN PACIFIC RAILROAD (1886)

California had a method of taxing corporate property that resulted in higher taxes than those placed on personal property. Southern Pacific objected, and the Court sided with the railroad. The decision is cited as having established that corporations are "persons" for purposes of applying the equal protection clause of the Fourteenth Amendment, which had been enacted to protect the newly freed slaves in the states of the former Confederacy. For the full story on this complex case, see chapters 9 and 10.

PEMBINA MINING COMPANY V. PENNSYLVANIA (1888)

In *Pembina,* the Court held that corporations are not citizens within the meaning of the privileges and immunities clause of the Constitution. The decision did not resolve the issue of whether a corporation is a person for purposes of the Fourteenth Amendment due process and equal protection clauses.

MINNEAPOLIS & ST. LOUIS RAILWAY COMPANY V. BECKWITH (1889)

The state of Iowa passed a law requiring railroad companies that failed to maintain fences to pay owners of livestock the value of livestock killed by trains. The Minneapolis & St. Louis Railway objected. Although the Court ruled against the railroad (on other grounds), the decision stated that corporations were persons under both the equal protection and the due process provisions of the Fourteenth Amendment. The Court stated that "corporations can invoke the benefits of provisions of the constitution and laws which guarantee to persons the enjoyment of property, or afford to them the means for its protection, or prohibit legislation injuriously affecting it."

CHICAGO, MILWAUKEE AND ST. PAUL RAILWAY V. MINNESOTA (1890)

Minnesota had created a rate-setting commission to govern railroad corporations that operated within the state, but the law did not allow railroads to appeal the decisions of the commission in state court. The Supreme Court ruled that the corporations were persons for purposes of applying the Fourteenth Amendment's due process clause; thus, Minnesota was required to allow railroad corporations to appeal decisions of the rate-setting commission in state courts.

NOBLE V. UNION RIVER LOGGING RAILROAD COMPANY (1893)

The Union River Logging Railroad had won federal approval for a right of way through public land. Later, the Interior Department concluded that Union River was actually a logging company rather than a railroad company, and the department rescinded the right of way. Union River went to federal court and claimed that under the Fifth Amendment, which entitles all "persons" to due process of law in federal matters, it was entitled to appeal the Interior Department's decision in federal court. The Supreme Court agreed with the company. This decision marks the first case in which the Court gave a corporation protection under one of the first ten amendments to the Constitution—the Bill of Rights. Whereas the Fourteenth Amendment says that all persons have a right to due process of law in state cases, the Fifth Amendment guarantees the same right in federal cases.

REAGAN V. FARMERS' LOAN & TRUST COMPANY (1893)

In this case, the Court ruled that the Fourteenth Amendment's due process clause requires that state economic regulatory legislation be subject to a reasonableness test by the courts. This buttressed the substantive due process doctrine, under which the Supreme Court invalidated numerous state laws regulating corporate behavior.

IN RE DEBS (1895)

Labor leader Eugene V. Debs, one of the organizers of the Pullman strike in 1894, refused to honor a court injunction ordering him to stop the strike. The Supreme Court ruled that the interstate commerce powers of the federal government gave it the power to stop the strike in the interests of the "general welfare." Although the case did not expand the definition of corporate rights, it illustrates the antilabor, procorporate tilt of the Court in the 1890s.

PLESSY V. FERGUSON (1896)

In 1892, Plessy purchased a first-class ticket on the East Louisiana Railway. Because he was one-eighth African and seven-eighths European, he was jailed for violating Louisiana's "separate but equal" accommodations law after he sat in the whites-only section of the train and refused to move. The Supreme Court ruled against Plessy, even though the Fourteenth Amendment specifically guaranteed "equal protection" for all persons under state law. The narrowness with which the Supreme Court interpreted the Fourteenth Amendment in this case—which involved an actual human being—stands in ironic contrast to the creative expansiveness of the interpretations of the same amendment in decisions involving corporate rights.

ALLGEYER V. LOUISIANA (1897)

A Louisiana law prohibited an individual from contracting with an out-of-state insurance company to insure property within the state. The Supreme Court overturned the law, ruling that it was a violation of the Fourteenth Amendment's "liberty" guarantee. In this case, "liberty" was interpreted to include the freedom to enter into contracts. The effect of *Allgeyer* was to allow the Supreme Court to strike down state labor laws using the contracts clause of the Constitution, which previously had applied only to federal law.

LOCHNER V. NEW YORK (1905)

New York had passed a law limiting the workweek of bakery employees to sixty hours. Lochner, the owner of an unincorporated bakery business, was convicted of violating the law. The Court overturned the conviction, ruling that the law impinged on the right of employees and employers to make contracts with each other. Although *Lochner* did not involve a corporation, it is seen as the epitome of the substantive due process doctrine under which the Court overturned numerous state laws regulating working conditions, wages, and other aspects of business. Justice Holmes wrote a brilliant and scathing dissent to the decision, but his position was ignored by the majority for another three decades. Holmes was vindicated by the Court's abandonment of the substantive due process doctrine in 1937.

HALE V. HENKEL (1906)

In pursuing a potential antitrust case against a group of tobacco corporations, a federal grand jury ordered Edwin Hale to produce a set of documents. Hale refused on the grounds that the corporation he worked for was entitled to protection under the Fourth Amendment ban on unwarranted searches and seizures, and under the Fifth Amendment right against self-incrimination. The Court split its decision—thumbs up to corporate enjoyment of the Fourth Amendment, thumbs down to corporate enjoyment of the Fifth Amendment.

ARMOUR PACKING COMPANY V. UNITED STATES (1908)

This case established the right of a corporation under the Sixth Amendment to receive a jury trial in a criminal case.

GOMPERS V. BUCKS STOVE AND RANGE COMPANY, AND LOEWE V. LAWLOR (1908)

These two decisions outlawed the use of boycotts as a pressure tactic by unions.

WESTERN UNION TELEGRAPH COMPANY V. KANSAS; SOUTHERN R.R. V. GREENE; PULLMAN COMPANY V. KANSAS; AND LUDWIG V. WESTERN UNION TELEGRAPH COMPANY (1910)

These four cases did not break new legal ground, but they had the effect of solidifying the "corporations are persons" formulation used by the Court in applying the Fourteenth Amendment.

HITCHMAN COAL & COKE COMPANY V. MITCHELL (1917)

This decision allowed courts to issue injunctions against unions that attempted to organize workers who had signed "yellow-dog" contracts—that is, company contracts in which workers promised not to join a union. With the aid of *Hitchman,* a judge could shut down an entire region to union organizing, as in 1927, when a single injunction barred the United Mine Workers from organizing in 316 Appalachian coal companies with over forty thousand workers.

TRUAX V. CORRIGAN; DUPLEX PRINTING COMPANY V. DEERING; AND AMERICAN STEEL FOUNDRIES V. TRI-CITY CENTRAL TRADES COUNCIL (1921)

This series of anti-labor decisions was issued by the Supreme Court shortly after William Howard Taft joined as chief justice. In the *Truax* case, a labor union's picketing had succeeded in reducing revenues at a restaurant. The Supreme Court ruled that the picket produced an intentional injury to the restaurant and that the restaurant had the right to recover its damages. The decision overturned an Arizona law that barred courts from issuing injunctions in most types of labor disputes. *Duplex Printing Company v. Deering* outlawed the use of secondary boycotts—that is, boycotts in support of a strike. *Tri-City Central Trades Council* limited picketing to one picket per plant gate.

THE CORONADO COAL CASES (1925)

These decisions prohibited unions under the Sherman Anti-Trust Act from striking in order to organize the unorganized segment of an industry.

LOUIS K. LIGGETT COMPANY V. LEE (1933)

In order to protect small businesses, Florida enacted a special set of taxes on chain stores. The Supreme Court ruled that such taxes were unconstitutional because they violated the chain stores' equal protection rights under the Fourteenth Amendment. Although this case did not create any new corporate rights, it demonstrates the way in which large corporations were able to use the Fourteenth Amendment to prevent states from intervening on the side of smaller businesses.

HOME BUILDING & LOAN ASSOCIATION V. BLAISDELL (1934)

In this case the Supreme Court upheld a Minnesota statute that gave relief to home-owners having trouble paying off their mortgages during the Depression. It was the first sign of a weakening in the substantive due process doctrine that the Court had used for fifty years to justify overturning state legislative attempts to regulate business.

WEST COAST HOTEL COMPANY V. PARRISH (1937)

The state of Washington had enacted a law fixing minimum wages for women and children. Previously, the Supreme Court had invalidated such laws under a social Darwinist interpretation of corporate rights. But now the Court upheld the law, putting an end to the substantive due process doctrine.

CONNECTICUT GENERAL LIFE INSURANCE COMPANY V. JOHNSON (1938) AND WHEELING STEEL CORPORATION V. GLANDER (1949)

These two cases are notable for their dissents by Justices Black and Douglas, respectively. Both justices argued that the *Santa Clara* decision had been mistakenly decided and should be reversed. In his dissent in the *Wheeling Steel* case, Douglas wrote, "It may be most desirable to give corporations this protection from the operation of the legislative process. But that question is not for us. It is for the people. If they want corporations to be treated as humans are treated, if they want to grant corporations this large degree of emancipation from state regulation, they should say so. The Constitution provides a method by which they may do so. We should not do it for them through the guise of interpretation."

UNITED SATES V. MORTON SALT COMPANY (1950)

After the Federal Trade Commission ordered Morton Salt Company and nineteen other salt companies to stop certain price-fixing practices, the FTC ordered the corporations to submit regular reports showing their compliance with the order. Morton Salt appealed the decision, claiming that the Fourth Amendment protected its privacy. In this decision, the Court did not overturn the Fourth Amendment protections granted earlier in *Hale v. Henkel* (1906), but it did narrow them. Specifically, the Court ruled: "Corporations can claim no equality with individuals in the enjoyment of a right to privacy."

Fong Foo v. United States (1962)

Standard Coil Products Company (with Fong Foo as a co-defendant) was accused of defrauding the government in connection with a multimillion dollar contract to supply weather-monitoring equipment. After seven days of what promised to be a long trial, the judge abruptly dismissed the case because of doubts about the credibility of the government's witnesses. Later, the government attempted to retry the case, but attorneys for the corporation claimed that the Fifth Amendment's statement "nor shall any person be subject for the same offense to be twice put in jeopardy of life or limb" applied to the defendant. The Court supported the argument that corporations were entitled to protection under the double jeopardy clause. The Court did not explain why the Fifth Amendment should apply to a corporation.

Ross v. Bernhard (1970)

This case established the Seventh Amendment right of a corporation to a jury trial in a civil case.

United States v. Martin Linen Supply Company (1976)

Martin Linen invoked the Fifth Amendment to avoid retrial in a criminal antitrust case. The case confirmed the earlier *Fong Foo* decision, which established that corporations enjoyed protection from double jeopardy under the Fifth Amendment.

Buckley v. Valeo (1976)

This case invalidated limits on the amount of money a candidate could spend on his or her own campaign. According to the Court, expenditures of money are so closely associated in a political campaign with political expression that limiting such expenditures is constitutional only if necessary to prevent corruption. Because people presumably cannot corrupt themselves, limiting their expenditures cannot be justified under the First Amendment. This case is notorious for its narrow conception of how money can corrupt the political process. For additional discussion, see chapter 13.

Marshall v. Barlow's, Inc. (1978)

Bill Barlow owned Barlow's, Inc., an electrical and plumbing installation in Pocatello, Idaho. When an inspector from the Occupational Safety and Health Administration arrived to conduct a routine inspection, Barlow demanded that he produce a search warrant, a step not required under the Occupational Safety and Health Act. The Supreme Court ruled in Barlow's favor, establishing that corporations enjoyed the protection of the Fourth Amendment: "The right of the people to be secure in their persons, houses, papers, and effects, against unreasonable searches and seizures, shall not be violated." Several justices dissented strongly, including Stevens, Blackmun, and Rehnquist.

First National Bank of Boston v. Bellotti (1978)

A consortium of major corporations, including the First National Bank of Boston, joined in a lawsuit against a Massachusetts law prohibiting corporations from spending money to influence the vote on political referendums. The Supreme Court sided with the corporations, stating that the First Amendment's free speech clause prevented the Massachusetts legislature from restricting this kind of political spending. For further discussion of this case, see chapter 13.

CENTRAL HUDSON GAS & ELECTRIC CORP. V. PUBLIC SERVICE COMMISSION OF NEW YORK (1980)

The New York Public Service Commission had instituted a ban on electric utility advertising to promote the use of electricity. The Court overturned the rule on the basis that corporations enjoy certain protections of commercial speech, defined in the decision as "expression related solely to the economic interests of the speaker and its audience." Although the Court recognized that the government could restrict certain kinds of commercial speech, such as fraudulent advertising or promoting unlawful activity, restrictions in general on commercial speech were not constitutional unless necessary to advance a specific public interest.

PACIFIC GAS & ELECTRIC V. PUBLIC UTILITIES COMMISSION (1986)

The California Public Utilities Commission ruled that unused space in the Pacific Gas & Electric bill should be available four times each year for messages from consumer advocacy groups. PG&E objected, and the Supreme Court backed the company. The decision framed a novel First Amendment right "not to help spread a message with which it disagrees." Once again, Justice Rehnquist disagreed vehemently with the majority. He wrote, "Extension of the individual freedom of conscience decisions to business corporations strains the rationale of those cases beyond the breaking point. To ascribe to such artificial entities an 'intellect' or 'mind' for freedom of conscience purposes is to confuse metaphor with reality." For further discussion of this case, see chapter 14.

AUSTIN V. MICHIGAN STATE CHAMBER OF COMMERCE (1990)

The Michigan Chamber of Commerce wanted to buy newspaper ads in support of a candidate for public office, but it was blocked by a state law prohibiting corporations from spending money from their general funds in connection with state elections. The law, however, did allow corporations to set up separate funds specifically for political purposes. And it allowed corporations to solicit "donations" from their own employees for such funds. The Supreme Court upheld Michigan's law, thereby establishing the narrow parameters within which states could regulate corporate political spending.

Note: The full text of all Supreme Court decisions since 1893 can be found at findlaw.com. A number of significant older cases are at tourolaw.edu/patch/SupremeCourtcases.html.

THE BILL OF RIGHTS AND THE FOURTEENTH AMENDMENT

Amendment I. Congress shall make no law respecting an establishment of religion, or prohibiting the free exercise thereof; or abridging the freedom of speech, or of the press, or the right of the people peaceably to assemble, and to petition the Government for a redress of grievances.

Amendment II. A well regulated Militia, being necessary to the security of a free State, the right of the people to keep and bear Arms shall not be infringed.

Amendment III. No Soldier shall, in time of peace be quartered in any house, without the consent of the Owner, nor in time of war, but in a manner to be prescribed by law.

Amendment IV. The right of the people to be secure in their persons, houses, papers, and effects, against unreasonable searches and seizures, shall not be violated, and no Warrants shall issue, but upon probable cause, supported by Oath or affirmation, and particularly describing the place to be searched, and the persons or things to be seized.

Amendment V. No person shall be held to answer for a capital, or otherwise infamous crime, unless on a presentment or indictment of a Grand Jury, except in cases arising in the land or naval forces, or in the Militia, when in actual service in time of War or public danger; nor shall any person be subject for the same offence to be twice put in jeopardy of life or limb, nor shall be compelled in any criminal case to be a witness against himself, nor be deprived of life, liberty, or property, without due process of law; nor shall private property be taken for public use without just compensation.

Amendment VI. In all criminal prosecutions, the accused shall enjoy the right to a speedy and public trial, by an impartial jury of the State and district wherein the crime shall have been committed; which district shall have been previously ascertained by law, and to be informed of the nature and cause of the accusation; to be confronted with the witnesses against him; to have compulsory process for obtaining witnesses in his favor, and to have the assistance of counsel for his defense.

Amendment VII. In Suits at common law, where the value in controversy shall exceed twenty dollars, the right of trial by jury shall be preserved, and no fact tried by a jury shall be otherwise re-examined in any Court of the United States, than according to the rules of the common law.

Amendment VIII. Excessive bail shall not be required, nor excessive fines imposed, nor cruel and unusual punishments inflicted.

Amendment IX. The enumeration in the Constitution of certain rights shall not be construed to deny or disparage others retained by the people.

Amendment X. The powers not delegated to the United States by the Constitution, nor prohibited by it to the States, are reserved to the States respectively, or to the people.

❖   ❖   ❖

Amendment XIV (Section One). All persons born or naturalized in the United States and subject to the jurisdiction thereof, are citizens of the United States and of the State wherein they reside. No State shall make or enforce any law which shall abridge the privileges or immunities of citizens of the United States; nor shall any State deprive any person of life, liberty, or property, without due process of law; nor deny to any person within its jurisdiction the equal protection of the laws.

Notes

Introduction

1   electric transit conversion: Jonathan Kwitny, "The Great Transportation Conspiracy," *Harper's*, Feb. 1981; The Industrial Reorganization Act: Hearings Before the Subcommittee on Antitrust and Monopoly of the Committee on the Judiciary United States Senate on S. 1167, Part 3, Ground Transportation Industries, 93rd Congress, 2nd session, 1974; "Corporations, Not Government, Drove Mass Transit Off the Cliff," *Dallas Morning News*, Aug. 6, 1996; Nicholas Von Hoffman, "Who Eliminated Old Transit Lines?" *Chicago Tribune*, Mar. 31, 1974.

1   By 1955, 88 percent: Bradford C. Snell, "American Ground Transport: A Proposal for Restructuring the Automobile, Truck, Bus, and Rail Industries," 1973, quoted in Paul Matus, "Street Railways: 'U.S. v. National City Lines' Recalled," *The Third Rail*, Sept. 1974.

5   "Did you ever expect a corporation": Edward, 1st Baron Thurlow, Lord Chancellor of England, member of Parliament at end of eighteenth century. *Oxford Dictionary of Quotations, 4th ed.* (New York: Oxford University Press, 1992), 697.

One: How Did Corporations Get So Much Power?

11 *Business Week* poll: Aaron Bernstein, "Too Much Corporate Power," *Business Week*, Sept. 11, 2000.

14 "We may congratulate ourselves": Letter to Col. William F. Elkins, Nov. 21, 1864, cited in Emmanuel Hertz, *Abraham Lincoln: A New Portrait, Vol. 2* (New York: Horace Liveright, 1931), 954.

15 "The belief is common in America. . . .": "The New York Gold Conspiracy," *Westminster Review*, 1870.

Two: From Street Fights to Empire

19 History of the London guilds: Sir Ernest Pooley, *The Guilds of the City of London* (London: Collins, 1947) 7–24; John P. Davis, *Corporations* (New York: Capricorn Books, 1961 [originally published 1904]), 211–225; H. L. Haywood, "Freemasonry and the Guild System," *The Builder*, Nov. 1923; Pamela Nightingale, *A Medieval Mercantile Community* (New Haven, Conn.: Yale University Press, 1995).

19 Fighting among the guilds: Pooley, 18–20; Nightingale, 255.

20 "brawn and mustard, capon boiled": Pooley, 34.

20 Fraternity of Pepperers, which begat: Nightingale, 237–238; John P. Davis, 224.

21 Since London had no police force: Nightingale, 570.

21 Guild control of London government: John P. Davis, 211.

21 sales of land were a primary avenue: Ron Harris, *Industrializing English Law: Entrepreneurship and Business Organization, 1720–1844* (Cambridge and New York: Cambridge University Press, 2000), 54.

21 James I and Elizabeth's use of charter renewals: Pooley, 22.

21 "searching and sealing patent": John P. Davis, 217.

21 Conflict between the Brewers' Guild and Elizabeth I: John P. Davis, 211.

21 Edward Darcy: Pooley, 22.

21 Statute of Monopolies: Harris, 46.

21 Charles I managed to raise £100,000: Harris, 47.

22 Origins of the Merchant Adventurers: Pooley, 24.

22 Financing models for early trading corporations: Harris, 40–45.

22 Drake's capture of a Portuguese galleon: John Keay, *The Honorable Company: A History of the East India Company* (New York: Macmillan, 1991), 11.

24 Use of joint-stock financing by Russia Company: Harris, 24–25.

24 Initially, this company raised capital one voyage at a time: Harris, 25.

24 Company use of stock in 1613, 1650: Antony Wild, *The East India Company: Trade and Conquest from 1600* (New York: HarperCollins, 1999), 63; Harris, 24–25.

24 General background on the East India Company: Ramkrishna Mukherjee, *The Rise and Fall of the East India Company* (New York: Monthly Review Press, 1974); James A. Williamson, *A Short History of British Expansion: The Old Colonial Empire* (New York: Macmillan, 1951); Keay, *The Honorable Company;* Maurice Collins, *British Merchant Adventurers* (London: Collins, 1942); Wild, *The East India Company* (New York: HarperCollins, 1999).

25 A third of Parliament owns stock in the company: Pat Regier, "Tempest in a Tea Pot," *Time Europe,* June 17, 2002.

26 "Sir Josiah Child": Mukherjee, 180.

27 "In the East, the laws of society, the laws of nature": Paul Langford, *A Quiet and Commercial People: England 1727–1783* (New York: Oxford University Press, 1989), 534.

27 "Indians tortured to disclose their treasure": John Micklethwait and Adrian Wooldridge, *The Company: A Short History of a Revolutionary Idea* (New York: Random House/Modern Library, 2003), 33.

THREE: THE ULTIMATE REALITY SHOW

30 General background on the Virginia Company: Joseph S. Davis, *Essays in the Earlier History of American Corporations* (Cambridge, Mass.: Harvard University Press, 1917), 33; Edmund S. Morgan, *American Slavery, American Freedom: The Ordeal of Colonial Virginia* (New York: W. W. Norton, 1975); Peter Linebaugh and Marcus Rediker, *The Many-Headed Hydra: Sailors, Slaves, Commoners, and the Hidden History of the Revolutionary Atlantic* (Boston: Beacon Press, 2000).

30 Excavations at the site of original James Fort: Karen E. Lange, "Unsettling Discoveries at Jamestown: Suffering and Surviving in Seventeenth-Century Virginia," *National Geographic,* June 2002.

31 "bringeth foorth all things": Morgan, 26–27.

31 "Adventurer" included anyone: Morgan, 45.

31 The list included Shakespeare: Linebaugh and Rediker, 14.

31 Drapers' Guild involvement: Pooley, 28.

31 glass, furs, potash: Morgan, 45.

31 Piracy as a motive for some investors: Morgan, 45.

31 Fomenting rebellion among the Cimarrons and Chichimici: Morgan, 28–30, 45.

32 Only one out of five ... survived: Lange, 78.

32 Among transported children, the survival rate: Linebaugh and Rediker, 59.

32 The scope of enclosure: Linebaugh and Rediker, 17.

32 Meanwhile, the English conquest of Ireland: Linebaugh and Rediker, 57.

32 Punishment of vagabonds under Henry VIII and Edward VI: Linebaugh and Rediker, 18.

32 The Beggar Act of 1598: Linebaugh and Rediker, 56.

32 During the Midlands Revolt: Linebaugh and Rediker, 19.

32 "prison without walls": Linebaugh and Rediker, 20.

32 "to ease the city and suburbs of a swarme": Linebaugh and Rediker, 16.

33 At the request of the company: Robert C. Johnson, "The Transportation of Vagrant Children from London to Virginia, 1618–1622," in Howard S. Reinmuth, Jr. (ed.), *Early Stuart Studies: Essays in Honor of David Harris Wilson* (Minneapolis: University of Minnesota Press, 1970).

33 "shall sweep your streets, and wash your dores": Linebaugh and Rediker, 59.

33 "driven in flocks": John Van der Zee, *Bound Over: Indentured Servitude and the American Conscience* (New York: Simon & Schuster, 1985), 210.

33 Regimentation and institutionalized cruelty in Virginia": Linebaugh and Rediker, 32; Morgan, 80.

33 "base and detracting": Morgan, 124.

33 Punishment of Thomas Hatch: Morgan, 125.

33 "Some he appointed to be hanged": George Percy, "'A Trewe' Relacyon—Virginia from 1609 to 1612," *Tyler's Quarterly Historical and Genealogical Magazine*, Apr. 1922, 3(4), 280.

33 "Almost all servants": Morgan, 126.

34 The survival of 12 children out of 165: Linebaugh and Rediker, 59.

34 The killings of Elizabeth Abbott and Elias Hinton: Morgan, 127.

34 Ill treatment of servants: Morgan 128–129.

34 Investor factions and Sandys plan: Morgan, 92–93.

35 Colonial legislative assemblies: John P. Davis, 196–210.

35 "The company reserved a 'quitrent'": Morgan, 94, 95, 123, 129.

36 Wrote's investigation of the Virginia Company and charter revocation: Morgan, 101.

36 Deaths of settlers: Lange, 78.

36 Bridewell children's revolt: Linebaugh and Rediker, 59.

36   "composed of great numbers of Sailors": Linebaugh and Rediker, 232.

37   Sons of Neptune: Linebaugh and Rediker, 235.

37   "was mixed up in every street fight": Esther Forbes, *Paul Revere and the World He Lived In* (Boston: Houghton Mifflin, 1942), quoted in Thom Hartmann, *Unequal Protection: The Rise of Corporate Dominance and the Theft of Human Rights* (Emmaus, Penn.: Rodale Press, 2002), 53.

FOUR: WHY THE COLONISTS FEARED CORPORATIONS . . .

38   Marchand: Roland Marchand, *Creating the Corporate Soul: The Rise of Public Relations and Corporate Imagery in American Big Business* (Berkeley: University of California Press, 1998); see pages 322–323 for Roosevelt's four freedoms speech and the fifth freedom ad campaign. Roland Marchand, *Advertising the American Dream: Making Way for Modernity, 1920–1940* (Berkeley: University of California Press, 1985).

39   Philip Morris Bill of Rights traveling exhibit: Howard Wolinsky, "Philip Morris and the Bill of Rights," *Priorities for Health* (American Council on Science and Health, 1991), 3(1).

39   Raphael: Ray Raphael, *A People's History of the American Revolution* (New York: The New Press, 2001).

39   Labaree: Benjamin Woods Labaree, *The Boston Tea Party* (New York: Oxford University Press, 1964).

40   "People of the same trade seldom meet together": Adam Smith, *The Wealth of Nations* (New York: Random House/Knopf [originally published 1776], 1994), Book I, Chapter 10, Part II.

40   Adam Smith's views of corporations: Smith, Book V, Chapter I, Part III.

40   Benjamin Franklin and the Physiocrats: Edwin R. A. Seligman, "Benjamin Franklin," *The Cambridge History of English and American Literature* (New York: Putnam, 1907), Vol. XVIII, Book III, Chapter XXIV, "Economists."

40   Prohibition on manufacturing iron pots: "Reasons Against a General Prohibition of the Iron Manufacture in His Majesty's Plantations" (ca. 1750).

41   Causes and circumstances of the Boston Tea Party: Labaree.

42   Quantity of tea destroyed: According to historian Labaree, the consumption of tea in the colonies is estimated at 1,200,000 pounds, of which 275,000 pounds was imported from England and the remainder was smuggled. See Labaree, 6–7, 144.

42   The financial crisis of the East India Company: Labaree, 6–62.

44   Governor Thomas Hutchinson's selection of consignees: John R. Alden, *A History of the American Revolution* (New York: Da Capo Press, 1989), 138.

44   a crowd of over five thousand: A. J. Langguth, *Patriots: The Men Who Started the American Revolution* (New York: Touchstone/Simon & Schuster, 1988), 176.

45   Crispus Attucks "would be enough": Linebaugh and Rediker, 237.

FIVE: . . . AND WHAT THEY DID ABOUT IT

46   Jefferson quote: Letter to Tom Logan, Nov. 1816, in Paul Leicester Ford, *The Writings of Thomas Jefferson, Vol. 10* (New York, 1892–1899), 69.

46   Only six nonbanking corporations: William G. Roy, *Socializing Capital: The Rise of the Large Industrial Corporation in America* (Princeton, N.J.: Princeton University Press, 1997), 49.

47   Involvement of Washington and Franklin in land companies: Peter Kellman, "Labor Organizing and Freedom of Association," *Rachel's Environment & Health News,* May 18, 2000, 697.

47   Fulton and canals: Anton Chaitkin, "The Chinese Model for America's Canals," *American Almanac,* Dec. 1989.

48   Constitutional Convention debates: Roy, 50; Ralph Nader, "The Case for Federal Chartering," in Ralph Nader and Mark J. Green, eds., *Corporate Power in America* (New York: Grossman Publishers, 1973), 74; Joseph S. Davis, 15–16; Edgar Lee Masters, "Implied Powers and Imperialism," *The New Star Chamber and Other Essays* (Chicago: Hammersmark Publishing Company, 1904).

49   Pennsylvania's dispute over issuing a charter to a coal company: Roy, 48.

49   "one of the most powerful, repetitious": Louis Hartz, *Economic Policy and Democratic Thought, 1776–1860* (Cambridge, Mass.: Harvard University Press, 1948), 69.

49   "We entirely disapprove": Susan E. Hirsch, *Roots of the American Working Class: The Industrialization of Crafts in Newark, 1800–1860* (Philadelphia: University of Pennsylvania Press, 1978), 86.

49   "the independent spirit": Howard B. Rock, *Artisans of the New Republic: The Tradesmen of New York City in the Age of Jefferson* (New York: New York University Press, 1979), 183–197.

50   "The unobtrusive work-shop": "Incorporating the Republic: The Corporation in Antebellum Political Culture," *Harvard Law Review,* 1989, 102.

50   A New Jersey editorialist: Richard Grossman and Frank T. Adams, *Taking Care of Business: Citizen and the Charter of Incorporation* (Cambridge, Mass.: Charter, Ink, 1993), 14.

50   "Every corporate grant": "Incorporating the Republic."

50   "We being journeymen": "Remonstrance of George W. Cushing & Others (1838)," quoted in "Incorporating the Republic."

51   Restrictions in corporate charters: Grossman and Adams, 8–12; Lawrence M. Friedman, *A History of American Law, Second Edition* (New York: Simon & Schuster, 1985), 190–191; Roy, 54–55; Adolph A. Berle, Jr. "Historical Inheritance of American Corporations," *Social Meaning of Legal Concepts 3* (1950), 196.

52   Restrictions on banking: Ronald E. Seavoy, *The Origins of the American Business Corporation, 1784–1855* (Westport, Conn.: Greenwood Press, 1982), 55; Grossman and Adams, 9.

52   *Ultra vires* restrictions: Morton J. Horwitz, *The Transformation of American Law, 1870–1960: The Crisis of Legal Orthodoxy* (New York: Oxford University Press, 1992), 77–79; Friedman, 518–519.

53   Pullman . . . divest itself of company-owned town: Louis Menand, *The Metaphysical Club* (New York: Farrar, Straus and Giroux, 2001), 316.

54   Charter revocation: Grossman and Adams, 10–13.

54   Number of corporations in 1800: Joseph S. Davis, 24–25.

54   Corporate formation in Pennsylvania: Stuart Bruchey, *The Roots of American Economic Growth: 1607–1861* (New York: Harper and Row, 1965), 130.

54 Growth of manufacturing: Stuart Bruchey, Enterprise: *The Dynamic Economy of a Free People* (Cambridge, Mass.: Harvard University Press, 1990), 151–152.

55 World rank of U.S. per capita manufacturing output: Paul Kennedy, *The Rise and Fall of the Great Powers* (New York: Random House, 1987), 149.

SIX: THE GENIUS

56 "An electric brain and cool quiet manner": Carl Sandberg, *Abraham Lincoln* (New York: Harvest Books, Harcourt Trade Publishers, 1989), 279.

56 The Central was nicknamed: Charles R. Geisst, *Monopolies in America: Empire Builders and their Enemies from Jay Gould to Bill Gates* (New York: Oxford University Press, 2000), 21.

56 Gould and Fisk: Matthew Josephson, *The Robber Barons* (New York: Harcourt, Brace & World, 1934), 134–135.

57 Adam Smith, Karl Marx: Smith, Book V, Chapter I, Part III. Karl Marx and Friedrich Engels, *The Communist Manifesto* (New York: Oxford University Press, 1998).

58 Origins of railroads as state-owned businesses: Roy, 83–96; Friedman, 178, 181, 193.

58 in the 1830s, the state supplied the locomotives: Friedman, 193.

58 Restrictions in the charter of the Pennsylvania Railroad: Roy, 84.

58 Opposition to the railroad: McClure, 123–124, 136, 142–143, 227. Veteran legislator A. K. McClure wrote, "It is difficult for our people in this progressive age," looking back on the early years of the Pennsylvania Railroad, "to understand the desperate resistance made by the people generally throughout the State to the introduction of railroads."

59 "When the contest had reached white heat": McClure, 227.

59 Biographical information on Tom Scott: Scott Reynolds Nelson, *Iron Confederacies: Southern Railways, Klan Violence, and Reconstruction* (Chapel Hill: University of North Carolina Press, 1999); T. Lloyd Benson and Trina Rossman, "Re-Assessing Tom Scott, the 'Railroad Prince'" (paper for the Mid-America Conference on History, 1995), see http://alpha.furman.edu/~benson/col-tom.html; Samuel Richey Kamm, *The Civil War Career of Thomas A. Scott* (doctoral dissertation, University of Pennsylvania Graduate School of History, 1940); A. K. McClure, *Old Time Notes of Pennsylvania* (Philadelphia: John Winston Company, 1905).

59 "Public sentiment was so strong": McClure, 138.

59 Scott's statewide organizing tactics: McClure, 141.

60 the ingenious device of allowing the railroad to divert taxes: Kamm, 13.

60 Defeat of pro-repeal legislators: McClure, 486.

60 Irrevocability of the tonnage tax repeal: Kamm, 13.

60 On one occasion he worked: McClure, 150.

60 He engineered the movement: Kamm, 164–174.

61 "For nearly twenty years": McClure, 150.

61 "a single force so formidable": Josephson, 89.

61 "At the bidding of the railroad": Josephson, 102–103.

61 The grand vision: Nelson, 74.

61 Use of slave labor to build railroads: Nelson, 16–19.

62 "Well into the 1850s": Nelson, 28.

62 any merger involving the North Carolina Railroad: Nelson, 143.

62 Scott's innovation of the holding company: Nelson, 7, 141–145.

63 "a complicated spree of leases": Benson and Rossman.

63 Creation of the Southern Railway Security Company: Nelson, 141.

63 Buying up Southern newspapers: Nelson, 153.

64 "we shall be unworthy": Nelson, 154.

64 Lack of coverage in Richmond: Nelson, 154.

64 Scott's relations with the Ku Klux Klan: Nelson, 163–166.

64 "theft of services": Nelson, 169.

64 Compromise of 1877: Philip S. Foner, *The Great Labor Uprising of 1877* (New York: Monad Press, 1977); Peter Kellman, *Building Unions: Past, Present and Future* (New York: Apex Press, 2001), 25; Mike Werner, "Property Picks a President," *By What Authority,* Spring 2001, 3(2); Nelson, 167; Benson and Rossman.

65 Strike of 1877: Benson and Rossman; Howard Zinn, *A People's History of the United States* (New York: HarperPerennial, 1995), 240–246; Foner.

65 "rifle diet": Richard O. Boyer and Herbert M. Morais, *Labor's Untold Story* (New York: Cameron, 1955), 61.

65 "trailed his garments across the country": Nelson, 74.

66 "Only a few months before Scott incorporated the Southern": Nelson, 146–147.

67 Cromwell's legal maneuvers in the Cotton Oil Trust case: Horwitz, 83–84.

67 New Jersey general incorporation statute: Horwitz, 83–85; Roy, 164–166, 201–203.

68 By 1901, 71 percent: *Manual of Statistics,* 1901, cited in Roy, 152.

68 "So many Trusts and big corporations": Horwitz, 84.

68 "race to the bottom": Horwitz, 84; Roy, 152, 166.

68 "the traitor state": Lincoln Steffens, "New Jersey: A Traitor State," *McClure's Magazine,* 1905, 41, 25.

68 A half-dozen other states: Roy, 152.

68 Some 2,650 separate firms disappeared: Louis Galambos, "The Emerging Organizational Synthesis in American History," *Business History Review,* 1970, 22, 279–290.

68 From $33 million to more than $7 billion: Roy, 4–5.

68 Figures on market concentration: Robert L. Heilbroner and Aaron Singer, *The Economic Transformation of America: 1600 to the Present, 2nd ed.* (New York: Harcourt Brace Jovanovich, 1984), 205.

69 Standardization of time zones: John Steele Gordon, "The Business of American Standard Time," *American Heritage,* July/August, 2001; Alan Trachtenberg, *The Incorporation of America: Culture and Society in the Gilded Age* (New York: Hill and Wang, 1982), 113.

SEVEN: SUPERPOWERS

72   In 1811, the first general incorporation statute: John P. Davis, ix.

72   Early general incorporation statutes: Friedman, 195; Roy, 48–50; Seavoy, 6–7.

73   almost half had done so by 1903: *Report of the Committee on Corporation Laws of Massachusetts* (1903), 162–164, cited in *Liggett v. Lee* (1933), dissent by Louis Brandeis, footnote 29.

73   The average Fortune 500 company's life span: Arie de Geus, *The Living Company* (Boston: Harvard Business School Press, 1997), 8.

74   Global 500 list: *Financial Times,* May 13, 2002.

74   Corporate involvement with fascist regimes: Isabel Vincent, "Who Will Reap the Nazi-Era Reparations?" *National Post,* Feb. 10, 1999; Michael Dobbs, "Ford and GM Scrutinized for Alleged Nazi Collaboration," washingtonpost.com, Nov. 30, 1999.

74   IBM: Paul Fiesta, "Probing IBM's Nazi connection," www.cnet.com, June 28, 2001; Edwin Black, "Final Solutions," *The Village Voice,* Mar. 27, 2002; Edwin Black, "The Ghosts in the Machine," *Forward,* Mar. 29, 2002; "IBM Statement on Nazi-Era Book and Lawsuit," www.ibm.com/press, Feb. 2001.

74   Canadian and American companies and slave labor: Frank Murray, "3 Large Companies Cited for Slavery Reparations," *Washington Times,* Mar. 27, 2002; James Cox, "Corporations Challenged by Reparations Activists," *USA Today,* Feb. 21, 2002.

75   "ability to disguise itself": Ralph Estes, *The Tyranny of the Bottom Line: Why Corporations Make Good People Do Bad Things* (San Francisco: Berrett-Koehler, 1996), 47.

75   "Its image befouled": Estes, 47.

76   "the corporation had torn free . . .": Friedman, 525.

76   Doctrine of *ultra vires:* Horwitz, 77–79; Friedman, 518–519. According to Friedman, the case that effectively finished off *ultra vires* was *Jacksonville, Mayport, Pablo Railway & Navigation Company v. Hooper* (1896).

76   Although *ultra vires* lingered in theory: Horwitz, 78.

76   "drove from her borders": William Cook, *A Treatise on Stock and Stockholders, Bonds, Mortgages, and General Corporation Law, Vol. II* (1894), quoted in Friedman, 524.

76   "the favorite state of incorporations" and "a Snug Harbor": Friedman, 524.

77   Laws allowing incorporation "for any lawful purpose": *Liggett v. Lee* (1933), dissent by Louis Brandeis, footnote 28.

77   Robotics: Isaac Asimov, "Runaround," *Astounding Science Fiction,* Mar. 1942.

78   Shareholder liability in England: L.C.B. Gower, "Some Contrasts Between British and American Corporation Law," *Harvard Law Review,* June 1956, 69(8), 19.

78   Shareholder liability in the United States: Grossman and Adams, 9–10; Roy, 158–164.

78   "As with constitutional law": Arthur S. Miller, *The Modern Corporate State: Private Governments and the American Constitution* (Westport, Conn.: Greenwood Press, 1976), 47.

79   "the faculty of taking resolves": Paul Vindograph, quoted in Gregory A. Mark, "Personification of the Business Corporation in American Law," *University of Chicago Law Review,* 1987, 54, 1476.

79   In the classic corporation: Mark, 1477.

79   "rule of unanimous consent": Horwitz, 88.

80   St. Louis decision: Roy, 108.

80   Main Flour Mills: Adolph A. Berle, Jr., *The Twentieth Century Capitalist Revolution* (New York: Harcourt Brace, 1954), 196.

81   Warren Court goals: Scott R. Bowman, *The Modern Corporation and American Political Thought: Law, Power, and Ideology* (University State Park: The Pennsylvania State University Press, 1996), 176.

82   "by virtue of their size": Bowman, 179.

82   Time-Warner acquisition: According to Mergerstat, a mergers and acquisitions tracking service, the total value of mergers and acquisitions from 1971–1978 was as follows: 1971: $24 billion, 1972: $16 billion, 1973: $17 billion, 1974, $12 billion, 1975: $12 billion, 1976: $20 billion, 1977: $22 billion, 1978: $34 billion, total: $157 billion.

82   Thirty-seven of the top one hundred economies: Martin Wolf, "Countries Still Rule the World, *Financial Times,* Feb. 6, 2002.

82   Sixty-six of the one hundred largest economic entities: Charles Gray, "Corporate Goliaths: Sizing Up Corporations and Governments," *Multinational Monitor,* June 1999.

82   among the top two hundred: Sarah Anderson and John Cavanagh, *Top 200: The Rise of Corporate Global Power.* Washington, D.C.: Institute for Policy Studies, 2000.

82   Nineteen of the top twenty-five: Global 2002 list, *Financial Times,* May 13, 2002.

83   "Nowadays, nobody finds it odd": John Micklethwait and Adrian Wooldridge, *The Company: A Short History of a Revolutionary Idea* (New York: Random House/Modern Library, 2003), xvii.

83   "The larger the corporation": Ron Harris, *Industrializing English Law: Entrepreneurship and Business Organization, 1720–1844* (Cambridge: Cambridge University Press, 2000), 113.

85   *Dartmouth College* case: All quotes from Menand, 239–242.

EIGHT: THE JUDGE

88   Dred Scott family and legal case: *Dred Scott v. Sanford* (1857).

89   Stephen Field biographical information: Howard Jay Graham, *Everyman's Constitution* (Madison: State Historical Society of Wisconsin, 1968) 14, 128–129; Carl Brent Swisher, *Stephen J. Field: Craftsman of the Law* (Washington, D.C.: The Brookings Institution, 1930); Paul Kens, *Justice Stephen Field: Shaping Liberty from the Gold Rush to the Gilded Age* (Lawrence: University Press of Kansas, 1997).

89   Stanford recommended Field to Lincoln: Gustavus Myers, *History of the Supreme Court of the United States* (Chicago: Charles H. Kerr & Co., 1912), 502n.

89   as did Field's brother David: Kens (1997), 96.

90   Field's estate value: Swisher, 446n.

90   "It seems to me": C. Peter Magrath, *Morrison R. Waite: The Triumph of Character* (New York: Macmillan, 1963), 259–260.

90 **Lucrative position for Pomeroy:** Pomeroy received $3,333 for a four-month retainer in 1882 and $2,500 for services on the *Santa Clara* case in 1883. According to Kevin Phillips, the average daily wages of a skilled working man were $2.16 in 1879, or about $500 per year. Kevin Phillips, *Wealth and Democracy: A Political History of the American Rich* (New York: Broadway Books, 2002), 41.

90 **Field secretly provided Pomeroy:** In a letter from Field to Pomeroy on March 28, 1883, Field writes: "Some weeks ago, I wrote you with reference to the San Mateo tax case telling you that its decisions would not be made until next term, and enclosing also certain memoranda which had been handed me by two of the Judges. Have you ever received these? They were, of course, intended only for your eye, and I should be glad to know that they have come to your hands." The Field/Pomeroy letters are collected in Graham, 101–109.

90 **"Judge Field will not sit":** Kens (1997), 226.

90 **Garfield–Reid exchanges:** Magrath, 239–242.

92 **"Indiana was really":** Magrath, 243.

92 **Matthews' work for railroads:** Myers, 556.

92 **"In behalf of":** Myers, 557–558.

93 **Matthews proved more independent:** Magrath, 247.

93 **Field's doctrines enjoyed majority:** Russell Galloway, *Justice for All? The Rich and Poor in Supreme Court History* (Durham, N.C.: Carolina Academic Press, 1991), 80–82.

93 **Railroads and graft:** Robert Justin Goldstein, *Political Repression in Modern America: From 1870 to 1976* (Urbana and Chicago: University of Illinois Press, 1978, 2001), 7.

93 **Grange movement:** Friedman, 447–448; Dorothy W. Hartman, "Life in the 1880's: Order of the Patrons of Husbandry—The Grange" (Indianapolis: Conner Prairie Museum, 2002).

94 **"Resolved, that the railways of the road":** Robert L. Heilbroner and Aaron Singer, *The Economic Transformation of America: 1600 to the Present, 2nd ed.* (New York: Harcourt Brace Jovanovich, 1984), 205.

94 **Field's development of Fourteenth Amendment doctrine:** Graham, 144–148, 392; Eli Pariser, "The Argument from Silence," unpublished thesis, 2001, ep@9-11peace.org.

95 **Chinese railroad laborers:** Kens (1997), 132–133.

95 **"You know I belong to the class":** Letter from Stephen J. Field to John Norton Pomeroy, Apr. 14, 1882, quoted in Graham, 105.

96 *In Re Ah Fong:* Pariser.

96 *In Re Parrott:* Pariser; Kens (1997), 215–217.

99 **"The truth cannot be evaded":** Horwitz, 70; emphasis in original.

99 **"Because an individual corporator":** Mark, 1474.

100 **"In the publicly held industrial corporations":** Mark, 1477.

NINE: THE COURT REPORTER

102 *Supreme Court Reporter:* St. Paul: West Publishing Company, 1886.

102 *United States Reports:* New York and Albany: Banks & Brothers Law Publishers, 1886.

103 In 1960, the following exchange of notes: Howard Jay Graham, *Everyman's Constitution: Historical Essays on the Fourteenth Amendment, the "Conspiracy Theory," and American Constitutionalism* (Madison: State Historical Society of Wisconsin, 1968), 560, 566–567; Magrath, 223–224.

104 The Library of Congress alone: Magrath, 322.

104 The exchange of notes was discussed: Magrath; David O'Brien, *Storm Center: The Supreme Court in American Politics* (New York: W. W. Norton, 1986); and Thom Hartmann, *Unequal Protection: The Rise of Corporate Dominance and the Theft of Human Rights* (Emmaus, Penn.: Rodale, 2002), 112.

105 Graham was shy, deaf: Leonard Levy, "Foreword," in Graham, viii.

106 "It seems almost inconceivable": Magrath, 224.

107 Davis biographical information and motives: Hartmann, 116–119.

108 "There is perhaps no better illustration": O'Brien, 149.

TEN: THE LAVENDER-BREASTED TURKEY GOBBLER

111 "the great egoist": Graham, 16.

111 "I have been afraid it would get you ill": Magrath, 270.

112 Fourteenth Amendment theory of Beards: Charles A. and Mary R. Beard, *The Rise of American Civilization, Vol. II* (New York: Macmillan, 1927), 111–114. Charles A. Beard, *An Economic Interpretation of the Constitution of the United States* (New York: Macmillan, 1935).

112 The book had been a best-seller: According to Charles Beard's biographer, Ellen Nore, the regular edition sold 70,000 copies and book clubs sold an additional 62,000. Ellen Nore, *Charles A. Beard: An Intellectual Biography* (Carbondale: Southern Illinois University Press, 1983), 124.

113 "endows the captains of a rising industry": Walton H. Hamilton, "Property— According to Locke," *Yale Law Journal,* 1932, 41, 864.

114 "a secret purpose": Justice Black's dissent in *Connecticut General Life Insurance Company v. Johnson* (1938).

114 Journal published in 1914 by Kendrick: Benjamin B. Kendrick, *Journal of the Joint Committee of Fifteen on Reconstruction, 39th Congress, 1865–1867* (New York: Columbia University, 1914).

115 Howard Graham's rebuttal: Howard J. Graham, "The Conspiracy Theory of the Fourteenth Amendment, Part I," *Yale Law Journal,* Jan. 1938; Howard J. Graham, "The Conspiracy Theory of the Fourteenth Amendment, Part II," *Yale Law Journal,* Dec. 1938; both are included in Graham, *Everyman's Constitution.* Note that the appendix to *Everyman's Constitution* reprints a transcript of Roscoe Conkling's argument in the *San Mateo* case.

ELEVEN: SURVIVAL OF THE FITTEST

118 Herbert Spencer and social Darwinism: Mike Hawkins, *Social Darwinism in European and American Thought, 1860–1945* (New York: Cambridge University Press, 1997), 83; Menand, 143, 194.

118 "the average vigour of any race": Herbert Spencer, *Principles of Biology* (New York: Appleton and Co., rev. ed., Vol. I, 1898), 531.

119 **"Pervading all nature":** Herbert Spencer, *Social Statics* (London: John Chapman, 1851), 289.

119 **"The original, mainly landholding masters":** Karen Orren, *Belated Feudalism: Labor, the Law, and Liberal Development in the United States* (New York: Cambridge University Press, 1991), 4.

120 **It was not until 1843:** Orren, 80.

120 **"By his instructions, the clergyman":** Charles Perrow, *Organizing America: Wealth, Power, and the Origins of Corporate Capitalism* (Princeton, N.J.: Princeton University Press, 2002), 67.

120 **"There were few areas":** Sidney Pollard, *The Genesis of Modern Management: A Study of the Industrial Revolution in Great Britain* (New York: Cambridge University Press, 1965), 163, quoted in Perrow, 67.

121 **His first employees:** Jack Beatty, *Colossus: How the Corporation Changed America* (New York: Broadway Books, 2001), 65.

121 **"As the first workers in the first American factories":** Beatty, 65.

121 **Blacklists:** Perrow, 80.

121 **Workers remained in perpetual debt:** Perrow, 80.

121 **"In every jurisdiction":** Orren, 74.

121 **Principle that labor was "entire":** Orren, 84–85.

121 **Relative liberty:** Orren, 92.

121 **"You have rules":** Barbara Ehrenreich, quoted in "Corporate Culture in the Age of Enron," *In These Times*, Dec. 23, 2002.

122 **Charles Dickens quotes:** Charles Dickens, *American Words for General Circulation* (New York: Penguin, 1985), 114–119, quoted in Beatty, 76–79.

122 **"benign phase":** Perrow, 67.

122 **Investigation of child labor in Manayunk:** Perrow, 54.

123 **Victory of eight-hour day movement:** Paul Kens, *Lochner v. New York: Economic Regulation on Trial* (Lawrence: University Press of Kansas, 1998), 20.

123 **Fourteen new unions emerged:** Goldstein, 25.

123 **Although laws had been passed:** Kens (1998), 21.

123 **Samuel Gompers' opposition:** Kens (1998), 24–25.

123 **The Paris Commune:** Graham, 124.

123 **American reaction to Paris Commune:** Goldstein, 26.

123 **"an uneasy feeling":** Goldstein, 9.

123 **In the wake of the Commune:** Quotes from Goldstein, 25.

124 **Crowds attacked by mounted police:** Goldstein, 27.

124 **Labor conflict:** David Helvarg, *The War Against the Greens* (San Francisco: Sierra Club Books, 1994), 172.

124 **"The alarming development":** Priscilla Murolo and A. B. Chitty, *From the Folks Who Brought You the Weekend: A Short, Illustrated History of Labor in the United States* (New York: The New Press, 2001), 122.

124 Knights of Labor: Murolo and Chitty, 123, 126.

124 Seven workers killed: Goldstein, 37.

124 Haymarket incident: Murolo and Chitty, 126–127; Goldstein, 36–41.

125 "Gentlemen of the jury": Murolo and Chitty, 126.

125 Pullman strike: Murolo and Chitty, 133.

125 Injunctions: William E. Forbath, "The Shaping of th American Labor Movement," 102 Harvard Law Review 1109 (1989).

126 "exposed to flour dust": Kens (1998), 9.

126 Leaders of the Bakeshop Act campaign: Kens (1998), 53–57.

127 "I congratulate you on the moderation of your demands": Kens (1998), 62.

127 Arrest of Joseph Lochner: Kens (1998), 89.

127 Field's strategy in developing substantive due process: Bernard Schwartz, A History of the Supreme Court (Oxford; New York: Oxford Univ. Press, 1993), 117–118, 181–182; Bruchey (1990), 304–305.

127 Contribution of Thomas Cooley: Kens (1998), 98.

128 The Field faction on the Court: Galloway, 80–82.

128 "morals, health, safety": Kens (1998), 155.

129 Oliver Wendell Holmes: Schwartz, 190–200; Kim Phillips-Fein, "Practically Speaking," In These Times, Oct. 15, 2001; Menand, 61–65. Oliver Wendall Holmes, The Common Law (Cambridge, Mass.: Harvard University Press, 1963 [originally published 1881]).

130 "Necessitous men": Charles A. Reich, Opposing the System (New York: Crown, 1995), 170.

130 "The power over a man's subsistence": Alexander Hamilton, The Federalist Papers, quoted in Arthur S. Miller, The Modern Corporate State: Private Governments and the American Constitution (Westport, Conn.: Greenwood Press, 1976), 45–46.

130 Supreme Court invalidation of state statutes: Mayer, "Personalizing the Impersonal: Corporations and the Bill of Rights," Hastings Law Journal, 1990, 41, 589.

130 "less than one-half of 1 percent": Dissent by Hugo Black in Connecticut General Life Insurance Company v. Johnson (1938).

130 Supreme Court injunction decisions: Goldstein, 183–184.

130 "We have to hit": Henry F. Pringle, The Life and Times of William Howard Taft: A Biography, Vol. 2 (New York: Farrar & Rinehart, 1939), 967.

131 The bonus army: Paul Dickson and Thomas B. Allen, "Marching on History," Smithsonian, Feb. 2003.

132 "If the process of concentration": Franklin Roosevelt speech in San Francisco, Sept. 23, 1932, quoted in Reich, 126.

132 Roosevelt, Justice Roberts, and the end of substantive due process: Schwartz, 234–235.

133 Dissent by Justice Hugo Black: Connecticut General Life Insurance Company v. Johnson (1938).

133   Dissent by Justice William O. Douglas: *Wheeling Steel Corporation v. Glander* (1949).

133   Roosevelt's "second Bill of Rights": Reich, 127–129.

133   History of human rights: Geoffrey Robertson, *Crimes Against Humanity: The Struggle for Global Justice* (New York: The New Press, 2000), 5–11.

134   H. G. Wells's writings: Robertson, 20–34.

134   Universal Declaration of Human Rights: Robertson, 26–34.

135   Distribution of wealth following the New Deal: Phillips, 79.

135   "Private economic power": John Kenneth Galbraith, *American Capitalism: The Concept of Countervailing Power* (New Brunswick, N.J.: Transaction Publishers, 1993 [originally published 1952]), 111–112.

TWELVE: THE REVOLT OF THE BOSSES

137   From 1968 to 1977: Alan Westin, "Good Marks But Some Areas of Doubt," *Business Week,* May 14, 1979.

137   "Order seemed to be unraveling": Christian Parenti, *Lockdown America: Police and Prisons in the Age of Crisis* (London and New York: Verso, 1999), 3.

137   Nixon's legislative proposals: David Vogel, *Fluctuating Fortunes: The Political Power of Business in America* (New York: Basic Books, 1989), 60, 63, 91.

138   Consumer and environmental groups and legislation: Vogel, p. 60 and chapter 4.

138   Wave of regulatory agencies: Jerome L. Himmelstein, *To the Right: The Transformation of American Conservatism* (Berkeley: University of California Press, 1990), 136.

138   Lewis Powell's memorandum: Jerry M. Landay, "The Powell Manifesto: How A Prominent Lawyer's Attack Memo Changed America," Mediatransparency.org, Aug. 20, 2002; see www.mediatransparency.org.

139   Profile of Ralph Nader: *Fortune,* May 1971.

140   Conference Board meetings: Vogel, 145.

140   Business support for early regulatory initiatives: Gabriel Kolko, *The Triumph of Conservatism: A Reinterpretation of American History, 1900–1916* (New York: The Free Press, 1963, 1970); Murolo and Chitty, 142–143; Mayer, 594–602.

140   Business opposition to women's suffrage: "Woman Suffrage," www.grolier.com; Carrie Chapman Catt and Nettie Rogers Shuler, *Woman Suffrage and Politics: The Inner Story of the Suffrage Movement* (Seattle: University of Washington Press, 1926).

141   Even in the 1930s: Marchand, 202–203.

143   The Business Roundtable and the Taft-Hartley Act: Vogel, 154–155.

143   Joseph Coors and the Heritage Foundation: Lee Edwards, *The Power of Ideas: The Heritage Foundation at 25 Years* (Ottawa, Ill.: Jameson Foundation, 1998), 7–11.

143   California Chamber of Commerce and the Pacific Legal Foundation: Alliance for Justice, "Justice for Sale," 1993, cited in Landay, 13.

143   Creation of "counterintelligentsia": William E. Simon, *A Time for Truth* (New York: Berkley Books, 1979), quoted in Himmelstein, 146.

143 **American Legislative Exchange Council:** "Corporate America's Trojan Horse in the States: The Untold Story of the American Legislative Exchange Council," Defenders of Wildlife and Natural Resources Defense Council, 2002; Karen Olsson, "Ghostwriting the Law," *Mother Jones,* Sept.-Oct. 2002.

144 **USA*NAFTA:** For a detailed account of the formation of this coalition, see John R. MacArthur, *The Selling of "Free Trade": NAFTA, Washington, and the Subversion of American Democracy* (Berkeley: University of California Press, 2000).

144 **Center for Tobacco Research and others:** Background and quotes from www.prwatch.org.

144 **Enron's membership in coalitions:** "A Most Favored Corporation," Center for Public Integrity, 2002.

145 **Astroturfing:** John Stauber and Sheldon Rampton, *Toxic Sludge Is Good for You! Lies, Damn Lies, and the Public Relations Industry* (Monroe, Me: Common Courage Press, 1995), 79.

145 **"fuck up the mega-machine":** Judy Bari, *Timber Wars* (Monroe, Me.: Common Courage Press, 1994), 98, 135, 178.

145 **SLAPPs:** Nader and Smith, 158–192.

145 **"frequently devastated":** George Pring and Penelope Canan, *SLAPPs: Getting Sued for Speaking Out* (Philadelphia: Temple University Press, 1996), quoted in "SLAPP Happy: Corporations That Sue to Shut You Up," *PR Watch,* 1997, 4(2).

145 **Oprah Winfrey show:** see www.prwatch.org.

146 **Judicial education seminars:** Joe Stephens, "Judges' Free Trips Go Unreported," *Washington Post,* June 30, 2000; *Nothing for Free: How Judicial Seminars are Undermining Environmental Protections and Breaking the Public's Trust* (Washington, D.C.: Community Rights Council, July 2000).

146 **Topics at Elkhorn Ranch seminar:** *Nothing for Free,* Appendix A: "FREE's 1996 Colloquium for Federal Judges."

146 **"totally altered their frame of reference":** *Nothing for Free,* 13.

147 **"As a result of":** *Nothing for Free,* 13.

147 **Tillman Act, Hanna scandal, and Taft-Hartley Act:** Anthony Corrado et al., eds., *Campaign Finance Reform: A Sourcebook* (Washington, D.C.: Brookings Institution, 1997), chapter 2.

147 **"There are two things that are important in politics":** Helen Dewar, "Campaign Reform's Uphill Fight," *Washington Post,* Oct. 7, 1997.

147 **"stake in the general prosperity":** George Thayer, *Who Shakes the Money Tree: American Campaign Practices from 1789 to the Present* (New York: Simon & Schuster, 1974), 2.

148 **Archer Daniels Midland:** In 1972, Dwayne O. Andreas, CEO and chairman, gave President Nixon's personal secretary Rosemary Woods an 8- by 14-inch expansion envelope containing a thousand $100 bills. Woods had her assistant put the envelope in the basement safe. See "Andreas Steps Down, ADM Chief Took Politics to a New Level," *Washington Post,* Jan. 1, 1999.

148 **$750,000 cash donation:** Joshua E. Rosenkranz, *Buckley Stops Here: Loosening the Judicial Stranglehold on Campaign Finance Reform* (New York: The Century Foundation Press, 1998), 23.

148 **SUN-PAC ruling:** Vogel, 119.

149 **"We talk about the PAC":** Dan Clawson, Alan Neustadtl, and Mark Weller, *Dollars and Votes: How Business Campaign Contributions Subvert Democracy* (Philadelphia: Temple University Press, 1998), 14.

149 **"If your boss comes to you":** Clawson, Neustadtl, and Weller, 14.

149 **Business PACs versus labor PACs in 1974 and 1984:** Himmelstein, 141.

149 **Coordination among business PACs:** Vogel, 208.

150 **Soft money:** "The Half-Billion Dollar Shakedown," *Common Cause,* Apr. 2001; see www.commoncause.org.

150 **"No corporation doing business in this state":** Jane Anne Morris, "Speaking Truth to Power About Campaign Reform," in Dean Ritz (ed.), *Defying Corporations, Defining Democracy* (New York: The Apex Press, 2001), 193.

151 **Number of corporate lobbyists:** Ken Silverstein, *Washington on $10 Million a Day: How Lobbyists Plunder the Nation* (Monroe, Me.: Common Courage Press, 1998), 18.

Thirteen: Speech = Money

152 **Bob Dylan quote:** From "It's All Right Ma (I'm Only Bleeding)."

153 **California "Nickel a Drink" Initiative:** California Commission on Campaign Financing, *Democracy by Initiative: Shaping California's Fourth Branch of Government* (Los Angeles: Center for Responsive Government, 1992), 265–291; Advocacy Institute, *Taking Initiative* (Washington, D.C.: Advocacy Institute, 1992).

154 **Montana history:** K. Ross Toole, *The Rape of the Great Plains: Northwest America, Cattle and Coal* (Boston: Little, Brown, 1976).

154 **Libby, Montana:** Andrew Schneider, "A Town Left to Die," *Seattle Post-Intelligencer,* Nov. 18, 1999.

155 **Initiative 125:** *Montana Chamber of Commerce v. Argenbright* 226 F. 3d 1049 (9th Cir. 2000).

156 **"American business and the enterprise system":** See Landay.

157 **Analysis of *Buckley v. Valeo:*** Rosenkranz, chapter 3.

159 **"the motley rabble . . .":** Linebaugh and Rediker, 232.

159 **"anarchia":** Linebaugh and Rediker, 235.

Fourteen: Judicial Yoga

161 **Corporate legal theory:** This chapter follows the scheme for organizing the evolution of legal corporate theory proposed by Carl J. Mayer, "Personalizing the Impersonal: Corporations and the Bill of Rights," *Hastings Law Journal,* 1990, 41, 609. See also Horwitz, "*Santa Clara* Revisited: The Development of Corporate Theory," *The Transformation of American Law, 1870–1960: The Crisis of Legal Orthodoxy* (New York: Oxford University Press, 1992); and Gregory A. Mark, "The Personification of the Business Corporation in American Law," *University of Chicago Law Review,* 1987, 54, 1441.

162 **Mortmain clauses:** Seavoy, 10.

164 **Otto Gierke and "group personality":** Horwitz, 71–72; Mark, 1441.

166 **Dewey on corporate personality:** John Dewey, "The Historical Background of Corporate Legal Personality," *Yale Law Journal*, 1926, 35.

166 **Supreme Court decisions after World War I:** Mayer, 629–639.

167 **Criticism of *Santa Clara* by Justice Douglas:** *Wheeling Steel Corporation v. Glander* (1949).

171 **ACLU position on the right of corporations to be free from compelled speech:** See the ACLU's amicus brief in *Board of Regents of the University of Wisconsin v. Scott Harold Southworth,* United States Supreme Court, October 1998 term, June 14, 1999. For additional commentary on the ACLU position on free speech, see Robert McChesney, *Rich Media, Poor Democracy* (New York: The New Press, 2000), chapter 6, "The New Theology of the First Amendment: Class Privilege Over Democracy," 257–280.

171 **Berle and Means book:** Adolph A. Berle, Jr., and Gardiner C. Means, *The Modern Corporation and Private Property* (New York: Macmillan, 1932).

174 **"most prominent and valuable of our constitutional ad ban allies":** Ogilvy & Mather, "Strategy to Combat Advertising Content Restrictions and Counter-Advertising Requirements," 1987. The memo is document ti0317733/7763 in the House Commerce Committee's Web-based archive of "39,000 Documents Released April 22, 1998." Quoted in David Tannenbaum, "Buying Votes, Buying Friends," *Multinational Monitor,* July-Aug. 1998, p. 17.

175 **Kasky case:** American Civil Liberties Union of Northern California, "The ACLU's Position in *Kasky v. Nike,*" www.aclunc.org; Reclaim Democracy, "*Kasky v. Nike:* Just the Facts," www.reclaimdemocracy.org.

FIFTEEN: CRIME WAVE

178 **Enron:** April Witt and Peter Behr, "Losses, Conflicts Threaten Survival," *Washington Post,* July 31, 2002; "Bigger than Enron," *Frontline* documentary; transcripts at www.pbs.org/wgbh.

178 **At least twenty-eight former governmental officials:** "A Most Favored Corporation," Center for Public Integrity, 2002.

179 **And on the recommendation:** Mary Gordon, "Bush Appointed Enron's Favorites to FERC Posts," Associated Press, Feb. 1, 2002.

179 **Three-quarters of the Senate:** "Enron: The Real Scandal," *The Economist,* Jan. 17, 2002.

179 **some $1.1 billion:** John Dunbar, Robert Moore, and Mary Jo Sylvester, "Enron Top Brass Accused of Selling Stock Were Big Political Donors," Center for Public Integrity, Jan. 9, 2002.

179 **Enron employees blocked from selling:** Dunbar, Moore, and Sylvester.

179 **Scandals at other companies:** Penelope Patsuris, "The Corporate Scandal Sheet," www.forbes.com, August 26, 2002.

180 **In 1980, the average CEO:** "Executive Pay," *Business Week,* May 6, 2002.

180 **Charles E. Wilson's salary in 1950:** Frederick Lewis Allen, *The Big Change: America Transforms Itself 1900–1950* (Westport, Conn.: Greenwood Publishing Group, 1983), quoted in Phillips, 76.

180 **Krugman's views:** Paul Krugman, "For Richer: Inequality in America," *New York Times Magazine*, Oct. 20, 2002.

181 **Ownership by top management expanded:** Robert Monks, "Where Were Enron's Owners?" Forbes.com, Feb. 11, 2002.

182 **Stock options created perverse effects:** John Cassidy, "The Greed Cycle: How the Financial System Encouraged Corporations to Go Crazy," *The New Yorker*, Sept. 23, 2002.

182 **"Too many corporations seem disconnected":** *San Francisco Examiner*, July 11, 2002.

182 **"destructive greed":** *The Guardian*, July 10, 2002.

183 **Bush and Harken Energy:** See Molly Ivens and Lou Dubose, *Shrub: The Short But Happy Political Life of George W. Bush* (New York: Random House, 2000), 27–33.

183 **Cheney and Halliburton:** Alex Berenson and Lowell Bergman, "Under Cheney, Halliburton Altered Policy on Accounting," *New York Times*, May 22, 2002.

183 **Business Roundtable statements:** "BRT CEOs Issue 'Best Practices' Roadmap for Excellence in Corporate Governance Guidelines Proposed to Increase Trust in U.S. Companies Post-Enron," Business Roundtable press release, May 14, 2002.

184 **$636 million to Republicans:** Arianna Huffington, "Corporate Reform: A Ship Sailing Nowhere," *Christabella, Inc.*, Aug. 9, 2002.

184 **1993 fight over stock options accounting:** Arianna Huffington, *Pigs at the Trough* (New York: Crown, 2003), 106–110.

185 **Private Securities Legislative Reform Act:** Jay Mandle, "Corporate Scandals/Congressional Complicity," *Democracy Matters*, Sept. 1, 2002.

185 **Conflicts of interest with auditors:** "Bigger Than Enron," *Frontline* documentary, June 20, 2002; transcripts at www.pbs.org.

Sixteen: Global Rule

187 **Hong Kong:** Center for Strategic and Constitutional Studies, "Hong Kong Update," www.csis.org, May 1998.

188 **Minor Cooper Keith and United Fruit:** Daniel Litvin, *Empires of Profit: Commerce, Conquest and Corporate Responsibility* (New York; London: Texere, 2003), 113–141.

189 **Union Minière:** Litvin, 155–169.

189 **ITT:** William Blum, *Killing Hope: U.S. Military and CIA Interventions Since World War II* (Monroe, Me.: Common Courage Press, 1995), 206–214.

190 **from $21 billion to $110 billion:** Ned Daly, "Ravaging the Redwoods," *Multinational Monitor*, Sept. 1994, cited in David Korten, *When Corporations Rule the World*, 2nd ed. (San Francisco: Berrett-Koehler and Bloomfield, Conn.: Kumarian Press, 2001), 163.

190 **China's economic expansion:** "Effect of China's Leap Is Felt Around the World," *Los Angeles Times*, Nov. 30, 2002; Kris Hundley, "China, Inc.," St. Petersburg Times, July 14, 2002.

191 **Information on transnational and American companies worldwide:** Jeff Gates, *The Ownership Solution: Toward a Shared Capitalism for the 21st Century* (Reading, Mass.: Perseus Books, 1998), 69, 70.

191 **Foreign-owned share of U.S.:** Phillips, 284.

191 **Overview of NAFTA and WTO:** Lori Wallach and Michelle Sforza, *Whose Trade Organization: Corporate Globalization and the Erosion of Democracy* (Washington, D.C.: Public Citizen, 1999).

191 **NAFTA articles:** Mary Bottari, "NAFTA's Investor 'Rights' A Corporate Dream, A Citizen Nightmare," *Multinational Monitor,* Apr. 2001, 22(4).

192 **Takings Project:** "The Takings Project: Using Federal Courts to Attack Community and Environmental Protections," Executive Summary (Washington, D.C.: Community Rights Counsel, 2002); William Greider, "The Right and U.S. Trade Law: Invalidating the 20th Century," *The Nation,* Oct. 15, 2001; Jon Margolis, "The Quiet Takings Project Is Trespassing on Democracy," *High Country News,* Aug. 2, 1999.

193 **"the best news":** "Happy Earth Day, Lake Tahoe!" *Takings Watch* (Community Rights Counsel), Apr. 2001.

193 **Pending claims of $13 billion:** Bottari.

194 **MetalClad case:** William Greider, "The Right and U.S. Trade Law: Invalidating the 20th Century," *The Nation,* Oct. 15, 2001; Michelle Swenarchuk, "The Chapter 11 Dossier: Corporations Exercise Their Investor 'Rights,'" *Multinational Monitor,* Apr. 2001, 22(4).

194 **Methanex case:** Transcript of "Trading Democracy," *NOW with Bill Moyers,* Feb. 1, 2002; Greider; Swenarchuk; www.methanex.com.

194 **Philip Morris and Canada:** Robert Weissman, "Philip Morris' Trade Card," *Multinational Monitor,* Apr. 2002.

195 **Opposition to the Multilateral Agreement on Investments:** "MAI Negotiations Collapse," Environmental News Service, Mar. 23, 1998; Naomi Klein, *No Logo: Taking Aim at the Brand Bullies* (New York: Picador USA, 2000), 443.

Seventeen: Fighting Back

197 **Reverend Billy:** Richard Baimbridge, "The Magic of Disney Meets the Wrath of Reverend Billy," Adbusters, Winter 2000.

198 **"the end of history":** Frances Fukuyama, *The End of History and the Last Man* (New York: The Free Press, 1992).

199 **Union membership:** Kellman, 5.

199 **Between 1979 and 1994, 97 percent:** Jeff Gates, "Towards a More Democratic Capitalism," *Blueprint,* 1998.

199 **By 1998, the top 1 percent of the American population:** Edward N. Wolff, "Recent Trends in Wealth Ownership, 1983–1998" (Jerome Levy Economics Institute, Working Paper No. 300, Apr. 2000), Table 2.

199 **If the wealth of the country were divided:** Wolff, Table 1.

199 **"We are ruled by Big Business":** Ronnie Dugger, "A Call to Citizens: Real Populists Please Stand Up!" *The Nation,* August 14–21, 1995; Ronnie Dugger, "Welcome to Our Future," speech at founding convention of the Alliance for Democracy, Hunt, Texas, Nov. 11, 1996.

200 **"a kind of collective 'click'":** Klein, 334.

201 **Wackenhut case:** Sheila O'Donnell, "Private Spooks: Wackenhut vs. Whistleblowers," in Eveline Lubbers, ed., *Battling Big Business: Countering Greenwash, Infiltration and Other Forms of Corporate Bullying* (Monroe, Me.: Common Courage Press, 2002), 107–113.

201 **McDonald's case:** Eveline Lubbers, "McSpying," in *Lubbers*, 86–97; Fanny Armstrong and Will Ross, "Using Libel Laws to Silence Critics," in *Lubbers*, 78–85; Klein, 387–391.

201 **"uncovering not an opposite meaning":** Klein, 281.

202 **"Seattle Man":** Paul Krugman, "'Seattle Man' Denies Globalization," *Seattle Post-Intelligencer*, Jan. 25, 2000.

202 **codes of conduct:** Klein, 430–437; Steve Greenhouse, "Plan to Curtail Sweatshops Rejected by Union," *New York Times*, Nov. 5, 1998; Steve Greenhouse, "Two More Unions Reject Agreement for Curtailing Sweatshops," *New York Times*, Nov. 6, 1998; Alan Howard, "Partners in Sweat," *The Nation*, Dec. 29, 1998.

203 **"But we blew it":** "Interview with Richard Grossman," *Corporate Crime Reporter*, Nov. 24, 1997.

203 **Grossman and Adams' pamphlet:** Richard Grossman and Frank T. Adams, *Taking Care of Business: Citizenship and the Charter of Incorporation* (Cambridge, Mass.: Charter, Ink, 1993).

204 **"In 1628, King Charles I granted a charter":** Richard Grossman, "Can Corporations be Accountable? Part 1," *Rachel's Environment & Health Weekly*, July 30, 1998, 609.

204 **POCLAD's lawyers filed a book-length complaint:** Robert Benson, *Challenging Corporate Rule: The Petition to Revoke Unocal's Charter as a Guide to Citizen Action* (New York: Apex Press, 1999).

205 **California suspended the charters:** Charlie Cray, "Chartering a New Course: Revoking Corporations' Right to Exist," *Multinational Monitor*, Oct.-Nov. 2002, 9.

205 **Once suspended, a California corporation:** California Corporations Code, Section 2205.

205 **Florida and New York revocation actions:** Cray, 8–9.

206 **False Claims Act:** "Defense Companies that Lobby for Weaker False Claims Act Have Defrauded Government, Study Finds," *Corporate Crime Reporter*, Feb. 28, 1994, 2–3.

206 **Alien Tort Claims Act:** David Corn, "Corporate Human Rights," *The Nation*, July 15, 2002; Shravanti Reddy, "Individuals Struggle to Hold Corporations Accountable for Abuses," *Digital Freedom Network*, August 8, 2002; "Energy Giants Sued for Third World Violence," *Independent News Desk*, May 13, 2002; see www.newsdesk.org.

207 **Farmer-Paellmann lawsuit:** John S. Friedman, "Corporate Bill for Slavery," *The Nation*, Mar. 10, 2003; "Farmer-Paellmann not afraid of huge corporations," *USA Today*, Feb. 21, 2002; Salim Muwakkil, "Paying Back the Slavery Debt," *Chicago Tribune*, Apr. 17, 2002; Mumia Abu-Jamal, "The Case for Reparations," www.millionsforreparations.com; Bill Rigby, "Blacks File Slavery Suits Against Firms," Reuters, Sept. 4, 2002; *Deadria Farmer-Paellmann vs. FleetBoston Financial Corporation, Aetna Inc., CSX, and Their Predecessors, Successors and/or Assigns, and Corporate Does Nos. 1–1000*, United States District Court for the Eastern District of New York, Mar. 26, 2002.

208 **"This Amendment enshrines":** Mayer, 661.

209 **"I'm not so naïve":** Hartmann, 252.

209 **Examples of Supreme Court reversals:** Rosenkranz, 80–83; Justice Douglas's dissent in *Wheeling Steel Corporation v. Glander* (1949).

210 **Porter Township:** Tom DiStefano, "Porter Township Ordinance Attracts National Attention," *Clarion News,* Feb. 13, 2003.

211 **"Too many organizing campaigns":** Grossman and Adams, 22.

211 **Dan Clawson and Alan Neustadtl:** Clawon and Neustadtl are the authors of two books on the topic of corporate political contributions: Dan Clawson, Alan Neustadtl, and Denise Scott, *Money Talks: Corporate PACs and Political Influence* (New York: Basic Books, 1992) and Dan Clawson, Alan Neustadtl, and Mark Weller, *Dollars and Votes: How Business Campaign Contributions Subvert Democracy* (Philadelphia: Temple University Press, 1998). Quotes from Clawson, Neustadtl, and Scott, 196.

212 **"nonreformist reform":** Clawson, Neustadtl, and Scott, 218.

213 **Populist Party:** See Lawrence Goodwyn, *The Populist Moment: A Short History of the Agrarian Revolt in America* (New York: Oxford University Press, 1978).

214 **Socialist Party:** See James Weinstein, *The Decline of Socialism in America, 1912–1925, rev. ed.* (Piscataway, N.J.: Rutgers University Press, 1984).

214 **Progressive movement:** See Martin J. Sklar, *The Corporate Reconstruction of American Capitalism, 1890–1916* (New York: Cambridge University Press, 1988).

215 **Palmer raids:** Murolo and Chitty, 167; Goldstein, 156–157.

215 **"I find you, Joyce":** Goldstein, 28.

216 **"grossly underestimated":** Philip Taft and Philip Ross, "American Labor Violence: Its Causes, Character and Outcome," in Hugh Graham and Ted Gurr, eds., *Violence in America* (New York: Bantam, 1969), 380.

216 **"American labor suffered":** Goldstein, 3.

216 **Bagdikian's book:** Ben Bagdikian, *The Media Monopoly, 6th ed.* (Boston: Beacon Press, 2000).

216 **Clear Channel Communications:** Eric Boehlert, "Radio's Big Bully," salon.com, Apr. 30, 2001; Eric Boehlert, "Radio's Giant Hits the Skids," salon.com, Aug. 7, 2002.

217 **all-expenses-paid trips:** McChesney, "Media Democracy's Moment," *The Nation,* Feb. 6, 2003.

EIGHTEEN: INTELLIGENT, AMORAL, EVOLVING

220 **International Labor Rights Fund lawsuit:** *John Doe I, John Doe II, etc. v. ExxonMobil Corporation,* United States District Court for the District of Columbia, 01-1357 CIV, "Complaint for Equitable Relief Damages," www.laborrights.org.

221 **ExxonMobil's revenues outrank the budgets:** Charles Cray, "Corporate Goliaths: Sizing Up Corporations and Governments," *Multinational Monitor,* June 1999.

221 **Competitors like British Petroleum:** Neela Banerjee, "Economic Interests Keep Drive for Renewable Energy Stuck in Neutral," *New York Times,* Aug. 20, 2002.

223 **"The science of politics":** Alexander Hamilton, *The Federalist #9;* quoted in Michael Hardt and Antonio Negri, *Empire* (Cambridge, Mass.: Harvard University Press, 2001), 161.

224 "provided human rights in the U.S.": Robertson, 11.

225 van Leeuwenhoek: Paul de Kruif, *Microbe Hunters* (New York: Harcourt Brace, 1926), 1–22.

227 "grey goo": Bill Joy, "Why the Future Doesn't Need Us," *Wired*, Apr. 2000, p. 238.

228 Three Laws of Robotics: Isaac Asimov, *I, Robot* (New York: Bantam reprint ed., 1994 [originally published 1950]).

NINETEEN: SO WHAT'S THE ALTERNATIVE?

230 Muhammad Yunus quote: Muhammad Yunus, *Banker to the Poor: Micro-Lending and the Battle Against World Poverty* (New York: PublicAffairs, 1999, 2003), 205.

231 Thirteen symptoms of fascism: Laurence Britt, "Fascism Anyone?" *Free Inquiry*, spring 2003, 23(2); see http://secularhumanism.org/library/fi/britt_23_2.htm.

233 Corporate influence on EU policy: See Belén Balanyá, Ann Doherty, Olivier Hoedeman, Adam Ma'anit, and Erik Wesselius, *Europe Inc.: Regional & Global Restructuring & the Rise of Corporate Power, 2nd ed.* (London: Pluto Press, 2003). Also see Corporate Europe Observatory, "Brussels: The EU Quarter," Nov. 2004, at www.corporateeurope.org/docs/lobbycracy/lobbyplanet.pdf.

233 T. R. Reid and Jeremy Rifkin have concluded: T. R. Reid, *The United States of Europe: The New Superpower and the End of American Supremacy* (New York: Penguin Press, 2004). Jeremy Rifkin, *The European Dream* (New York: Jeremy Tarcher, 2004).

233 European restrictions on children's advertising: Lionel Wijesiri, "TV Ads and Children: Areas of Concern and Policy Implications," *Daily News*, Oct. 26, 2002; see www.dailynews.lk/2002/10/26/fea07.html.

234 European campaign spending and advertising: Ruth Levush, *Report for Congress: Campaign Financing of National Elections in Selected Foreign Countries* (Washington, D.C.: Library of Congress, Law Library, LL 97-3, 97-1552), May 1997.

235 Green Bay Packers ownership structure: see http://www.packers.com.

235 Community-owned teams in the minor leagues: Gar Alperovitz, *America Beyond Capitalism: Reclaiming Our Wealth, Our Liberty, and Our Democracy* (Hoboken, N.J.: Wiley, 2005), 92.

235 Community-owned retail stores: Stacy Mitchell, "Home Shopping Networks," *AlterNet*, Mar. 17, 2004; see www.alternet.org/story/18158/.

236 60 percent of economic activity is local: Alperovitz, 126.

236 Krugman quote: Paul Krugman, *Pop Internationalism* (Cambridge, Mass.: MIT Press, 1996), 211.

236 Number and assets of ESOPs: Alperovitz, 82.

236 Comparison between number of workers in ESOPs and unions: Alperovitz, 81, citing Bureau of Labor Statistics for 2003.

236 From 38 to 68 percent: Alperovitz, 86.

236 Philadelphia Contributionship: David J. Thompson, "Happy Anniversary: 250 Years of Cooperation in America" (Madison: University of Wisconsin Center for Cooperatives, 2002); see www.wisc.edu/uwcc/info/history/ben_franklin.html.

236 Statistics on cooperatives: "Consumer Cooperatives: Part of Our America Fabric" (Washington, D.C.: Consumer Federation of America, n.d.); see www.consumerfed.org/coop.pdf.

237 The wealthiest 1 percent of the population owns almost as many corporate shares as the other 99 percent: Wolff's estimate in 2002 was that 47 percent of stock, bond, and other investments are in the hands of the wealthiest 1 percent. Edward Wolff, *Top Heavy: The Increasing Inequality of Wealth in America and What Can Be Done About It* (New York: The New Press, 2002), 8–9.

237 "It is a striking anomaly . . .": David Schweickart, *After Capitalism* (Lanham, Md.: Rowman & Littlefield, 2002), 16.

237 Mondragon: Schweickart, 67.

237 Grameen: Yunus, 158–164, 215–231.

238 Grameen's medley of business models: Yunus, 124.

238 Rate and salary comparisons between SMUD and PG&E: Dan Berman, "SMUD: What's Not to Like?" *Davis Enterprise,* Jan. 23, 2005. Coalition for Local Power, "Estimated Annual Compensation, 1998–2003" at http://www2.dcn.org/orgs/localpower/PGE_Compensation.html.

239 "separate rating agencies, financial institutions . . .": Yunus, 251.

239 New financial infrastructure: Stephen Lydenberg, *Corporations and the Public Interest: Guiding the Invisible Hand* (San Francisco: Berrett-Koehler, 2005), 92–94, 113–114, 120–121.

240 Schweickart's transition scenario: Schweickart, 170–179.

241 A mixture of institutional forms: Schweickart, 45–56, 170–177.

References

Alperovitz, Gar. *America Beyond Capitalism: Reclaiming Our Wealth, Our Liberty, and Our Democracy.* Hoboken, N.J.: Wiley, 2005.

Bagdikian, Ben. *The Media Monopoly* (6th ed.). Boston: Beacon Press, 2000.

Bakan, Joel. *The Corporation: The Pathological Pursuit of Profit and Power.* New York: Simon & Schuster, 2004.

Balanyá, Belén, Ann Doherty, Olivier Hoedeman, Adam Ma'anit, and Erik Wesselius. *Europe Inc.: Regional & Global Restructuring & the Rise of Corporate Power* (2nd ed.). London: Pluto Press, 2003.

Beatty, Jack (ed.). *Colossus: How the Corporation Changed America.* New York: Broadway Books, 2001.

Benson, Robert. *Challenging Corporate Rule: The Petition to Revoke Unocal's Charter as a Guide to Citizen Action.* New York: Apex Press, 1999.

Benson, T. Lloyd, and Trina Rossman. "Re-Assessing Tom Scott, the 'Railroad Prince.'" Paper presented at the Mid-America Conference on History, 1995.

Berle, Adolph A., Jr. *The Twentieth Century Capitalist Revolution.* New York: Harcourt, Brace, 1954.

Berle, Adolph A., Jr., and Gardiner C. Means. *The Modern Corporation and Private Property.* New York: Macmillan, 1932.

Bowman, Scott R. *The Modern Corporation and American Political Thought: Law, Power, and Ideology.* University State Park: The Pennsylvania State University Press, 1996.

Bruchey, Stuart. *The Roots of American Economic Growth, 1607–1861.* New York: Harper & Row, 1965.

Bruchey, Stuart. *Enterprise: The Dynamic Economy of a Free People.* Cambridge, Mass.: Harvard University Press, 1990.

Carnoy, Martin, and Derek Shearer, *Economic Democracy.* White Plains, N.Y.: Sharpe, 1980.

Clawson, Dan, Alan Neustadtl, and Denise Scott. *Money Talks: Corporate PACs and Political Influence.* New York: HarperCollins/Basic Books, 1992.

Clawson, Dan, Alan Neustadtl, and Mark Weller. *Dollars and Votes: How Business Campaign Contributions Subvert Democracy.* Philadelphia: Temple University Press, 1998.

Dan-Cohen, Meir. *Rights, Persons, and Organizations: A Legal Theory for Bureaucratic Society.* Berkeley: University of California Press, 1986.

Davis, John P. *Corporations: A Study of the Origin and Development of Great Business Combinations and Their Relation to the Authority of the State.* New York: Capricorn Books, 1961 [originally published 1904].

Davis, Joseph S. *Essays in the Earlier History of American Corporations.* Cambridge, Mass.: Harvard University Press, 1917.

Derber, Charles. *Corporation Nation*. New York: St. Martin's Press, 1998.

Dewey, John. "The Historical Background of Corporate Legal Personality," *Yale Law Journal*, 1926, 35.

Draffan, George. *The Corporate Consensus: A Guide to the Institutions of Global Power*. New York: Apex Press, 2002.

Drutman, Lee, and Charlie Cray. *The People's Business: Controlling Corporations and Restoring Democracy*. San Francisco: Berrett-Koehler, 2004.

Dugger, William M. *Corporate Hegemony*. New York: Greenwood Press, 1989.

Estes, Ralph. *The Tyranny of the Bottom Line: Why Corporations Make Good People Do Bad Things*. San Francisco: Berrett-Koehler, 1996.

Fligstein, Neil. *The Transformation of Corporate Control*. Cambridge, Mass.: Harvard University Press, 1990.

Foner, Philip S. *The Great Labor Uprising of 1877*. New York: Monad Press, 1977.

Friedman, Lawrence M. *A History of American Law* (2nd ed.). New York: Simon & Schuster, 1985.

Galambos, Louis. "The Emerging Organizational Synthesis in American History," *Business History Review*, 1970, 22.

Galloway, Russell. *Justice for All? The Rich and Poor in Supreme Court History*. Durham, N.C.: Carolina Academic Press, 1991.

Gates, Jeff. *The Ownership Solution: Toward a Shared Capitalism for the 21st Century*. Reading, Mass.: Perseus Books, 1998.

Geisst, Charles R. *Monopolies in America: Empire Builders and Their Enemies from Jay Gould to Bill Gates*. New York: Oxford University Press, 2000.

Goldstein, Robert Justin. *Political Repression in Modern America: From 1870 to 1976*. Urbana and Chicago: University of Illinois Press, 2001 [originally published 1978].

Goodwyn, Lawrence. *The Populist Moment: A Short History of the Agrarian Revolt in America*. New York: Oxford University Press, 1978.

Graham, Howard Jay. *Everyman's Constitution: Historical Essays on the Fourteenth Amendment, the "Conspiracy Theory," and American Constitutionalism*. Madison: State Historical Society of Wisconsin, 1968.

Greider, William. *The Soul of Capitalism: Opening Paths to a Moral Economy*. New York: Simon & Schuster, 2003.

———. *Who Will Tell the People? The Betrayal of American Democracy*. New York: Simon & Schuster, 1992.

Grossman, Richard, and Frank T. Adams. *Taking Care of Business: Citizenship and the Charter of Incorporation*. Cambridge, Mass.: Charter, Ink, 1993.

Greenwood, Daniel J. H. "Essential Speech: Why Corporate Speech Is Not Free," *Iowa Law Review*, 1998, 995.

Hacker, Andrew (ed.). *The Corporation Take-Over*. New York: Harper and Row, 1964.

Handlin, Oscar, and Mary Handlin. "Origins of the American Business Corporation," *Journal of Economic History*, 1945, 5.

Harris, Ron. *Industrializing English Law: Entrepreneurship and Business Organization, 1720–1844.* New York: Cambridge University Press, 2000.

Hartmann, Thom. *Unequal Protection: The Rise of Corporate Dominance and the Theft of Human Rights.* Emmaus, Penn.: Rodale, 2002.

Hartz, Louis. *Economic Policy and Democratic Thought: Pennsylvania 1776–1860.* Cambridge, Mass.: Harvard University Press, 1948.

Hawkins, Mike. *Social Darwinism in European and American Thought, 1860–1945.* New York: Cambridge University Press, 1997.

Himmelstein, Jerome L. *To the Right: The Transformation of American Conservatism.* Berkeley: University of California Press, 1990.

Horwitz, Morton J. *The Transformation of American Law, 1870–1960: The Crisis of Legal Orthodoxy.* New York: Oxford University Press, 1992.

Huffington, Arianna. *Pigs at the Trough.* New York: Crown, 2003.

Hurst, James Willard. *The Legitimacy of the Business Corporation in the Law of the United States, 1780–1970.* Charlottesville: University Press of Virginia, 1970.

"Incorporating the Republic: The Corporation in Antebellum Political Culture," *Harvard Law Review,* 1989, 102.

International Forum on Globalization. *Alternatives to Economic Globalization.* San Francisco: Berrett-Koehler, 2002.

Jensen, Derrick. *The Culture of Make-Believe.* New York: Context Books, 2002.

Josephson, Matthew. *The Robber Barons.* New York: Harcourt, Brace & World, 1934.

Kamm, Samuel Richey. "The Civil War Career of Thomas A. Scott." Doctoral dissertation, University of Pennsylvania Graduate School of History, 1940.

Keay, John. *The Honorable Company: A History of the East India Company.* New York: Macmillan, 1994.

Kellman, Peter. *Building Unions: Past, Present, and Future.* New York: Apex Press, 2001.

Kelly, Marjorie. *The Divine Right of Capital: Dethroning the Corporate Aristocracy.* San Francisco: Berrett-Koehler, 2002.

Kens, Paul. *Justice Stephen Field: Shaping Liberty from the Gold Rush to the Gilded Age.* Lawrence: University Press of Kansas, 1997.

Kens, Paul. *Lochner v. New York: Economic Regulation on Trial.* Lawrence: University Press of Kansas, 1998.

Klein, Naomi. *No Logo: Taking Aim at the Brand Bullies.* New York: Picador USA, 2000.

Korten, David C. *The Post-Corporate World: Life After Capitalism.* San Francisco: Berrett-Koehler and Bloomfield, Conn.: Kumarian Press, 1999.

Korten, David C. *When Corporations Rule the World* (2nd ed.). San Francisco: Berrett-Koehler and Bloomfield, Conn: Kumarian Press, 2001.

Labaree, Benjamin Woods. *The Boston Tea Party.* New York: Oxford University Press, 1964.

Lasn, Kalle. *Culture Jam.* New York: HarperCollins, 1999.

Licht, Walter. *Industrializing America: The Nineteenth Century.* Baltimore: The Johns Hopkins University Press, 1995.

Linebaugh, Peter, and Marcus Rediker. *The Many-Headed Hydra: Sailors, Slaves, Commoners, and the Hidden History of the Revolutionary Atlantic.* Boston: Beacon Press, 2000.

Litvin, Daniel. *Empires of Profit: Commerce, Conquest and Corporate Responsibility.* London: Texere, 2003.

Lubbers, Eveline (ed.). *Battling Big Business: Countering Greenwash, Infiltration and Other Forms of Corporate Bullying.* Monroe, Me.: Common Courage Press, 2002.

Lydenberg, Steven. *Corporations and the Public Interest: Guiding the Invisible Hand.* San Francisco: Berrett-Koehler, 2005.

Magrath, C. Peter. *Morrison R. Waite: The Triumph of Character.* New York: Macmillan, 1963.

Mander, Jerry. *In the Absence of the Sacred.* San Francisco: Sierra Club Books, 1991.

Marchand, Roland. *Creating the Corporate Soul: The Rise of Public Relations and Corporate Imagery in American Big Business.* Berkeley: University of California Press, 1998.

Mark, Gregory A. "The Personification of the Business Corporation in American Law," *University of Chicago Law Review*, 1987, 54, 1441.

Mayer, Carl J. "Personalizing the Impersonal: Corporations and the Bill of Rights," *Hastings Law Journal*, 1990, 41.

McChesney, Robert W. *Rich Media, Poor Democracy: Communication Politics in Dubious Times.* New York: The New Press, 2000.

McClure, A. K. *Old Time Notes of Pennsylvania.* Philadelphia: John Winston, 1905.

McIntosh, Wayne, and Cynthia Gates. "Advancing Speech Rights of Corporations: The Changing First Amendment." Paper prepared for the annual conference of the American Politics Group, University of Essex, United Kingdom, Jan. 2002.

Menand, Louis. *The Metaphysical Club.* New York: Farrar, Straus and Giroux, 2001.

Micklethwait, John, and Adrian Wooldridge. *The Company: A Short History of a Revolutionary Idea.* New York: Random House/Modern Library, 2003.

Miller, Arthur S. *The Modern Corporate State: Private Governments and the American Constitution.* Westport, Conn.: Greenwood Press, 1976.

Mokhiber, Russell, and Robert Weissman. *Corporate Predators: The Hunt for Mega-Profits and the Attack on Democracy.* Monroe, Me.: Common Courage Press, 1999.

Monks, Robert A. G. *The Emperor's Nightingale: Restoring the Integrity of the Corporation in the Age of Shareholder Activism.* Reading, Mass.: Addison-Wesley, 1998.

Monks, Robert A. G., and Nell Minow. *Power and Accountability.* New York: HarperCollins, 1991.

Morgan, Edmund S. *American Slavery, American Freedom: The Ordeal of Colonial Virginia.* New York: W. W. Norton, 1975.

Mukherjee, Ramkrishna. *The Rise and Fall of the East India Company.* New York: Monthly Review Press, 1974.

Mumford, Lewis. *The Myth of the Machine I: Technics and Human Development.* New York: Harcourt, Brace, 1967.

Murolo, Priscilla, and A. B. Chitty. *From the Folks Who Brought You the Weekend: A Short, Illustrated History of Labor in the United States.* New York: The New Press, 2001.

Myers, Gustavus. *History of the Supreme Court of the United States.* Chicago: Charles H. Kerr, 1912.

Nader, Ralph, and Mark J. Green (eds.). *Corporate Power in America.* New York: Grossman Publishers, 1973.

Nader, Ralph, and Wesley J. Smith. *No Contest: Corporate Lawyers and the Perversion of Justice in America.* New York: Random House, 1996.

Nelson, Scott Reynolds. *Iron Confederacies: Southern Railways, Klan Violence, and Reconstruction.* Chapel Hill: University of North Carolina Press, 1999.

Nightingale, Pamela. *A Medieval Mercantile Community: The Grocers' Company & the Politics & Trade of London, 1000–1485.* New Haven, Conn.: Yale University Press, 1995.

O'Brien, David M. *Storm Center: The Supreme Court in American Politics.* New York: W. W. Norton, 1986.

Orren, Karen. *Belated Feudalism: Labor, the Law, and Liberal Development in the United States.* New York: Cambridge University Press, 1991.

Pariser, Eli. "The Argument from Silence." Unpublished thesis, 2001; eli.pariser@moveon.org.

Perrow, Charles. *Organizing America: Wealth, Power, and the Origins of Corporate Capitalism.* Princeton, N.J.: Princeton University Press, 2002.

Pertschuk, Michael. *Revolt Against Regulation: The Rise and Pause of the Consumer Movement.* Berkeley: University of California Press, 1982.

Phillips, Kevin. *Wealth and Democracy: A Political History of the American Rich.* New York: Broadway Books, 2002.

Pooley, Sir Ernest. *The Guilds of the City of London.* London: Collins, 1947.

Raphael, Ray. *A People's History of the American Revolution.* New York: The New Press, 2001.

Reich, Charles A. *Opposing the System.* New York: Crown, 1995.

Reid, T. R. *The United States of Europe: The New Superpower and the End of American Supremacy.* New York: Penguin Press, 2004.

Rifkin, Jeremy. *The European Dream.* New York: Jeremy Tarcher, 2004.

Ritz, Dean (ed.). *Defying Corporations, Defining Democracy.* New York: The Apex Press, 2001.

Robertson, Geoffrey. *Crimes Against Humanity: The Struggle for Global Justice.* New York: The New Press, 2000.

Rosenkranz, E. Joshua. *Buckley Stops Here: Loosening the Judicial Stranglehold on Campaign Finance Reform.* New York: The Century Foundation Press, 1998.

Roy, William G. *Socializing Capital: The Rise of the Large Industrial Corporation in America.* Princeton, N.J.: Princeton University Press, 1997.

Schofield, Michael. "Muzzling Corporations: The Court Giveth and the Court Taketh Away a Corporation's 'Fundamental Right' to Free Political Speech in *Austin v. Michigan Chamber of Commerce," Louisiana Law Review,* Nov. 1991, 52.

Schwartz, Bernard. *A History of the Supreme Court.* New York: Oxford University Press, 1993.

Schweickart, David. *After Capitalism*. Lanham, Md.: Rowman & Littlefield, 2002.

Seavoy, Ronald E. *The Origins of the American Business Corporation, 1784–1855*. New York: Greenwood Press, 1982.

Silverstein, Ken. *Washington on $10 Million a Day: How Lobbyists Plunder the Nation*. Monroe, Me.: Common Courage Press, 1998.

Sklar, Martin J. *The Corporate Reconstruction of American Capitalism, 1890–1916*. New York: Cambridge University Press, 1988.

Stauber, John, and Sheldon Rampton. *Toxic Sludge Is Good for You! Lies, Damn Lies, and the Public Relations Industry*. Monroe, Me.: Common Courage Press, 1995.

Stone, Christopher. *Where the Law Ends*. New York: Harper and Row, 1975.

Swisher, Carl Brent. *Stephen J. Field: Craftsman of the Law*. Washington, D.C.: The Brookings Institute, 1930.

Vogel, David. *Fluctuating Fortunes: The Political Power of Business in America*. New York: Basic Books, 1989.

Wallach, Lori, and Michelle Sforza. *Whose Trade Organization? Corporate Globalization and the Erosion of Democracy*. Washington, D.C.: Public Citizen, 1999.

Wolff, Edward. *Top Heavy: The Increasing Inequality of Wealth in America and What Can Be Done About It*. New York: The New Press, 2002.

Yunus, Muhammad. *Banker to the Poor: Micro-Lending and the Battle Against World Poverty*. New York: PublicAffairs, 2003.

Zinn, Howard. *A People's History of the United States*. New York: HarperPerennial, 1995.

Index

Page numbers appearing in italics refer to table entries.

About the Author

W HILE WORKING FOR THE U.S. FOREST SERVICE during high school,
Ted Nace learned about the plans of several major corporations
to develop coal strip mines and other energy projects near his hometown
of Dickinson, North Dakota. During graduate school, Nace worked for
the Environmental Defense Fund, where he helped develop computerized
simulations that demonstrated the investor and ratepayer benefits of replacing coal-fired power plants with alternative energy programs. The
EDF simulations led to the cancellation of a multi-billion-dollar coal-
based power complex proposed by two California utilities. After com-
pleting his graduate studies, Nace worked for the Dakota Resource
Council, a citizens' group concerned about the impacts of energy development on agriculture and rural communities.

Nace moved to California, where he wrote and edited for *PC World,*
Macworld, and other computer magazines and book publishers. Hoping
to create a more supportive environment for authors like himself, he
founded Peachpit Press. Under Nace's leadership, Peachpit developed a
number of innovative book series, including Little Books, Visual Quick-
Start Guides, and Real World Guides. The company won renown for its
harmonious and creative arrangements with authors, and it produced
dozens of best-sellers. Peachpit outpaced older and larger publishing
companies to become the world's leading source of books on computer
graphics and desktop publishing.

After eleven years as publisher, Nace sold Peachpit Press to British conglomerate Pearson Plc, and he returned to freelance writing. In seeking
to understand the institutional structure of power in America, he inves-
tigated the historical roots of the corporation, as well as reflected on his
own experiences as a community organizer and a publishing entrepreneur. *Gangs of America* is the result of that research and reflection.

For more information go to: www.GangsofAmerica.com

About Berrett-Koehler Publishers

Berrett-Koehler is an independent publisher dedicated to an ambitious mission: Creating a World that Works for All.

We believe that to truly create a better world, action is needed at all levels--individual, organizational, and societal. At the individual level, our publications help people align their lives and work with their deepest values. At the organizational level, our publications promote progressive leadership and management practices, socially responsible approaches to business, and humane and effective organizations. At the societal level, our publications advance social and economic justice, shared prosperity, sustainable development, and new solutions to national and global issues.

A major theme of our publications is "Opening Up New Space." They challenge conventional thinking, introduce new points of view, and offer new alternatives for change. Their common quest is changing the underlying beliefs, mindsets, institutions, and structures that keep generating the same cycles of problems, no matter who our leaders are or what improvement programs we adopt.

We strive to practice what we preach—to operate our publishing company in line with the ideas in our books. At the core of our approach is *stewardship*, which we define as a deep sense of responsibility to administer the company for the benefit of all of our "stakeholder" groups: authors, customers, employees, investors, service providers, and the communities and environment around us. We seek to establish a partnering relationship with each stakeholder that is open, equitable, and collaborative.

We are gratified that thousands of readers, authors, and other friends of the company consider themselves to be part of the "BK Community." We hope that you, too, will join our community and connect with us through the ways described on our website at www.bkconnection.com.

A BK Currents Title

This book is part of our BK Currents series. BK Currents titles advance social and economic justice by exploring the critical intersections between business and society. Offering a unique combination of thoughtful analysis and progressive alternatives, BK Currents titles promote positive change at the national and global levels. To find out more, visit www.bkcurrents.com.

Be Connected

Visit Our Website

Go to www.bkconnection.com to read exclusive previews and excerpts of new books, find detailed information on all Berrett-Koehler titles and authors, browse subject-area libraries of books, and get special discounts.

Subscribe to Our Free E-Newsletter

Be the first to hear about new publications, special discount offers, exclusive articles, news about bestsellers, and more! Get on the list for our free e-newsletter by going to www.bkconnection.com.

Participate in the Discussion

To see what others are saying about our books and post your own thoughts, check out our blogs at www.bkblogs.com.

Get Quantity Discounts

Berrett-Koehler books are available at quantity discounts for orders of ten or more copies. Please call us toll-free at (800) 929-2929 or email us at bkp.orders@aidcvt.com.

Host a Reading Group

For tips on how to form and carry on a book reading group in your workplace or community, see our website at www.bkconnection.com.

Join the BK Community

Thousands of readers of our books have become part of the "BK Community" by participating in events featuring our authors, reviewing draft manuscripts of forthcoming books, spreading the word about their favorite books, and supporting our publishing program in other ways. If you would like to join the BK Community, please contact us at bkcommunity@bkpub.com.